Faithful Nurturing

MOTHERING FROM THE HEART, TO THE HEART

By Mary Illions Wilde, MD

Mary Illions Wilde

bless you in your
creative journey

Faithful Nurturing: Mothering from the Heart to the Heart

ISBN: 978-1534625181

To my inspiring, insightful sister
To my wise & loving mother
May you bloom and grow forever...

CONTENTS

Note to reader:

Though partly a memoir, this book is not presented chronologically. Because *Faithful Nurturing* was written over the course of several years, the number of my children and their ages vary from story to story. Also, my mom's health and independence seem to vary, when in actuality it steadily declined over years with a sudden major decline after her strokes.

INTRODUCTION

This October I went on a pilgrimage from Minnesota to Illinois. I packed a small rental car with necessities and drove my eighth baby, then two months old, to see his grandma at least once before seasons change. Over the last decade, my sister and I have made this trip back and forth many times—usually to transport our mother as we take turns caring for her, but also to gather as a family.

My mom's hospital bed is situated in a bright sunroom at my sister's with views of a backyard birdfeeder and its colorful visitors. This time, like the birds, I will visit only briefly—just two days—but will accomplish my purpose. My mother seems increasingly frail and difficult to reach. Since her last stroke she can move only her right arm and she is elaborately propped with pillows. Her body is stuck, but it seems her soul is on its way somewhere else. I place my new baby on her chest and his soft, round head rests against her cheek for the first time. During the visit, I hug and kiss her, hold her hand, and sing her a song she used to sing to me. She looks at me with clarity just once, but for several minutes, and I consider this chance for connection a gift. I marvel that just sitting in her presence and hearing her rhythmic breathing soothes my soul.

Motherhood itself is a pilgrimage—a journey to a holy place, one of intimate connection, vulnerability, and transformation.

My own searching questions about motherhood came when I already had four children, at the close of my medical residency. For years I had been navigating the combined rigors of medical training mixed with motherhood, and at the program's end, I felt like one emerging from a dense wood into a sudden clearing—at once both liberated and lost. Now that I had the opportunity to be consistently home with my kids, what exactly would I do? What was my primary objective or core purpose as a mother? Because I considered motherhood my greatest work and now could focus wholly upon it, I pondered the issue deeply, sought advice, read stacks of parenting books, reflected upon my own childhood, studied scripture, and prayed.

The parenting books never seemed to tell the whole story—most were too theoretical, too simplistic, or too focused on outcomes that did not seem central to me. At first, with so many recommendations to sift through, I felt paralyzed—almost any course of action would be violating *some* parenting theory. Seeing other mothers who looked so assured, I wondered whether it was because of their wisdom or oblivion. In Dostoevsky's *Notes from Underground,* the narrator describes sitting behind an imaginary wall that only exists by his creation; his awareness of complexities impedes him while others obliviously, yet successfully, pass through. Was I creating such a quandary for myself?

When I asked several exemplary women how they had navigated motherhood, they gave varied but often vague answers. Perhaps I caught these mothers off-guard with my questions, but their silence was also wisdom: their personal lessons could not be transmitted in a few words or in casual conversation. Motherhood, like life in general, is schoolhouse to the soul; the learning comes experientially. The unsettling reality is that we must keep being mothers while still learning how—it is the only way one really *does* learn how.

My ongoing contemplation about mothering has resulted in both flashes of insight scrawled on the nearest scrap of paper and more slowly emerging conclusions as I specifically sat down to write. There has been a certain urgency to this process, because ideas don't wait (not in full detail), *and* because my younger children, with their toddler instinct to rip paper randomly, put all recorded ideas at peril. A kind, well-meaning friend assured me, "There is no rush. These insights of yours will be there—they are not going anywhere." But, as Louise Erdrich states in her book *A Blue Jay's Dance: Writings of a Birth Year,* "On pharmacy prescription bags, dime-store notebooks, children's construction paper, I keep writing."[1] The time to write is now—certainly not for convenience, but for integrity—because it is now, as a mother with small children that I stand and look at this particular, beautiful landscape.

French Impressionist Claude Monet painted his lily pond in all different lights: at dawn, at dusk, and at high noon. In so doing, he could accurately discover and capture how the light reflected off the water; he painted what he saw, even if that made water red, yellow, or purple. This is my book of impressions and I say it like I see it, as it looks from where I am and in this certain light.

Stopping to look closely enough to translate what I see into words has given me a more detailed view of my children and myself as a mother. After years of pediatric training, studying parenting and child development theories, and being humbled by parenthood itself, I have come home to a simpler truth I already knew. Rather than outward technique, it is the internal landscape of the heart that affects parenting more than anything else. Mothering is about being, as far as possible, in the right state of soul to nurture and nourish another person.

The ultimate locus of knowing how to parent is not outside of us in some parenting book or in the teaching of some "expert," but is within us, honed over time, inspired by a loving God who wants every good thing for us and our families. The best parenting book is our own story—the discoveries, miracles and successes day to day; it is our book of life. Still, it helps to compare notes. That is why I keep reading and why I took the time to write this book. Though we walk individual paths shaped by our own families, cultures, and experiences, we are part of a grand community of women often wishing for and working for the same things.

I am a member of the Church of Jesus Christ of Latter-day Saints, but my life has been enriched by faithful people from many backgrounds. In *Faithful Nurturing*, while I address general principles embraced by devoted mothers of any denomination, I reference illustrative passages from my own religious tradition[*]—in spiritual matters, it is my own mother tongue. I write from my faith context and trust that you will read from yours.

Faithful Nurturing began as a record of personal insights and questions and has somehow grown over the years into a large manuscript. It is a record of my journey as I have tried to parent with faith and intention, learning lessons from everyday interactions with my children. Chapters 1-17 explore foundations that prepare us to nurture; chapters 18-23 explore what nurturing is; chapters 24-39 suggest specific methods; and chapters 40-42 discuss how to find happiness in the process.

While the ideas I share in this book have been useful to me, they represent my hopes and sustained effort rather than consistent mastery. Just as our children keep growing, so do we—our books will never, ever be done.

MW

---

[*] For further explanation of LDS beliefs, see www.mormon.org. For LDS references (including King James Version of the Bible, Book of Mormon, Doctrine and Covenants, and *Ensign* articles), see www.lds.org.

I. ATTRIBUTES OF MOTHERHOOD

On vision and symbols

1 ~ TIME FLOWS IN TWO DIRECTIONS

In recent years, responsibility for my mother's house has fallen to me—a time capsule that I have had the opportunity and burden to open. While sorting through things in the basement, I found a small floral suitcase in which I had toted toys as a young girl. I unzipped it and found a 30-year-old pretending game, half-played. There were homemade tickets made of orange construction paper, a coin purse with pennies, a Polaroid photo of my sister and me, and a few assorted small toys. At some point in a day, I had set the suitcase aside and had not picked it up again, until just now. I remembered the words to an old song:

> I've been sifting through the layers,
> Dusty books and faded papers.
> It tells a story I used to know,
> One that happened so long ago.
> It's gone away, yesterday—
> Now I find myself on the mountainside
> Where the rivers change direction
> Across the Great Divide.[1]

At that moment I stood at a figurative Continental Divide, watching the currents of my experience flow both forward and back—as if time itself flowed in two directions. I thought of how my six-year-old son might carry around just such a suitcase, pretending to be leaving on the next train. For a moment I remembered how real those games could be. Now it is my turn to be the mother, rather than the child.

Another recent discovery from an old box of photos was a beautiful picture of a young mother and her daughter in a garden. The mother is in a pink dress and black heels sitting on a decorative stool and reaching out toward a little girl who leans against her knee, and sunlight glows through the leaves behind them. It is my mom and my sister before I was born.[*] Looking into this photo is like looking through a window at people I love—like watching my own kids play outside as I stand washing dishes at the kitchen sink. Yet, the exact mother in the picture is someone I never met and someone I'll never completely know. My current memory relies on a childhood lens, positioned just a few feet off the ground and pointing

---

[*]This photo is on the book's cover.

outward at everything. If only I could go back to play the scenes again, this time more closely watching my mother's face—perhaps then I could guess her thoughts and how she arrived at the wisdom she did.

Now things have come full circle. She is back living with us—half the year with me and my family, half the year with my sister and hers—because, as my son says, she's "too wobbly" to live alone. I rush home to show my mom the picture, but she seems less captivated or surprised by it than I am. To herself, she is as much or more the woman in the picture than the elderly woman in the recliner holding it. She's dressed again in pink, but the dress and heels have given way to sweats and socks with traction. Now I am the one who bathes *her*; as I rinse her hair I remember how she used to sing to my sister and me while rinsing our hair with water poured from a cup. I am the one who feeds *her*; I prepare the meals and dish up the food while she and my husband and children wait. Some days her hands are too shaky to scoop the food, so I spoon it to her, between eating my own meal, feeding the baby in the highchair, and everything else—the dishing and fetching, the quieting of seven hungry boys.

But what is "now" keeps changing, the currents of time keep flowing. Years have again passed. Now I have eight boys. Now my mom has had two massive strokes and my sister and I provide her nourishment through a feeding tube. Now I have moved with my family back into my childhood home. I am back where I started. I carry lessons from the past and press forward the best I can. Time flows on.

Reflect or discuss:

1) Have you had any moments where vivid recollections of your childhood have surprised or deeply affected you?

2) How does your childhood affect your present experience as a mother?

2~ BEING AND DOING

On the score for his great choral mass *Missa Solemnis,* Beethoven inscribed the following message to the performers: *Von Herzen—möge es wieder—zu Herzen gehen,* or "From the heart, may it go to the heart." To me as a singer, these words capture the essence of true musicianship—the ability to internalize and then meaningfully share a piece of music. The phrase, like a wish or a prayer for connection, also applies to motherhood: from the heart I send love and lessons, which I hope my children will receive. My heart, or core identity, does much to influence my children—it cannot be pretended to those so intimate.

Volumes have been published on child development, yet little research exists on "mother development," though surely it occurs. As time and experience teach us, certain qualities persist and others fall away. Mercifully, the repetitive tasks of motherhood hold the blessing of multiple chances. We develop partly by our own calculated intent, but also steadily and naturally, even if we ourselves are too close to see it.

What is a mother to be?

Washing hair, clipping toenails, packing lunches, reading stories, navigating feelings, ideas, and battlegrounds. I have so many people to be tender with right now that sometimes I forget how. Yet I know motherhood is about *being* something to someone, not just doing certain tasks *for* them. My expectation of what a mother is comes largely from my fortunate childhood experience with my own mother. But being a child at the time, I didn't always know what went on "behind the scenes," and my attempt to apply what I saw comes many years after I observed it.

Like a mother's love, memory has grace of its own, glossing over minor ups-and-downs. We recall our mothers in essence and episode, and this too is how our children will remember us: "She was like this . . ."; "She would always . . ."; and, "I remember once. . ." The memories come in flashes of small experiences—conversations or interchanges—that support the overall character. Our children learn our true character over time and will hold onto those experiences that are truly representative. The rest becomes less prominent or even drops away.

Some of our memories are more experiential impressions rather than words or narratives—the raw elements that have shaped us. One day while visiting home as adults, my sister and I rested on my mom's bed to talk. She played for me a recording of her own children in a choir singing *Baby Song of the Four Winds*, based on a poem by Carl Sandburg, in which a baby invites the wind to rock and care for him.[2] While we listened, we were surrounded by the same floral wallpaper that had always been there in my mother's room; the small handle on her headboard tap-tapped with any small movement as it always had; the sheer white curtains softened the light from outside with a familiar glow. My memory flashed back to a time many years before, when in this very spot wearing braids and a flannel nightgown, I listened while my mom read me a Trixie Belden mystery. For that moment I symbolically, yet tangibly returned to the comforting presence of my mother.

A person's essence is made up of attributes—qualities that belong to, define, or are characteristic of that individual. Inherent qualities or attributes are at the core of what we are to "be" as mothers and define the influence we are ultimately able to have. In the end, good mothering is much more dependent on *who we are* than the specific behavioral or parenting techniques we have employed.

Several years ago, after being asked to formally share my thoughts on "important qualities to develop in preparation for motherhood," I wrote this list in my journal: *charity, joyfulness, responsiveness, skillfulness,* and *firmness.* While such a list of attributes seems quite two-dimensional, it does serve as a starting point.

Charity is a crowning virtue made up of other attributes: "Charity suffereth long, and is kind; . . . beareth all things, believeth all things, hopeth all things, endureth all things" (I Corinthians 13:4-7). *Joyfulness* encompasses hope and implies a genuine delight in and appreciation for the opportunity of motherhood. *Responsiveness* requires an openness to spiritual promptings and to our children—their hopes, ideas, strengths, discoveries, fears, needs, and problems. (In many ways these go hand in hand. As it has been said, "The more faithfully you listen to the voice within you, the better you will hear what is sounding outside."[3]) *Skillfulness* involves knowing how to do things to care for a family—how to communicate and have relationships, how to set reasonable expectations for children according to their developmental level, how to obtain food and prepare it, how to organize (time, efforts, and surroundings), how to promote health and wellness, and so on. *Firmness* is conviction—the ability to stick to something that's right even when it's hard, because wise parental acts are often poorly received.* It is also personal integrity—the strength and discipline to live up to what we are asking our children to live up to.

We cannot demand respect or persuasively talk others into respecting us—even the attempt decreases credibility. But as we are respectable and honorable, as we are loving and wise as mothers, over time we will have our children's respect. As Emerson said, "As much virtue as there is, so much it appears; as much goodness as there is, so much reverence it commands. . . . God is described as saying 'I AM.' The lesson which all these observations convey is Be, and not seem."[4] The scriptures say "God is love"; there is no schism between the attribute in its fullest application and who God is (1 John 4:16); through divine grace and help and our own personal effort, this can be more and more true of us (see 2 Peter 1:4, 1 John 3:2).

Attributes of motherhood are qualities of the heart. Being who we need to be as mothers helps us effectively nurture. This process is part intentionality (striving toward ideals) and part preservation project. We must notice what's already there—what is perfectly present—and guard and maintain it.

Once I told my husband that I felt like a failure because I wasn't getting the kids places on time, our house was a mess, and I hadn't finished certain things I'd hoped to finish. Later in the conversation, I described the fun we had had on an outing: I had taken the kids and my elderly mom to a flower show at an upscale department store downtown. My mom had needed to sit down to rest and I wondered how the little kids would do with waiting for her—especially after the long lines they had already endured. We happened to be near the hat section, so I had the kids put on a little hat "fashion show" for their grandma. We were trying on wide-brimmed fancy hats, small sailor caps, fluffy winter hats, and laughing and parading around. We were careful with the hats, reasonably quiet (and didn't get thrown out of the store), and everyone was happy. As I related this story to my husband, he said, "Mary, *this* is where you shine." I realized I had been focusing on just my weak areas. But the delightful things that come easily and naturally to us are also part of the work we do as mothers and must not be left out of the equation. Much of what we need and want to be as mothers, we already are.

---

* See Hebrews 12:11.

18

Reflect or discuss:

1) What have you learned about motherhood from your mother? Who else has most influenced your attitude and approach toward mothering?

2) What attributes do you consider central to mothering?

3) What are your strengths as a mother? What are you best at? Where do you "shine"?

What is a mother to do?

Can one ultimately separate being from doing? Ideally, there would be no schism between the two and what we "do" would flow seamlessly from who we "are." In one sense, our actions can be nothing more or less than a reflection of our true character. Another reality, however, is that we are always in the process of becoming; therefore, what we do in a given instance doesn't always equate with what we ultimately know to do.

From my voice teacher I have learned profound lessons which, though originally given in context of vocal pedagogy, have held much wider application. One day she said to me, "Mary, be patient with yourself. You think because you intellectually 'get it' [understand this new technique] you should be able to immediately do it, but your body needs to be completely retrained in this point. It will come, but it will take time." This was like a shot of pure wisdom to me. I realized that also in spiritual matters I was often very impatient with myself; when my mind understood a certain truth about needing to *be* different in a certain way, I felt I should be immediately successful in applying it. But at times our *spirits* need to be completely retrained. It will come, but it takes time and practice. My voice teacher calls practice "woodshedding" (gathering, splitting and storing); she says that if we want the warmth later, we need to do the work now.

Mother is not only a noun, but also a verb and implies an object, or as the author Saint-Exupery might call it, someone to "tame." His profound children's book *The Little Prince* tells of a magical character who lives on a tiny planet and tends a single rose. Later in his travels, the Little Prince is shocked to find a garden with hundreds of roses. He says to them, "An ordinary passerby would think that my rose looked just like you . . . but in herself alone she is more important than all the hundreds of you other roses: because it is she that I have watered." His friend the fox, says, "It is the time you have devoted to your rose that makes your rose so important

. . . you are responsible, forever, for what you have tamed."[5] Those who we tend and water become our roses. The *way* we tend and water is important, but it is the fact that *we* were the ones who *did* the tending and watering that will make us "unique in all the world"[6] to them, and they to us.

Once at a community function I sat with a woman whose children were running circles around her. She seemed quietly exasperated and asked rhetorically, "What is a mother to do?" The question resonated in my ears: what *is* a mother to do? The same main acts of mothering are going on under roofs all over town and all over the world. They are common acts, but only because the needs they address are universal. By feeding, clothing, washing, and ministering, we raise the next generation and forge bonds that give meaning and framework to our lives.

The natural work of motherhood is made up of saving acts. They are acts that physically "save" others and spiritually save us. Christ taught: "Then shall the King say unto them on his right hand, Come, ye blessed of my Father, inherit the kingdom prepared for you from the foundation of the world: For I was an hungered and ye gave me meat; I was thirsty and ye gave me drink; I was a stranger and ye took me in; naked, and ye clothed me; I was sick and ye visited me. . . . Inasmuch as ye have done it unto one of the least of these my brethren, ye have done it unto me" (Matthew 25:34-40). He also told His disciples, "If I . . . your Lord and Master, have washed your feet; ye also ought to wash one another's feet" (John 13:13-15). Motherhood involves feeding the hungry, clothing the naked, ministering to the sick, washing feet—and all these things many times over. This type of service is built into motherhood. Once someone asked me, "Don't you wish you had a clone of yourself to do some of the work?" I thought about it but replied, "No. If I did, I think I'd throw her out." *I* want to do this work of motherhood; it is a holy work. What a wonderful gift that if we do those daily tasks before us, following that natural path necessitated by active motherhood, we will be found at the right hand of God (judged favorably by Him). That mothering involves ongoing, repetitive tasks is a hidden blessing; it provides us multiple chances to practice and learn to nurture with love.

Reflect or discuss:

1) Consider everything you have done in the last 24 hours, both big and small tasks. Notice that though it may not have exactly paralleled your mental "to do" list, it is likely longer! Notice how much you really do for those around you.

2) Repeat this exercise as needed (when you feel particularly convinced that you're "not accomplishing anything" or when others' appreciation seems particularly lacking or insufficient).

3~ ESTABLISHING VISION

Vision is a sketch, a path, and a vantage point. When as mothers we can stay in tune with why we are doing all that we are doing, the process of mothering holds much greater meaning. Though certain aspects of life may proceed differently than we initially hope or expect, much can unfold according to our greatest efforts and wishes, especially when we have an ideal in mind.

Any vision begins as a preliminary sketch—a vital beginning, but without full depth or detail. As a young girl, I had simple, happy views of motherhood, much like the sentiments expressed in this children's song:

> When I grow up I want to be a mother and have a family. . .
> One little, two little, three little babies of my own . . .
> And I will love them all day long
> And give them cookies and milk and yellow balloons.
> And cuddle them when things go wrong
> And read them stories and sing them pretty tunes.[7]

Though all of these things have come to pass, I now know that motherhood isn't all milk, cookies and cuddling. There are lessons to teach, boundaries to hold, problems to avert, and tasks to accomplish. Life's profound joys and messy complexities have filled in my initial sketch with both bright and shadowed contours, adding depth and richness to the picture.

Even more than a realistic depiction, however, vision takes us beyond our current reality—not in flighty, arbitrary daydreaming, but toward deeply held, inspired views of who we are and what we can become. As author James Allen states, "Dream lofty dreams, and as you dream, so shall you become. Your Vision is the promise of what you shall one day be; your Ideal is the prophecy of what you shall at last unveil."[8]

Vision leads us down a path to develop certain attributes, but attributes also contribute to vision. 2 Peter 1:5-9 teaches that without qualities such as diligence, faith, virtue, knowledge, temperance, patience, godliness and kindness, we lack true vision: "But he that lacketh these things is blind, and cannot see afar off" (1:9). In contrast, when we apply such virtues in the context of mothering, the vision we hold for our families can become less like a whimsical wish and more like a revelation, bringing in view the promises "afar off" (Hebrews 11:13).

"Where there is no vision, the people perish,"[9] but with vision, we gain purpose and stamina. Moses gained inspired vision about his role and possibilities for his people on Mount Horeb (also called Sinai). We too can gain vision of the vital role we will play as mothers and the possibilities for our families. As with Moses, moments of expanded vision in our lives are mountaintop experiences; we are suddenly able to gain true perspective as if from a vantage point. Not only does vision allow us to look up more closely at inspired, lofty possibilities, but also to look down to understand our present reality with more perspective.

Yet nobody climbs a mountain to stay at the pinnacle. Having once stood there, we gain context and perspective, but then we must descend and get to work. Day-to-day ups and down of parenting still occur despite our goals and ideals. The instant of realization is not the only high moment, but also its everyday application and culminating fruit.

A recurring mountaintop experience in our family has been meeting each new baby for the first time. Our boys gather around to see their tiny new brother and reverence the chance to hold him. As the months pass, however, the novelty of a new sibling intermittently gives way to moments of annoyance: babies grow into toddlers who crumple homework, knock down Lego towers, or accidently pee on the rug. There are waves of teasing, tripping, poking, hitting, and I am the weary referee. Then I stumble upon something magical: my toddler and preschooler sitting together each with an arm around the other on the bottom stair, or my teenage son listening to the radio and doing air guitar with his three-year-old brother. The family just might turn out okay, after all!

Once we are part of a family, vision is created much in tandem with others—especially one's spouse. Shared vision brings unity and power; distinct vision offers balance and complement. While my husband and I share many underlying hopes for our family, he brings a different emphasis, which I appreciate. The kids also have their own emerging vision. Our vision, therefore, naturally expands as our lives become more intertwined with others. Personal vision has generational influences as well—there is a legacy effect in the scope of our vision, be it broad or narrow, which is ours to build upon. The apostle Paul alludes to this in his letter to Timothy: he writes, "The unfeigned faith that is in thee . . . dwelt first in thy grandmother Lois, and thy mother Eunice" (2 Timothy 1:5) . . . . "Continue thou in the things which thou hast learned" (2 Timothy 3:14).

Reflect or discuss:

1) What is your personal vision of motherhood? What are some experiences or episodes that have shaped or captured this vision? How do other family members influence or enhance it?

2) What are your wishes for your family? (In other words, which qualities do you most want your family to have?) What efforts and choices are you currently making to support this vision? What outcomes have you seen? What are the most important next steps?

3) What roles do prayer and inspiration play in establishing or clarifying vision?

4~ Discovering personal metaphors

In the process of creating a detailed mental picture of our ideals for motherhood, powerful symbols may emerge. We may recall certain instrumental experiences or realizations that have inspired us. As we discover these central influences, we can select ways to represent them in our physical surroundings to keep us in tune with our goals on a daily basis.

My house is filled with symbols, though a person walking through the door may not recognize them. Two symbols relating to my vision of mothering are a Mary Cassatt painting over the piano and a heart-shaped rock sitting in a clay pot on my dresser. Though I don't always consciously notice them, when I do, I feel more centered and connected with my goals.

Mary Cassatt, an American Impressionist painter born in the mid 1800's, created multiple works depicting mothers and children. Her painting, *The Bath*, particularly struck me after I had just read Matthew 25 in a new way, realizing that the common acts of mothering—feeding, clothing, caring for sick children, and even welcoming children into our lives in the first place—were exactly those things mentioned in the scripture that qualify us to be on God's "right hand." Cassatt's painting, a mother washing her daughter's feet in a basin, came to symbolize this concept for me (in conjunction with John 13:13-17, where Jesus washes His disciples' feet). This was a powerful, unifying moment where I saw the interconnectedness of the purposes in my life: I was not an individual trying to please God *and* care for my family, I was an individual trying to please God *by* caring for them. When I see the painting hanging above our piano in the living room, it connects and elevates the small daily acts in which I'm engaged.

As for the heart-shaped rock, it was a gift, but one I had to make efforts to claim. On one of the first warm days of spring, when we could no longer be contained inside, I walked with my then five-year-old, Elias, and his two younger stroller-riding brothers to the park. He found the treasure of a mauve-colored, roughly heart-shaped rock and said it was going to be his present to me. He set it safely on the picnic table while we played, but when we left quickly to meet the next crop of brothers coming home on the bus, the rock was forgotten. About a block from home Elias suddenly wailed, "My rock!" At the next opportunity, after greetings and snacks and school day inquiries, we turned back for the park. Because there was little time for such a rescue mission with music lessons and dinner looming, Elias rode in the stroller and I jogged. While I jogged, I thought how it was a bit funny that I was doing all the work to retrieve a present for myself (though really it was so Elias could happily give it). I knew the rock might not even be there anymore, especially since other observant children had surely passed that way. But the rock *was* there. Elias jumped out of the stroller once we were near and dashed ahead to discover it.

Three days later was Mother's Day. I woke early with our two-year-old, Malachi, who was sick and crying in the night. I rested with him on the couch and soon heard the four older boys bustling in the kitchen. I opened my eyes occasionally when I heard certain suspicious noises or argument, but stayed put. Soon they said, "Mom, get back in bed!" Malachi had fallen asleep in my arms, so I gently set him down and climbed back under my own covers. The boys came in with big smiles and a cookie sheet for a breakfast tray. On the tray was a smiley-face made of toast and eggs (two fried eggs for eyes and toast cut out for a mouth), a cup of root beer, an origami flower, and, of course, the heart-shaped rock.

To me, the rock symbolizes many things. Just as I had to put forth effort to go back for the rock despite not knowing it would be there, much of the love we give as mothers requires work and the returns are never guaranteed. We give love with hope that it will be fully received and returned.

The "heart" is often used to refer to our core state of being or deepest feelings. A favorite book of mine, *A Heart Like His* by Virginia Pearce, describes how we can better recognize the state of our hearts from moment to moment—that a heart ready to receive and transmit God's love feels "enlarged, soft, open, [and] warm," whereas one less ready feels "shriveled, small, hard, closed, [and] cold."[10] Pearce compares the open-hearted feeling to her experience as a young girl doing creative dance in a flowing gown. I too remember the swelling, joyful feelings I had as a little girl dancing to classical music in my living room—I imagined I was a famous ballerina doing fancy leaps and pirouettes. Maria Callas, an opera singer known for her heartfelt rendition of each major role, recalled a stage director telling her, "Your hands should only do those things which are an extension of your heart and mind." Like any art form, our mothering can extend sincerely from the heart. Colossians 3:23 states, "And whatsoever ye do, do it heartily, as to the Lord, and not unto men." In this scripture, "heartily" literally means "with heart"—with effort, purpose, and love.

26

"Heartiness" also connotes strength, endurance and resilience, which motherhood will also require.

All of my treasured items relating to motherhood have their own story: drawings and notes from the kids, pressed and framed Mother's Day flowers, statues, quotes, old-fashioned irons used as bookends, and family photos. But the greatest symbols of all my mothering efforts to this current moment are my children themselves. They keep growing out of their shoes and they have light in their eyes, which must mean that some of my nurturing is going right. My husband and children are not blocking my way to some lofty personal ideal; they are major players in it.

Wishing for beautiful futures must not blind us to the beauty that is now. My youngest son is eighteen months. He has soft pink cheeks, light brown curls, and a rounded belly. His laughter is music—there is nothing more wonderful. To God, time is an eternal now; all is before Him in panoramic view. He looks over His creation, each aspect holding intricate histories and potentials, and says, "It is good." In fullness of vision, we too would see the present with appreciation, the past with understanding, and the future with hope.

Reflect or discuss:

1) Which symbols could represent your vision for mothering? Have any experiences, objects, photos, or quotes emerged as particularly meaningful to you?

2) Consider how these symbols could be displayed in a meaningful place to offer you reminders, inspiration, and perspective. Take steps to personalize your mothering space by decorating with some of these items.

II. Boundless Charity

On loving wisely

5~ CHARITY: THE GREATEST OF ALL

The scriptures tell us that of all attributes we could develop, charity is the greatest. Charity remains kind despite a long, difficult day; charity thinks well of others; charity responds wisely and well; charity rejoices, hopes, and endures. Charity is the essence of nurturing. As pure and enduring love, "Charity never faileth" (1 Corinthians 13:4-8); it is a key to success in parenting and all other areas of life.

Relying on our own personal resolve to love others or their inherent lovability, however, eventually may fail. Difficult situations arise that we may not be able to get our hearts around unless we seek God's help. Whether it is an exasperating moment with a child or a long-term, ongoing trial, the answer is the same. As we experience God's love in personal ways, we become more able to reflect it to others. [1] Mother Theresa, who formally dedicated her life to charitable service, described praying each morning until she felt God's love and then spending her day trying to share it.[2]

Even without an extreme situation or a named relief effort, we can develop charity. In the course of a normal day, multiple opportunities for charity present themselves. Also in the course of a day—especially certain days, there will be room for improvement. As we practice charity regularly, our capacity for charity will grow.

If always wishing for grander or more pleasant venues in which to serve, we limit our ability to engage in present opportunities.[3] For instance, at times I'm swelling with generous feelings in the abstract—I'd take in an orphan or go across the world and help with disaster relief—but I can't seem to pick up someone's sock (whose owner I've already committed to love) without intense irritation. We all have a primary sphere in which to labor; it is ours and ours alone. It is in this main sphere where our most vital exercise of charity must occur—as limited, unpublished or problematic as it may be.

Charity as seeing clearly

Most of us have grand views of loving, yet sometimes have difficulty loving the people right in front of us. Really loving others becomes easier when we are seeing clearly, as God sees. Paul's discourse on charity in 1 Corinthians 13 states, "For now we see through a glass, darkly; but then face to face" (v. 12). Similarly, the blind man experiencing healing through Jesus initially has clouded vision: he says, "I see men as trees, walking" (as indistinct moving forms or shadows). When Christ puts His hands a second time upon the man's eyes, "he saw every man clearly" (Mark 8:22-25). With God's help, we too can have our sight perfected to see others more clearly and love them more completely.

I was once told a story by the owner of a neighborhood flower shop reflecting a great lesson she had learned running her own business. She said that one day a salesman came to her shop selling a product she was not interested in. She declined, but offered kind encouragement. Years later, the same man came in, though she did not initially recognize him, to order wedding flowers with his fiancée. He said, "We are in your shop instead of any other floral shop in town because, several years ago when I worked as a salesman, you were kind to me. On a particularly difficult day, you were the only person who treated me like a human being." The flower shop owner told me, "Everyone deserves to be treated well—they are real people with homes and families. That's how I run my business and that's how I run my life."

Charity has everything to do with parenting, because it is by kindness that the deepest loyalties are won. Rather than seeing "through a glass, darkly," the flower shop owner saw "face to face": the people who walked through the door of her shop were real to her, not shadowed forms. While strangers may seem distant and therefore either unreal or romanticized, sometimes our own family seems too close to clearly see with any lens. But of all the people we should know are "real" with "homes and families" are those within our *own* families.

It has been said that "the highest type of discernment . . . perceives in others and uncovers for them their better natures, the good inherent within them."[4] Like a prism that finds "beautiful red and green and purple" even within plain light,[5] when we see others as God's children with infinite potential, our vision enlarges them and brings out their best. There is true transformative power in this, even a perceptible change in the recipient: the brightness illuminated cannot be hidden from a bystander's view. As a pediatrician, I have seen many families parading in and out of the clinic and at times have been struck by a child's particular "shine." It is as if all the loving care he or she has received becomes, for a moment, clear and tangible. These children may be sick, with tired eyes and the unceremonious dress of rumpled hair and crusted pajamas, but this light of a mother's love shines through.

Seeing clearly part II: celery and a cell phone . . .

In addition to seeing *people* clearly, charity also requires perceptiveness to situations and needs. Often, the "patterned" type of giving we do is based on perceived common wishes or universal needs. But more customized expressions of charity, which may be especially meaningful, come naturally to those who care enough to pay close attention.

In the early weeks of our dating, my now-husband caught me off-guard by his individualized kindnesses. Rather than the stereotyped roses or other more formal bouquets, he once brought me a small brown sack filled with freshly picked snapdragons. He had seen them growing outside a vacant building and remembered that I said my mom taught me how to "snap" (open and close) the "jaws" of such flowers during our walks together when I was a little girl. Another time he brought me a bouquet of celery. I had mentioned that I was making a recipe that required celery but realized I was out. His thoughtful attention got *my* attention!

Like a bouquet of roses, another example of "patterned" giving is the tradition of bringing meals to assist a family when a new baby has arrived. I have participated in this wonderful tradition both at the giving and receiving end. Still, there is power in noticing needs beyond such established traditions. With one pregnancy, I casually expressed my worries to a friend that I'd go into labor and not be able to contact my husband, since we owned no cell phone. I didn't expect anyone to resolve this problem for me—women had been having babies for millennia without cell phones, and I figured things would work out. My friend, however, insistently offered the use of her extra cell phone for the week. It was a simple thing, but it meant even more than the meals, the receiving blankets, and the baby outfits.

Meals, bedtimes, laundry, diaper changes, rides—the "patterned" giving of mothers—often seems repetitive and thankless in its performance. But is vital, like breathing, for it bestows upon children an overall sense of well-being. Still, the episodes that may allow our children to *feel* especially loved are the moments where even minute, unique needs are perceived and met. Having a larger family, sometimes I feel less able to meet customized needs of individuals; I must rely on inspiration and intuition to know when special attention is required.

Charity as generosity

Love is always a risk. What if we love our children more than they end up loving us? What if we care for others better than they care for us? What if we dedicate everything to our families and don't get the results we hoped for?

The scriptures say, "Cast thy bread upon the waters: for thou shalt find it after many days" (Ecclesiastes 11:1). Though some may say that, by then, the bread would be either soggy or moldy, I have found that often, miraculously, it is neither. I have also found that just as my "castings" more often come in pieces (small, individual acts of generosity) rather than whole loaves, it is also how the blessings most often return. The phrase "after many days" is also significant. After "many days" of underlying generosity and kindness to our children (which add up to weeks and years), we will see glimpses of its return, not only in isolated acts, but in their core being.

It is important to understand that if we equate the "return" of our charitable efforts toward a child with their complete compliance, we have no guarantees. Though God blesses us abundantly, His generosity never takes anything away—not our agency, our ability to learn, or our opportunity to prove ourselves. Truly generous action on our part will respect others' agency and foster their growth. Recently, when one of my sons particularly bemoaned having to do his Saturday work, I nearly came to his rescue, but then decided against it. On that occasion such supposed "generosity" would have robbed him of the lessons he needed most—that he could face large tasks and even gain a sense of satisfaction from completing them.

Sometimes our casting comes in forgiveness and repentance. In preparation for Yom Kippur, the "Day of Atonement," the Jewish tradition of *tashlikh* involves casting pieces of bread into a stream and watching the current carry them swiftly away, a symbol for past wrongs forsaken. The repentance process reminds us that we are in a continual state of reliance upon God's generosity. Part of being generous with others and ourselves is allowing the process of change and improvement piece by piece. It is recognizing someone "afar off"* and believing that a better version of them or ourselves is possible. To these future hopes we also cast our bread.

One risk-taking aspect of generosity is the willingness to "love first." Christ offered love that was not contingent upon being received—it was simply there. Such generosity in love inspires natural reciprocation. The Apostle John says of Christ, "We love him, because he first loved us" (1 John 4:19). How can we be "first" to love our children and spouse? In every situation or interchange, *someone* has to be.

Loving someone despite their shortcomings or "for no good reason"[6] means more in the long run than any affection that is won or earned. "For if ye love them which love you, what reward have ye? Do not even the publicans the same?" (Matthew 5:46). It is not easy to maintain fresh love for an uncooperative, thrashing child, a screaming teenager, or an occasionally insensitive spouse. Loving them more than the moment warrants will be our crust to cast.

Charity as goodwill

One who gave more than a crust to undeserving family members was Joseph in Egypt. After enduring much hardship including years of slavery and imprisonment—a path initiated by his brothers' jealous act many years earlier—Joseph finds himself in the position to rescue them from famine. He has become a ruler in Egypt and these very brothers come, not recognizing him, to beg for the chance to buy grain. Rather than taking the opportunity to punish his brothers or relish in their dependent position, he provides for them generously, though initially anonymously: "Then Joseph commanded to fill their sacks with corn, and to restore every man's money into his sack, and to give them provision for the way: and thus did he unto them" (Genesis 42:25). This first act of Joseph's goodwill comes after a point of personal realization and wrenching decision: he leaves his brothers' presence and weeps (v. 24). Later, he and his brothers fully reconcile—a process which includes more deep emotion and is enabled only by his pure goodwill toward them where there could have been

---

* This concept of promises "afar off" persuading and encouraging us comes from Hebrews 11:13. Consider also the story of the prodigal son: the father sees his son "when he was yet a great way off" and runs to welcome him (Luke 15:20).

vindictiveness: "And Joseph nourished his father, and his brethren, and all his father's household, according to their families" (Genesis 47:12).[7]

In the King James Version of 1 Corinthians 13, "suffereth long, and is kind" is written as one phrase, denoting a very special and enduring sort of kindness despite or in the midst of suffering. Jesus Christ consistently sought the blessing of those around Him, even those who caused Him to suffer. This was dramatically exhibited at the end of His life as He healed the servant's ear (cut off by Peter in His defense) and in His later plea, "Father, forgive them, for they know not what they do" (Luke 23:34). In speaking of His atonement, Jesus states, "[I] have suffered these things for all, that they might not suffer if they would repent" (D&C 19:16). Though we cannot rescue our children from all suffering, we can seek their good always, even in the midst of our own suffering, and even if they are a partial cause of it.

Charity as unselfishness

Charity "seeketh not her own"—at least not at the expense of others. This statement does not advocate giving up identity or becoming transparent, but rather forging an identity that includes a willingness to sacrifice for the best causes. The ultimate desired end is our soul "saved" (not given away), though we are reminded that any natural tendency to compete against others to achieve it will backfire: "For whosoever will save his life shall lose it; but whosoever shall lose his life for my sake . . . the same shall save it. For what shall it profit a man, if he shall gain the whole world, and lose his own soul? Or what shall a man give exchange in for his soul?" (Mark 8:35-37).

There are martyrs whose legacies instruct and inspire, but most of us are called to *live* for the cause. It has been stated that "we can lay down our lives for those we love not by physically dying for them but rather by living for them—giving of our time; always being present in their lives; serving them; being courteous, affectionate, and showing true love for those of our family and to all men."[8] We do not need compensation or recognition for this—it is our privilege. Of course, there are both wise and foolish sacrifices even on behalf of others, and discernment is required. In service of our children, we would wisely give up time, attention, pride, vanity, selfishness, materialism, and unhealthy habits. Yet sacrificing relationship with spouse for alliance with children, trading our own health or overall family functioning to meet whims or demands of a single family member, or skipping needed mentorship to preserve calm in the moment may be foolish.

Certain moments may be harder than others as we strive to demonstrate charity, particularly in the context of our own physical discomfort, fatigue, or sadness. Christ Himself faced such struggles. Right after He learns of the death of His cousin John, Jesus attempts to go "by ship to a desert place apart" (Matthew 14:13), but a multitude follows Him. Rather than sending them away, He is "moved with compassion toward them" (14:14) and heals the sick among them. The disciples then suggest dismissing the crowd, but Jesus miraculously provides a meal for all 5,000 of them from a mere five loaves and two fishes. Likewise, we will have miraculous moments when, despite our own extremity, we will nourish and carry others.

Reflect or discuss:

1) In what ways have you been able to feel God's love for you? How can you more fully or regularly experience and share this?

2) When have you experienced charity or pure love from another person? How did this make you feel?

3) Think of and record specific examples of charity you have witnessed, given, or otherwise experienced that demonstrate the components of seeing clearly, generosity, goodwill, and unselfishness.

6~ HOW IS CHARITY OBTAINED?

The scriptures contain directives and implications about how one obtains attributes such as charity. Though it is a gift, charity can be sought. We are told to "seek earnestly the best gifts" (D&C 46:8). Earnest seeking includes learning about, praying for, qualifying for, and choosing.

Learn. One important preliminary and ongoing way to "seek" is to study. In the scriptures we have not only definitions and exhortations about charity, but perfect patterns of it. Once I was trying to figure out how to make a sewing project for which I had no pattern or written instructions. Despite being quite inexperienced in sewing, I was able to comprehend the necessary process by taking apart an old item with similar construction—I never would have guessed the shapes of the pieces required. Similarly, scriptural examples of applied charity have profound significance and relevance. In the Christian tradition, we have the perfect pattern in Jesus Christ—one who exemplified and embodied charity. Studying Christ's life, teachings, and interactions will allow deeper comprehension than reading about love in the abstract. Similarly, we can observe and learn from the charitable acts of those around us.

The scriptures direct us to learn "by study and also by faith" (D&C 88:118). To have any impetus for study, we first need to believe charity is something worthwhile and possible to acquire. If Saul could become Paul, if Alma the younger could go from rebellious son to prophet and wise father, we too can make major transformations through divine grace and personal will. We too can "have this hope" that, more and more, "we shall be like him" (Moroni 7:48). Right before Moroni's wonderful discourse on charity, he teaches, "Christ hath said: If ye will have faith in me ye shall have power to do whatsoever thing is expedient in me." Moroni goes on to ask, "Has the day of miracles ceased? . . . Behold I say unto you, Nay; for it is by faith that miracles are wrought." (Moroni 7: 33, 35, 37).

Perhaps the greatest miracle is personal transformation. In the book of Ezekiel, the Lord gives a promise to the latter-day house of Israel: "A new heart also will I give you, and a new spirit will I put within you; and I will take away the stony heart out of your flesh, and I will give you an heart of flesh" (Ezekiel 36:26). You and I can be part of this promise.

Pray. We are specifically instructed that one necessary step in "seeking" a gift is praying for it. Not just wishing for it, but asking for it—

and not just as a casual request. Moroni teaches, "Wherefore . . . pray unto the Father with *all the energy of heart*, that ye may be filled with this love [charity]" (7:48, emphasis added). On several occasions, when I have been in the midst of a difficult interaction with my kids, I have offered a silent prayer to be blessed with charity. When I have remembered to do this, it has always helped. In my morning and nighttime prayers, though somewhat removed from the thick of that day's experience, I speak with God about who I wish to become and ask for guidance and help. Charitable inclinations do not necessarily come naturally to me or anyone else; *wanting* to *want* to be charitable sometimes is the first step.[*]

Qualify. After stating that we should pray for charity with full energy of heart, the above verse goes on to say that this type of love is "bestowed upon all who are true followers of his Son, Jesus Christ," which implies that charity can come as a natural product of discipleship. If we really are "true followers," we can more likely qualify to obtain charity (yet note that charity is still "bestowed," not earned). Charity is always a gift, always something more than we can obtain on our own. We cannot force feelings of charity within us, but such inclinations will be more likely to rest upon us if we qualify. In Galatians chapter 5, we learn that love is a "fruit" of the Spirit; if we are worthy of the companionship of the Holy Ghost in a given moment, one fruit (product or result) of that may be an associated sense of charity within us. In one scripture, the Lord states, "Be faithful and diligent in keeping the commandments of God, and I will encircle thee in the arms of my love" (D&C 6:20, see also John 15:10). Following God not only qualifies us, but also provides experiential learning. Jesus taught, "If any man will do [God's] will, he shall know of the doctrine" (John 7:17). As we practice or "exercise" charity, as we pay the price for it over time, our love can become more and more similar to God's love—"brighter and brighter until the perfect day" (D&C 50:24).

Choose. We may be worthy of charity and have the gift available, but still we need to choose to receive it. Several scriptures emphasize our active

---

[*] The Book of Mormon contains a wonderful discourse on building faith, which applies to building other attributes as well: "If ye will awake and arouse your faculties, even to an experiment upon my words, and exercise a particle of faith, yea, even if ye can no more than desire to believe, let this desire work in you, even until ye believe in a manner that ye can give place for a portion of my words" (Alma 32:27). If we exercise a particle of charity, or have a desire for charity, this can grow within us.

role in the process of obtaining charity. Colossians 3:14 states, "And above all these things, *put on* charity"; elsewhere we are directed, "*Clothe yourselves* with the bond of charity, as with a mantle [cloak]" and "*Clothe [thy]self* with charity."[9] It seems significant that *we* are the ones directed to do this "clothing." Though charity is partly a gift, it is also dependent on our initiative. Sometimes our hearts will be changed suddenly and dramatically, but more often in small increments by compiled daily acts and choices. To continue to grow in charity, though it may have become part of our nature, we must keep choosing it over and over again.

How can we foster charity even with all the demands and realities of life? Alma 5: 26 asks, "If you have experienced a change of heart, and if ye have felt to sing the song of redeeming love, . . . can ye feel so now?" If you have felt charity swelling within you in the past, can you feel so *now*—now when your kids are fighting, the dinner is burned, your husband is late, or whatever the situation may be? And these are rather trivial matters, but what about even larger ones? "Who shall separate us from the love of Christ? Shall tribulation, or distress, or famine, or nakedness, or peril, or sword?. . .Nay, in all these things we are more than conquerors through him that loved us. For I am persuaded, that neither death, nor life. . .nor things present, nor things to come. . . shall be able to separate us from the love of God" (Romans 8:35, 37-39).

When I began studying voice with my most recent teacher, she had me practice only exercises for months. She said that until I could learn to "get the sound right," the words, the rhythms, and other details of the music would distract me from proper technique. I saw there was an upcoming vocal department recital and I wanted to try to prepare a piece for it, but she said I wasn't ready. When I later started on my first arias, she would sometimes insist I walk away from my music (even if it meant making up the words) so I would learn to trust what I knew and not get so fixated on counting and pronunciation. When I worried about small mistakes or inaccuracies, she'd say, "Music is not about that, you are going about it in the wrong way. The *sound* is what's most important." An audience could be moved by any beautiful melody, if beautifully sung.

For me, this idea of "getting the sound right" translated very personally into a metaphor for charity. Loyalty to technique and sound were akin to loyalty to principle and action. Like "getting the sound right," I wanted to consistently "abide in his love" (John 15:10)—to stay there and operate from there—rather than possess a fragile kindness that could suddenly turn sour or crumble in an instant.

Companion virtues and virtuous companions

Charity does not operate as an isolated virtue, but comes hand in hand with others, particularly faith and hope. In a discourse comparing the relationship between faith, hope, and charity to the legs of a stool, which together give a stable foundation and lead to good works, Dieter Uchtdorf states, "Faith, hope, and charity complement each other . . . as one increases, the others grow as well."[10]

As we seek these companion virtues, it can be immensely helpful to have a circle of supportive family and friends who seek common goals. I have the blessing of a good and supportive family and have been surrounded by friends who inspire the best in me by their own goodness and generosity. One friend, who I met several years ago when we chaperoned a class fieldtrip to the zoo, brought my mother flowers after hearing that her sister had died. My next-door neighbor, an active 70-year-old and former nun, gave me keys to her house and car and said, "My house is your house, my car is your car." My childhood friend, who has nine kids and now lives over an hour away, brought me dinner when I had a baby. Another childhood friend, already working more than full-time as a certified nursing assistant, helped me in caring for my mom after her stroke. I have met several inspiring friends through the Relief Society—a women's group within The Church of Jesus Christ of Latter-day Saints whose motto is "Charity never faileth." Founded in March 1842, this international organization has millions of members who work in their local areas to provide "relief" within their own congregations and the wider community. In this group, I have had the opportunity to learn and formally teach, to serve and be served.

Once when my husband was out of town, I somehow lost my keys during church. I was stranded there with six children, one of whom was supposed to sing in a choir festival at a church across town right after our meeting. I was literally encircled by several women offering assistance. One dropped my son off at his choir festival. Several others helped me search for the keys. Another, who had driven to church separately from her husband, offered me her car so I could go with my older boys and hear my son perform in the festival. Another offered to take my two youngest children home with her for a couple of hours despite having four boys of her own and company coming for dinner. Others called and offered additional help. When my husband returned two days later, I told him about the whole thing and even got my purse and turned it upside-down to show him how there were no keys—and the keys fell on the carpet in front of me. I felt embarrassed and humbled, but mostly just grateful for the great kindnesses I had received. I'm sure that strongly supportive organizations exist in other denominations and in other communities, but feel blessed to be part of the amazing LDS Relief Society in my own small congregation in Minnesota!

Evolution of charity

Both in specific situations and overall, charity often emerges in the shape of an hourglass. In its early stages, it is wide and hopeful and vulnerable—an idealistic wish to "save the world." When the details of this good wish hit up against limiting realities within individuals and contexts, then comes a point of constriction—a realization that one cannot do everything. Within this narrow segment often comes a crisis of character, where one must face and overcome tendencies toward disengagement, despair or burnout. When the opening is found, there is a possibility of wiser, more directed service that is particularly efficient and productive. What allows this freeing expansion are wise boundaries. I am still learning this.

When I was nine months pregnant with my fifth son, Malachi, I felt strongly about gathering in as a family; our time together felt measured since I knew my attentions would soon be concentrated on the new little one. School had just let out and a new family moved in across the street. The kids seemed to watch us from the window: as soon as we set foot outside, they would come over. Just like my kids, they wanted to tell me their thoughts and be pushed on the swing; they too needed motherly reminders not to run with sticks or fight over toys. The parents were never around and I was sheepish about seeking them out only to ask them to teach or enforce social boundaries with their children. Other neighborhood kids saw the action at our house and came too. I felt like I was running a daycare—which would have been okay if I had chosen to.

One reason I felt so conflicted is that I love children and I saw that these kids were needy, but right then I wanted to be focusing on connecting with my own children. I tried to process it with my husband, but he didn't feel the conflict and would say things like, "So send them

41

home," or "Does it really cause that much of a problem to have them around? The kids all seem happy playing together." I felt guilty sending them home because I worried it was a mean or selfish thing to do, so it seemed that doing it would ruin my afternoon anyway. I even remember one day taking the kids out to play and, upon seeing the neighbors making their bee-line over, saying, "Kids, we are going to the store." So there I was, dragging the kids shopping unnecessarily to escape from the neighbors.

I saw how ridiculous this was. I wanted to be giving and loving without limits; I wanted to model kindness and a welcoming attitude and did not want to be an angry person. Yet I felt conflicted, because something I valued was being thoughtlessly taken away. I anguished over this seemingly little situation because it was a test of my heart and generosity. I prayed over it and received answers piece by piece. One night, saying what I thought was an unrelated prayer for help as a mother to have a heart big enough to welcome and love all the children God sent to our family, I realized that these neighbor children had been sent to our family too, in their own way. Their intersection at the edges of our family was tangential, yet I wanted my heart to expand to be able to welcome and love them. Talking with my sister helped me distill truth from this inward crisis—she could relate to my struggle and felt protective of me. She said, "This is a special time. Guard it. It *does* take something away from your kids to have to share you right now." She was right. To the neighbor kids, these few days were like any others; but to me they were historic—the ending of one era and ushering in of another.

Though I initially hadn't been able to stand up for myself, I took courage from my sister's wise advice and set some boundaries. I requested that the neighbors *ask* if we were available to play before coming over, and I gave myself permission to tell them no. I realized too that my husband's comments, which initially to me had seemed unsupportive and dismissive, were also part of my answer—they gave perspective for the times we did decide to have the neighbor kids over. I was able to say to myself, "Even if the kids are sharing me and I am sharing them right now, yes, it really is not much of a problem to have them here and, yes, we are all happily playing."

Not every moment was perfect. Once they headed over when we started roasting hot dogs for a special family night. After I told them we were unavailable to play, they laid in the grass at the edge of our yard and watched us all evening. Though I recognized I could not control everything, it gave me peace to know that I could control some things, including choosing to love these children and creating boundaries that made it more possible. Through this incident I was able to clarify other important boundaries, such as communicating and upholding our own family rules with whoever was in our home or yard. In setting these boundaries, I was able to regain my loving feelings—and therefore model kindness, but also sincerity, conflict resolution and the upholding of standards.

Some opportunities to love and serve we can't afford to miss, particularly within our own family and in special cases where we feel divine direction or assignment. These bounds provide focus more than limitation; with them the effectiveness and meaning of our service expands. To honor our pre-existing commitments, we may need to forego others. In his short, wise text entitled *Arriving at Your own Door*, psychologist Jon Kabat-Zinn writes, "Saying 'yes' to more things than we can actually manage to be present for with integrity and ease of being is in effect saying 'no' to all those things and people and places we have already said 'yes' to, including perhaps our own well-being."[11]

We each have a primary sphere—our very own land of opportunity, in which we are already positioned to serve. As Mother Theresa taught, one doesn't need to go to the leper colonies in India to find someone to minister to. The greatest serving and proving ground is the one we are in. It is sufficient. Taking on or wishing for projects from other pastures while neglecting our own is a sad mistake. If you have ever dreamed of crossing the globe in a relief effort, start by repackaging your generosity and applying it to your present sphere. Your own family warrants the firstfruits of your energy, generosity, patience and love. It is okay to save some "precious oil" for those you love best (see John 12:3-8)—they will not always be with you, but for now they are yours to love and care for.

Perfect charity at home cannot be made prerequisite for wider service in the neighborhood, the community, or the world, or we'd never do any— but charity at home must not be neglected or sacrificed for charity outside it. Mordecai Ueshiba, founder of the Japanese martial art *aikido* (translated as "the art of peace") said, "Heaven is right where you are standing, and that is the place to train."[12] Our primary sphere does not have to be our only sphere, but it is our most important one, because there we are irreplaceable.

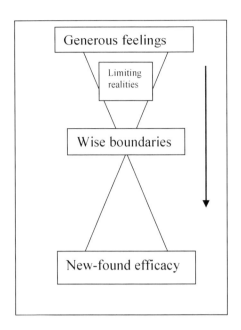

Reflect or discuss:

1) What have you done to seek charity? What has been the result? What more would you like to do?

2) At this time in your life, which part of the above hourglass diagram do you identify with the most?

7~ FINDING AND SETTING BOUNDARIES

God's love is boundless.[13] It is unlimited in depth: "God so loved the world, that he gave his only begotten Son" (John 3:16). It is unlimited in scope: "For he maketh his sun to rise on the evil and on the good, and sendeth rain on the just and on the unjust" (Matt 5:45). It is unlimited in duration: "Yea, I [the Lord] have loved thee with an everlasting love" (Jeremiah 31:3). Though we can seek to emulate God's perfect love, as humans we are limited by our mortal condition. Our expression of love *will* have bounds.

Anne Morrow Lindbergh observed, "My life cannot implement in action the demands of all the people to whom my heart responds."[14] Acknowledging this truth offers realistic hope, allowing us to see the many needs around us without reflexively dulling our heart's response. When observing another's need, possible responses may include providing direct help, orchestrating help, praying on another's behalf, or merely feeling compassion without direct involvement. Any of these may be reasonable and appropriate depending on our role in a given situation. A limited response to the needs of others could reflect uncharitable tendencies, but in certain contexts it may reflect necessity or wisdom. Honestly discerning the factors that govern our placement of boundaries will allow us to draw them more wisely.

In finding boundaries, we must be surveyors of our own emotions, abilities, and desires, as well as God's desires for us. Just as the irregular borders of countries often have complex histories and wind around established landforms, our boundaries will be affected by facts of our past, present and future. The borders of our own lands will never exactly match those of another. My Jewish grandmother had twelve kids and often made three different menu choices for each meal to keep everyone happy. In contrast, I pander to tastes only on special occasions and often find myself saying things like, "Too bad, that's what's for dinner." Each of us has reasons for laying the boundaries as we do. Like the occasional shifting borders of countries, states, and territories, new circumstances may also require revision of personal boundaries. We may need to draw them more widely or narrowly than we have in the past to apply lessons we have learned.

Discernment of healthy boundaries can be challenging because a sense of stretch does not always indicate the error of overdoing; sometimes it is a merely a growing pain. C. S. Lewis stated, "If our charities do not at all pinch or hamper us, I should say that they are too small."[15] Quite often, meaningful giving *will* stretch us. We cannot reasonably wish for a bigger heart while entirely resisting this stretch. Rarely when I decide to do a service for someone, let alone make dinner for my own family, is it completely convenient and smooth. Still, when service results in irritation or grumpiness, displaces our children (takes away not only what they want but what they need), or significantly disrupts the structure that enables our healthy functioning, we likely have crossed an important line. Often we learn only in retrospect, by missing the ultimate "prize" or seeing we have made a foolish trade; but fortunately, this information can inform future choices.

Valuable information can be obtained from our inward reactions to situations. Certainly, if our default interpretation of any troublesome interaction is always that we have to give or accommodate *more*, we run the risk of accepting or allowing unhealthy behaviors of those around us. An older woman once told me that her several grown children "hadn't amounted to much." She said, "When my children were young and growing I tried to do everything for them. I tried to be loving and accepting in everything, but I was wrong in this. They became rude and irresponsible children and now are rude and irresponsible adults." Hearing her story reminded me that maintaining reasonable expectations of others does fall within, not outside of, the context of charity.

Negative or pinched feelings (tension, resentment, or anger) may be a warning that something is wrong—and not always within *us*. Sometimes something needs to be taught, changed, confronted or communicated.[*] Ultimately, it is most charitable to others to hold them to certain standards. Though perhaps less comfortable at the time, it maintains vision and charity for who they can become, not only who they currently are. It fosters growth, rather than stagnation or dependence.

---

[*] Though overlooking weaknesses may be a component of charity, some behaviors simply cannot be accepted, and some self-protection may be warranted until true repentance and change are exhibited. We do not need to wait until a person changes to forgive them, but we likely should wait to trust them.

Our inward *positive* reactions also instruct and direct us about how to enact charity. If not distracting from central purposes, some embellishments—those that utilize our personal gifts, respond to another's unique preferences, or allow expressions of devotion—can elevate a task to pure joy. Sometimes it is difficult to predict what will bring joy and what will feel like drudgery, but since our energy is limited, we might as well choose to serve in ways we enjoy (or to a point where enjoyment is still possible, and where we could still feel to give more)—unless particular need or divine direction point us elsewhere. Service joyfully given will more naturally be joyfully received.

Acts of service tend to remain enjoyable when we proceed with honest diligence, yet not "run[ning] faster than we have strength." Our "strength" in a certain area at a certain time may be influenced by experience, skill, health, and simultaneous demands on our time and resources. Learning to pace ourselves requires a certain meticulousness and loyalty to primary purposes. My husband, a distance runner, periodically checks his pace by counting steps over time; he knows his approximate stride and can estimate his speed even over a small segment of a race. Even though some guesswork is involved because multiple factors play into speed and endurance on a given day—trail conditions, weather conditions, and his state of health—this careful pacing still keeps him within range of his goals. If in our lives we have enthusiasm without thoughtful strategy, we may forfeit the best "prize" by expending energies on areas of lesser importance.

Once I taught a lesson in church for which I spent hours preparing. I had a beautiful display of visual aids and intricate handmade handouts. But when I stood to speak, I only fumbled through—I had not pondered the topic sufficiently to speak with clarity on it. I was embarrassed and disappointed, realizing that I had focused on the outward display while neglecting the main task of teaching. "Extras" can be nice if time and energy allow—particularly when they are expressions of love and share special gifts—but they cease to be so if they are done at the expense of more important things. We must let go of unnecessary elaborations that distract us from the "weightier matters" (Matthew 23:23).

Limits that are drawn with divine guidance preserve our energy for the best good we can do. We have the ongoing privilege to seek God's help and direction. Sometimes there is no clear heavenly guidance on a matter despite its being sought, and then we must act according to known principles and reason. As my mom would tell me, "God has given us our minds, so we should use them." The scriptures direct us to "be anxiously engaged in a good cause, and do many things of [our] own free will, and bring to pass much righteousness" (D&C 58:26-27). We can choose to be someone who notices and responds to needs, who pitches in, who lifts and encourages, who relates to others in a loving rather than a hurried way. Many opportunities for good are very simple and arise right along our path. May we pray for eyes to see them.

Honoring boundaries

Once we have discerned important boundaries, how do we communicate and honor them? Boundaries are best expressed personally, clearly (giving accurate expectations), honestly (as soon as known), respectfully, and confidently (though revisions may come later). *The Caregiver Helpbook* states, "Because only you know what your limits are, setting your limits is up to you. Setting limits is a form of self-respect and honesty."[16]

There is a natural tendency to emotionally "push away" what we can't deal with at the moment—especially if we feel bad for saying no or making someone wait. In such situations, our wishes to love more and better can somehow translate into anger, avoidance or awkwardness. Feeling unable to demonstrate care in a certain way, we briefly lose the sense of care—like a lost hope. In these instances, if we could let go of the preconceived idea of what the outward charitable act must be or "look like," perhaps we could hold on to the inward charitable feeling. For example, when my husband gets home I try to greet him enthusiastically rather than with discouraged apology, even if I wish I'd prepared or accomplished more things.

When opportunities to serve exceed our capacity, we still can maintain a loving, compassionate heart—a wish for others' good—and draw boundaries confidently, without guilt or despair. No justifications, apologies, or detailed explanations are needed (or prudent, especially because they may invite argument!). In Mosiah chapter 4, we are told we must not judge or turn away a "beggar" (recognizing that we all rely on God for our very breath and all are "beggars" before Him), but that if we have nothing to give, we can say in our hearts, "I give not because I have not, but if I had I would give" (v. 24).

When we *do* have something to give, it is one of the choicest opportunities of life. To be on God's errand is to come to know Him better and to see Him in the faces of those around us. This truth, taught in Matthew 25:31-40, is also conveyed by 19th century poet James Montgomery:

> A poor wayfaring man of grief
> Hath often crossed me on my way,
> Who sued so humbly for relief
> That I could never answer, Nay.
> I had not power to ask his name,
> Whither he went, or whence he came,
> Yet there was something in his eye
> That won my love, I knew not why.

Subsequent stanzas describe encountering others in different contexts of need—hunger, thirst, poverty, injury, imprisonment and these needs being answered: "But my free spirit cried, 'I will!'" The final stanza reads,

> Then in a moment to my view
> The stranger darted from disguise;
> The tokens in His hands I knew,
> My Savior stood before my eyes!
> He spake; and my poor name he named:
> 'Of Me thou hast not been ashamed;
> These deeds shall thy memorial be;
> Fear not, thou didst them unto me.'[17]

Another 19th century writer advised, simply, "Be kind; everyone you meet is fighting a hard battle."[18]

My third son, Spencer, is named after Spencer W. Kimball, the former LDS Church leader who taught, "God does notice us, and he watches over us. But it is usually through another person that he meets our needs."[19] One evening shortly after I had my fifth baby, my then four-year-old Spencer said, "Mom, I want to make you some soup." He gathered vegetables from our garden and spices from the cupboard. I sat back and rested and advised. He painstakingly chopped carrots with a butter knife because I wouldn't let him use anything sharper. We boiled the soup in a large pot for the family dinner that night. To me, it tasted like pure charity.

The best boundaries:
> *are guided by our values and priorities
> *take into account our emotions and inward responses
> *help preserve health, well-being and balance
> *are informed by context, common sense, and divine guidance
> *do not rob others of growth experiences

Important for limit setting:
> *choice and personal responsibility
> *honest introspection
> *clear communication
> *early recognition

Reflect or discuss:

1) Are there areas in which you need to clarify your boundaries to yourself or others?

2) How can you better honor limits that protect your health, safety, and growth and promote these in others?

3) Are there any areas in which you have prematurely drawn boundaries that may restrict your growth?

III. MOMENTS OF MOTHERHOOD

On darkness and light

8~ MOMENTS MATTER

I have heard it said that, "The joy in motherhood comes in moments."[1] Many of the tests of motherhood come in moments, too—vital moments that can turn the tone and tide of our families, perhaps just for a day or week or month, but possibly even for generations.

I remember ten years ago, sitting and rocking my two boys in a big, soft recliner, singing a familiar and poignant song: "Turn around and you're two, turn around and you're four, turn around and you're a young boy going out of the door."[2] I stopped singing then because of my tears: my oldest son *was* four at the time, and according to the song, the next step was "out of the door." Now that same four-year-old is a teenager. Last week when he asked for the car keys to help load up the family after church, he commented with a smile that, given another year, he'd also be able to drive away.

Before I knew that I was pregnant with my seventh child, and as my 18-month-old wriggled out of my arms and toddled away, I thought maybe that was the end of my child-bearing. I felt in near-mourning for the days of that slow, steady rocking where there is no pushing away. Later, realizing that I was again expecting, I considered it God's mercy to anticipate at least one more little baby to rock. But I have come to know over time that there are many ways to rock a baby: playing soccer in the backyard, listening to a story idea, passing over a moody comment. The way of relating is constantly transitioning into something new, which in time will also pass.

In her book, *Being the Mom: 10 Coping Strategies I Learned by Accident Because I Had Children on Purpose,* Emily Watts writes of her surprise to calculate that she had likely made over 9,125 peanut butter sandwiches in the course of her mothering years.[3] Despite the work involved, realizing that a finite number could be placed on my remaining family meals, I felt sentimental rather than overwhelmed. Though certain interactions seem endless, they are not; we have only a limited number of opportunities to rock a sick baby, give a bath, walk to the park, and share in mealtime and bedtime. Sometimes our children are the ones to wisely recognize that endings come. One night my eight-year-old pleaded to be able to sleep on the floor in his next older brother's room; he said, "*Please,* Mom. We're playing this really fun pretend game that we've been playing all day. And I think I'm about to be done with pretend games. Pretty soon I'll be old enough that they might not be so fun." Despite how it delayed bedtime, that night I opted to let them continue the game.

Our family has the tradition around Christmastime of reading together in the evenings—not only the Christmas story in Luke 2, but also other classics like Dickens' *A Christmas Carol*. On this particular night we had read the personal account of a weary 19th century public servant, who described the cheer he received from late night Christmas Eve carolers who came to sing under his window. Later, after finally getting the kids in bed and feeling the full weight of my accumulating fatigue, I heard my older boys call, "Mom, Mom, come here!" While my first inclination was to give an exasperated "It's bedtime" speech, I held my tongue and walked upstairs. My boys sang "The First Noel" to me with their pure, young voices. While they sang, they smiled like sheepish angels. And to think I almost missed it!

One of my favorite days with my boys was an autumn walk to a neighborhood creek. My oldest son Jacob's goldfish had died and he got the idea to send it down river on a burning bier in true Viking style. My husband was out of town—I could have said no to the whole thing, but I said yes. We walked about a mile to the creek with the two youngest riding in the stroller and Jacob's fish wrapped in aluminum foil in the stroller basket. He constructed his boat out of bark and sticks and, though his fish was too soggy to burn as dramatically as he had envisioned, the kids felt it was momentous enough. After the ceremony, the boys ran up and down the banks of the shallow creek and claimed islands, gathered rocks, and found other natural treasures. It was a joy to watch them play, so creative and carefree. When my newly potty-trained son wet his pants, we had to go home, but it had been a grand afternoon.

I always know I am in a good frame of mind—one free of stress and rightly focused—when I want to linger: to watch my children sleeping, to sing them one more song, to hold them just a little longer. Our desire to stretch the moment is a way to mark and appreciate all that it uniquely and beautifully contains. Often I wish I could just enjoy my kids and let them "be kids," rather than always having to try to make them behave, follow through, or demonstrate something. For example, though I feel a tugging duty for safety's sake and for teaching respectful treatment of furniture, I admittedly love watching the joyful faces of my children when they jump on the bed. (Have they noticed that sometimes I pause before I stop them?) Though we cannot abandon propriety to the point of irresponsibility, and though choosing to let a given moment stretch *too* long can lead to complications later (compression of important future moments), savoring the moment sometimes requires that we suspend protocol. One can always find *some* reason to put a stop to anything: "you might get dirty," "you are wasting [supplies, water, etc]," "you will ruin the furniture," "you are missing sleep," "you will get off schedule," "you should be doing [homework, chores, practicing, etc.] instead." Unfortunately, it can be easy to get caught in patterns of rushing or scolding rather than savoring. Spending time in emotional distance or persistent annoyance—time that otherwise could have been spent encouraging, sharing, or expressing love—this is the ultimate waste.

When I have no patience to linger, when I have a tense heart, when I feel completely out of touch with the idea of savoring—these are *not* times I'm in tune with the greatest truths of life. My interactions in such contexts not only ruin themselves, but often spill into others in their aftermath. At such times, I feel like the laborer who fails at the last hour (Matthew 24: 46-50)—I hold out and hold out in patience and cheerfulness, but then all of a sudden, my patience runs out. The tones are harsher than I'd wish, the words less faithful or true, and my movements more brusque. Of course, it is not really the "last hour" when these moments occur, but being the sudden impetus prompting self-reflection and disappointment, it's the most recent thing to have happened.

A few summers ago we went as a family to Yellowstone. After several stops to see relatives, a night of camping at Grand Teton National Forest, and more than 36 cumulative hours in a tightly packed Suburban, we sat in the ring of tourists watching and waiting for the moment that Old Faithful would blow. This geyser, discovered and named in 1870, erupts every 35 to 120 minutes when pressure builds up sufficiently to send the water as high as 185 feet above its opening.[4] Though predictions can be made, no one ever knows exactly when the spray will come. Much of the area just around Old Faithful and other geysers is blocked off, because boiling water lies just beneath a thin-crusted surface. In this geyser I saw a piece of myself that disappointed me—an intermittent brittleness of mood and unpredictable (even to myself) caustic sprays of emotion. Do geysers ever calm or die out? If so, how?

When I read the book *I Didn't Plan to Be a Witch*, by parenting expert Linda Eyre, I felt comforted but a bit disillusioned at her admission: "I keep thinking that I will get over these witch attacks [out of control moments], but even though I must admit they are happening less often, I'm still susceptible."[5] Though we can theorize about "geyser moments"—these flashes of surfacing, unfiltered frustration or impatience—when all is rosy and under control, we all know that such moments feel desperate and not fully within the realm of reason. Perhaps geyser moments cannot be circumvented once and for all, but certain strategies can diffuse them somewhat, either making them less out of control or less frequent. If we can begin to identify the triggers that start us simmering, we will less likely be suddenly blindsided by our own strong emotions. And if we can identify resources early, perhaps we will feel less desperate in the moment.

"Anyone can become angry—that is easy," Aristotle writes, "but to be angry with the right person, to the right extent, at the right time, with the right motive, and in the right way—that is not [easy]."[6] Furthermore, what we often label as "anger" is rather our common-pathway experience of *various* negative emotions. As a mother, I find that much of what feels to me like anger is actually rooted in other emotions: worry, fear, disappointment, frustration, or a sense of powerlessness. As stated in *The Caregiver Helpbook,* "Emotions serve a purpose. They are messages, telling us to stop, look, and listen, to pay attention to what is going on."[7] If interpreted accurately and responded to effectively, even negative emotions can alert us and enable us to more fully understand and accomplish our true aims. Our selection of which feelings to foster and how to give them expression shapes our character and our experience.

Recently, I agreed to take two of my boys back to the neighborhood creek to release some crayfish they had caught the previous day. The creek was down a short path from the road and I hadn't thought to bring a stroller for the two younger brothers. My four-year-old was mad at me because I said "no" to doughnuts on our previous stop and he refused to get out of the car, so I allowed the older two boys to go ahead to the creek. It was not terribly deep or fast flowing so I didn't worry too much for their safety. But I knew the magnetic powers of that creek; though I had clearly said this was just to be a quick crayfish drop, soon the shoes and socks would come off, then the boys would be in, waist deep.

My almost-two-year-old cried to get out of his car seat, so I took him out and held him at the roadside. Soon, he wanted to get out of my arms and run—a developmentally appropriate wish, but I was six months pregnant and couldn't chase him well, and it was getting harder and harder to hold him. So I strapped him back into the car seat (not well-received). As I watched the minutes roll by, I started fuming on behalf of my crying toddler as much as myself. I tried calling to the older boys, but could not be sure they heard me. I also could not physically carry or contain both younger boys along the path (normally, my four-year-old would just come along, but I couldn't assume it today, given his sour mood).

Leaving kids in the car went completely against my usual judgment, but finally I decided my only recourse was a fast trip down the path alone. I jumped out, locked the car doors, and jogged down to the creek. Indeed, the boys were wading in the creek. I said very firmly and clearly, "Your brothers are crying in the car. You were not to get in the creek. Come NOW!" and I jogged back to the car. Then I waited again, and fumed again, and wondered what in the world I should do to them when they returned.

After ten more minutes they came running down the path, shoes and socks in hand. But in that ten minutes, I had come to some conclusions. They were young boys—it was hard for them to let the crayfish go and, though the wait was long and inconvenient for the rest of us, they likely felt they really had hurried and prematurely wrenched themselves away from the creek. My anger had stemmed mostly from conflicting wants and needs and the difficulty enduring them. As for the younger boys waiting with me in the car, they had quickly recovered. My four-year-old Malachi had wisely suggested, "Why don't you turn on some music?" They were smiling and bobbing around in their car seats to Jazz 88.5 by the time their brothers returned. So what I said was, "How was the creek? How did it feel to let the crayfish go?" And then simply, "It was very hard to wait in the car all that time. I wish you had been faster." They offered sincere apologies and we moved on. It was enough.

Though I could have appropriately given the kids a consequence for dawdling, such as making up the extra time taken, in this instance I chose not to. More important than the exact arrangement was: 1) shifting to take into account their perspective, 2) accurately stating my feelings about the impact of their actions, and 3) avoiding an overblown response.

Child psychologist Haim Ginott wisely taught,

> There is a place for parental anger in child education. In fact, failure to get angry at certain moments would only convey to the child indifference, not goodness. Those who care cannot altogether shun anger. This does not mean that children can

56

withstand floods of fury and violence; it only means that they can stand and understand anger which says: 'There are limits to my tolerance.'"[8]

He goes on to acknowledge that anger is a "costly emotion," but its productive expression can bring about insight and resolution. Though strong negative emotions occasionally have their place, none of us wants them to take a very big place. None of us wants to go through the parenting experience too frequently downcast or defeated, irritated or irate.

As mothers, we often must sort through our emotions while "in motion," since family life does not easily pause. If not addressed, negativity, stress, hurry, sadness, disappointment, and confusion can impair our ability to nurture.

A sacred dream is told of a prophet who sees himself in a dark and dreary place. He prays for God's mercy and then sees across a field a beautiful, white tree "whose fruit was desirable to make one happy." He goes to partake of the fruit and it is the sweetest thing he has ever tasted; it fills his soul with joy. He looks around for his family and calls to them to come also and taste this fruit. He sees many others coming along the path to the tree, but some become lost in obscuring mists of darkness, others leave the path after heeding mocking voices from a crowd in a large ornate building, and others fall into a polluted river that runs along the field. Only those pressing forward, clinging to an iron rail leading to the tree, are able to finally reach it. They fall down and then eat the ripe, wonderful fruit. A heavenly messenger tells the meaning of the dream: the tree and the fruit represent the love of God, "the most desirable above all things" and "the most joyous to the soul."[9]

Could this joyous, nourishing place be found, not just as an ending or culmination, but as a place from which to operate? What forces obscure our path? How can we overcome these obstacles and preserve our ability to feel God's love and nurture our children? The following chapters suggest ways to identify and cope with stressors, in part by utilizing resources, making changes, and maintaining perspective.

Reflect or discuss:

1) What are some moments you cherish or have cherished as a mother? Consider taking time to record the details of these memories in your journal.

2) Which situations present the greatest challenge?

9~ Specific triggers and tools

Why give attention to, rather than ignore, disappointing interactions? "To predict a geyser's next eruption," the Yellowstone website states, "observers analyze past information such as intervals between eruptions, length of eruption, and the character of an eruption." Though difficult interactions may seem baffling or unpredictable, acknowledging patterns allows early recognition, preparation, and demystification. As we develop awareness and skill, we can begin to recognize escalation, work to resist or reverse it, and, over time, develop increased temperance—the ability to withstand intense pressure without behaving "unseemly."[10]

While no model completely captures human experience, organized analysis helps us better understand it and respond to it. In my work as a physician, for example, one important model used with pediatric asthma patients is the "asthma action plan," which compares symptom severity and required treatment to a traffic light. If such an "action plan" were used to characterize emotional state rather than ease of breathing, it may look something like the table on the following page:

"Addressing Stress" Action Plan ("ASAP")		
	You may feel:	You may need:
Green Zone	Relaxed, happy, fully functional	To KEEP GOING . . . Continue in maintenance mode nourishing mind, body, and spirit.
Yellow Zone	Tired, tense, moody, jumpy, over-serious	To SLOW DOWN . . . Consider -taking a nap -stepping away -doing something that refreshes you (possible activities:_____ _____) Purpose: to return to maintenance mode activities in the Green Zone.
Red Zone	Desperate, extreme, paralyzed, tearful, volatile	To STOP AND. . . -Make an important change -Get help (trusted resources:_____ _____) -Cancel unnecessary plans/commitments Purpose: to make your way through the attentive Yellow Zone, and then back to the comfortable Green Zone

Asthma patients can typically identify specific triggers that set off their symptoms such as colds, allergens, or environmental irritants like smoke. Similarly, we can often identify triggers that threaten our emotional state, such as sleep deprivation, negative thinking, or over-scheduling. If we address stress right away, often we can work to alleviate it or anchor ourselves to weather it.

The following chapters identify emotionally disruptive "triggers" including negative thoughts, overwhelming demands, and deep disappointments, and offer strategies to surmount them. These tools focus primarily on personal response, because this is where our control lies, yet change, accommodation, and repair are often warranted in others too.

Though in every scenario we have choices to make and actions to take, we are not alone in this. God is always there and accessible in the moment through prayer; His help is always pertinent Also, other strong women have overcome similar challenges and can mentor and support us along our way.

Reflect or discuss:

1) Create your own version of the "addressing stress" action plan. Which activities refresh you? When needed, who can you go to for help?

2) As you read chapters 11-13 discussing specific triggers and tools, particularly note those that best relate to your experience, as well as others that may come to mind.

10~ Overcoming negative thoughts

At every moment we are presented with both darkness and light. Unlike optical illusions where perspective can flip between one interpreted image and another with neither being more correct than the other, certain life perspectives are more healthy and true than others. Though negative emotions, such as grief over loss or anger over injustice, have their rightful place in life, negative thought processes tend to be false and destructive, only detracting from, interrupting, or sabotaging our deepest wishes.

My kids have a dress-up box for play stocked with costumes and hodge-podge props of superheroes, knights, cowboys, and uniformed workers. One Halloween, my son was putting together a costume and selected from the box a scary "grim reaper" mask attached to a black hood—I've always hated it. Though sheer black fabric covered his face, my son could see through the mask in the light of day. But when, against my advice, he tried to wear it to go out trick-or-treating, he couldn't see a thing and nearly tripped down the front steps. That convinced him to take it off. We as mothers should also stop in our tracks when we notice dark views taking over. A shroud of darkness makes even nice days unpleasant, and hard days nearly unbearable.

We live in a time of high expectation for outward performance and appearances, a time of criticism and sarcasm, a time of impersonal and disconnected living. Even if we don't embrace societal trends, they affect us. We are increasingly faced with inward battles of "despair, discouragement, despondency, and depression."[11] The scriptures foretell a time of "seducing spirits" or philosophies (1 Timothy 4:1) and "perilous times" (2 Timothy 3:1) when "men's hearts shall fail them" (D&C 45:26-29). Social science literature confirms that such trends are now occurring: "International data show what seems to be a modern epidemic of depression, one that is spreading side by side with the adoption throughout the world of modern ways."[12] While some teeter at the edge of negative mood—and in this position must actively cling to health by attending to important needs, such as ensuring sleep, decreasing stressors, and reaching out for support and nurturance—others suffer major depression, a deep affliction requiring professional help.* These are particular challenges of our day: "For we wrestle not against flesh and blood, but against principalities, against powers, against the rulers of the darkness of this world" (Eph 6:12). How we fare in this struggle affects our children as well as ourselves. Psychologist Michael Yapko has coined the phrase "hand-me-down blues" to represent the way negative thinking can be passed from parent to child. Inheritance is not just about genetics, but also about modeled choices and perspectives. We as parents frame the perspectives of our children; *our* voices will have contributed to create the inner dialogues of thought that echo in *their* heads.

Discerning the truth

One day, approaching the checkout line at Costco after passing a near-life-sized R2D2 robot, my five year-old began wailing, "*My* robot! *My* robot!" Despite an upbringing that I think has discouraged materialism, the sight pushed him over the edge where he could not contain his longing. At that point, my newborn woke up and began screaming to be fed. My two-year-old just started crying, because it seemed to be what everyone else was doing. With all eyes on me, I felt particularly dumpy in my sweats. Since our departure had been jump-started by my elementary school-aged kids missing the bus and needing a ride, I hadn't had time to shower before running out the door to start my whirlwind of errands. According to all outward appearances, I wasn't doing so well—but an inside observer may have said I was doing splendidly. After all, it was before noon and I had already fed and clothed six children, participated in family prayer and scripture study, overseen morning chores and instrument practice, gotten the school-aged kids off to school (bundled for sub-freezing weather—no small feat), and taken the younger ones along on necessary errands, all the while feeling generally hopeful and cheerful inside.

Judging situations honestly—with compassion rather than harshness toward ourselves and others—can help to combat dark thoughts. Compassionate honesty is a more godly perspective and takes intentions,

---

* Though it is not the purpose of this text to address depression in depth, one distinction between low mood ("dysthymia") and major depression is the degree of functional impairment and risk to safety caused by one's emotional state. Recommendations from caring and skilled professionals, wisely applied, can be very helpful. (See also "A Broken Vessel" by Jeffrey R. Holland *Ensign,* Nov 2013).

effort, and context into account. "For man looketh on the outward appearance, but the Lord looketh on the heart" (I Samuel 16:7).

Each moment can be "framed" or interpreted in multiple ways. Paintings in an art museum are placed within ornate, beautiful frames for a reason—it accentuates and becomes part of the art. The scenes of our lives should similarly be placed in the best and most fitting frames, not consigned to ugly, unflattering ones. Ultimately, it doesn't matter what anyone around us thinks is going on, it doesn't even matter so much how we ourselves reflexively judge what is going on. The real truth takes everything into account: context, intents, and outcomes. Divine guidance can help us get a clearer view of the best frame or interpretation: "For the Spirit speaketh the truth and lieth not. Wherefore, it speaketh of things as they really are, and of things as they really will be; wherefore, these things are manifested unto us plainly, for the salvation of our souls" (Jacob 4:13). In most cases, the hopeful perspective is the true perspective.

As a pediatrician, I have heard all kinds of negative, misguided parental interpretations of childhood behaviors. Once a new mother said to me, "My six-week-old is lazy. All she does is sleep or sit around and watch TV." I tried to help this mother see the wonderful things her newborn could already do and her role in providing a stimulating, nurturing environment. When I am able to teach parents more accurate developmental expectations and thereby "reframe" their perspectives, it helps them care for their children better and love them more easily. As a mother I am also learning these things day by day.

I remember a night when my older kids had brought me to frustrated tears by being uncooperative and difficult. I had a newborn at the time and toted him around through all my herding and scolding. I looked at his pure face and said to him quietly, "*You* are my innocent one." But hearing my own words caused me to pause—suddenly I saw how innocent we all were. It has never been hard for me to know this about very young children; regardless of my fatigue level, I have never seen malicious intent in a crying baby or even an exploratory toddler. But, until that moment, I hadn't acknowledged a similar innocence in myself or my older children. It was true for all of us: usually we do the best we know at the time.

Martin Seligman, psychologist, author, and pioneer in the positive psychology movement, notes how many of us have ingrained habits of "automatic" thoughts and styles of explaining situations that affect our overarching mood and perspective. For example, those who judge negative events as temporary rather than permanent in duration, specific rather than pervasive in scope, and impersonal rather than personal in source have more success at maintaining a positive outlook.[13] He advocates "thought catching," an ongoing awareness of the explanations we are creating about the events around us, and greater self-accountability for accurate, fair assessments.[14] Similarly, branches of psychotherapy, such as narrative therapy, emphasize the importance of the underlying story we inwardly tell ourselves to explain our life's course. For example, our stamina may be affected by the degree to which we acknowledge God's hand in our lives, find underlying purpose or meaning, and perceive our own power to navigate.

Of course, care must be taken in explaining events. Just "thinking positively" does not repair real deficits or problems; often there is also work to be done. Long-standing or pervading problems may require coping mechanisms, support systems, and endurance. Problems stemming from mistakes may require forgiveness and change. Still, positivity is more than just a descriptive angle; positivity carries transformative power.

Assuming positive intent, for example, often helps inspire others to own or adopt it.* In her book *Happy Kids, Happy You,* Sue Beever presents an interesting hypothetical scenario. Having just come upon your child being less than gentle with the new baby, how will various responses affect outcome? If you assume he is jealous and trying to harm the baby, you will likely send him away, which perpetuates further negative feelings and behaviors. Instead, if you assume positive intent—that the child wants to interact with the baby but just doesn't know how, you react very differently. Perhaps you invite him to gently hold the baby, involve him appropriately in the baby's care, and show him which toys the baby may like. The author goes on to explain, "Whether your assumption about your child's intention is right or not, it influences you to behave in ways that reinforce it."[15] The self-fulfilling nature of positive expectancy helps bring about our own success as well.

We can reinforce positive thinking not only by our chosen focus, but also in the words we use to describe our experience and the people with whom we choose to discuss it. Blanket statements like "everything is going

---

* Such self-fulfillment occurs on the negative side as well; accusations of negative intent also influence others' interpretation of events and self-perception.

wrong," are rarely true; we can revise such assessments to be more specific and accurate.

Once when feeling inadequate and overwhelmed, I gained peace by creating a list of reconciling statements:

I cannot make my children turn out a certain way, but I can influence them, love them, and patiently teach them.

I cannot ensure my children's continual health, safety, or comfort, but I can teach and adopt healthy behaviors and safe practices. Even difficulty will teach them, as it teaches me.

I cannot supervise or monitor my children every minute, but I can provide responsible, reasonable supervision and trust that God also watches over them. I can trust them to learn even from mistakes.

Sometimes the highest mood we can achieve in a given moment is neutrality, with our heads just above sea level. Sometimes bare bones affirmations are all that apply: "at least the house didn't burn down"; "at least my two-year-old is healthy and strong enough to constantly run away from me"; "at least yesterday ended and the sun is rising."

All internal and external communication bears fruit; certain thoughts spoken bring productive change, while others only injure and sabotage our intentions. Often what we term "venting" does not purge negativity, but rather feeds it. Brigham Young taught,

> In all your social communications, or whatever your associations are, let all the dark, discontented, murmuring, unhappy, miserable feelings—all the evil fruit of the mind, fall from the tree in silence and unnoticed; and so let it perish, without taking it up to present to your neighbors. But when you have joy and happiness, light and intelligence, truth and virtue, offer that fruit abundantly to your neighbors, and it will do them good, and so strengthen the hands of your fellow-beings.[16]

But how do we work through or rid ourselves of negative thoughts, aside from just choosing to "drop" them? What if this unwanted "fruit" won't fall? "Strong feelings do not vanish by being banished,"[17] but not every feeling needs to be acted upon. Sometimes restraint or filtering is warranted so our actions remain in line with our deeper objectives.

Healthy processing of difficult emotions can occur while pondering (perhaps while doing something else like cleaning or exercising), journaling, or praying. In any context, prayer is a pertinent, reliable resource. Not only does God offer perfect guidance at the right time and in the best way, He is always available and has real power to change hearts and situations. There also may be a place for a carefully-chosen confidante or wise advisor—ideally, a supportive person objective enough not to complicate the problem, someone you trust to give the advice you know you need, or perhaps even better, one who will express confidence and provide encouragement, saying, "You'll figure it out; you can do it."

My sister Laurie has always been one I can talk to. We share history and perspective, and often seem to be having parallel challenges. Our conversations build layer upon layer, insight upon insight, and I always seem to learn something. During one particular discussion, Laurie shared insights she had gained from the scriptures about discerning truth. She first pointed out that, because not every perspective leads to healthy, worthwhile ends, we should "believe not every spirit [or philosophy], but try the spirits whether they are of God . . . for love is of God" (1 John 4:1-8). She then referred to several other verses she had found about delineating between darkness and light. Darkness confuses and distracts, diminishes confidence and potential, damages, limits, invites poor choices, bears poor fruit, erodes faith, estranges from God, and leaves us empty. In contrast, light clarifies, edifies and strengthens, invites goodness, bears good fruit, builds faith, brings us to God, and satisfies and fills. As Paul writes to the Thessalonians, "Ye are all the children of light, and the children of the day; we are not of the night, nor of darkness. . . . Prove all things; hold fast that which is good" (I Thessalonians 5:5, 21). (See endnotes for Laurie's scriptural references on light[18] and darkness.[19])

Discernment, the gift to rightly judge truth from error, is a universal endowment instilled through our divine parentage—one that can be fostered or suppressed by the patterns we establish.[20] From the beginning, the God of creation separated light from darkness (Genesis 1:4), and so must we in our own sphere, over and over again.

Discipline

After having "proven" or discerned light from darkness, next comes the disciplined choice to "hold fast." We have power to resist and reject false ideas and negative forces; we must resist the temptation *not* to hope.[21] Choosing to foster thoughts and actions that bring desired results is like strengthening the right muscles for good posture. As a result, we "that were sometime alienated and enemies in [our] minds" will be able to "continue in faith grounded and settled" (Col 1: 21-23).

God does not force change, but enables it according to our desires and willingness. Regardless of the setbacks we face, over time our character and ability will reflect our deepest wishes. As the poet has said,

> You will be what you will to be;
> Let failure find its false content
> In that poor word, "environment,"
> But spirit scorns it, and is free. . . .
> The human Will, that force unseen,
> The offspring of a deathless Soul,
> Can hew a way to any goal,
> Though walls of granite intervene.[22]

Reflect or discuss:

1) Select an area in which you currently struggle to feel positive. Divide a paper into three columns, the first entitled "What I'm feeling," the next "What is true," and the last "What is productive" and record your responses.

2) Who are your trusted advisors—those who encourage and empower you? How can you increase your interactions with such individuals?

3) What pursuits enliven you and bring you joy? How could you more regularly bring these energizing, uplifting influences into your life?

11 ~ DEALING WITH DEMANDS

As the main character states in the novel *These is My Words*, "My life feels like a book left out on the porch, and the wind blows the pages faster and faster, turning always toward a new chapter faster than I can stop and read it."[23] Sometimes it feels like life is going too fast to process, let alone appreciate.

The baby is crying, the dinner is burning, the phone is ringing, the kids need shuttling, the errands need running, and my projects remain undone—all this sense of busyness and press and a simultaneous sense of standstill, as if nothing is getting accomplished. Our time proceeds with multiple interruptions and interjections; always doing or "about to do" something, we can no longer identify which tasks interrupt which. Facing multiple demands, we lose context—everything coming at us feels noxious, even the good things. We may feel momentary resentment toward anyone requiring or requesting anything, and perhaps toward ourselves for our struggle. It is difficult to be kind and patient in spite of personal desperation.

Demands become overwhelming when high in number or intensity, or when our current state limits our ability to meet them. Stakes feel higher in demanding situations—we have less tolerance for things not going right, for things getting undone and needing to be redone, for gifts or services given at high cost but then unappreciated. Unfortunately, all of these scenarios are commonplace in parenthood.

As mothers, we cannot even begin to chronicle or predict the unbelievable situations that do or may arise. One day, I took my mom to a routine doctor's appointment at a large medical complex. Her physician decided he wanted to order several tests, which necessitated traveling to multiple locations within the complex. Because I had my baby and toddler in the stroller, and my mom couldn't go long distances with her walker, a transport aide came to push my mom in a wheelchair while we walked alongside. The time of the appointment had stretched much longer than expected and it was approaching time for me to leave to meet my kindergartener at the bus stop. After the EKG (which I reviewed and saw nothing terribly alarming), the nurse said my mom could not leave before results were reviewed by the ordering physician. I explained that, if so, I'd have to leave my mom for a short time to quickly meet my five-year-old son, who'd be dropped off on a street corner in 30 minutes. She said, "You're not going to leave your mother alone, are you?" At this point, I could not contain my tears. I politely told her, "I am only one person." Not only was the appointment already stressful on many levels, but the compounding demands were irreconcilable. There was no one to easily call to come to the rescue.*

Some trying moments for me have occurred with the discovery of mischievous or "exploratory" deeds and their aftermath at already overwhelming times—scenes one would expect of a vandal or an untrained puppy. I remember one day trying to have a special time with one particular child—a neighbor had given him some rhubarb, and he wanted to make a strawberry-rhubarb pie and freezer jam. We set out the ingredients, but when the time came to add the strawberry Jell-O for the jam,[24] it was missing. My first thought was honestly, "Oh great, I bet someone [namely, my two-year-old at the time] is wandering through the house and sprinkling it around" It was an extreme thought and I knew it probably couldn't be true; but as I went to investigate, it was true. Red Jell-O powder was everywhere, especially on my white comforter cover that I loved. And in the humidity of a Minnesota summer, the powder had started to liquefy. It felt like more than I could do to face this, but I sighed a very big sigh, soaked the linen, resumed pie-making with my older son and then spent the rest of the afternoon de-jelloing my house. Though I usually have kids help clean up messes they have made, this time I thought better of it.

We all face demands, but what makes them suddenly seem overwhelming or too much? It may be a sense of ineffectiveness, the stacking of multiple demands all at once, fragility in the moment, or seeming irreconcilability. Many factors, sometimes simultaneously, contribute to our feeling suddenly overwhelmed and often patterns arise. (See the table on the following page.)

---

* The happy ending was that I left for 45 minutes to pick-up my son and grab lunch for all of us while my mom read magazines in the waiting room. We were finally released (after all the tests and discussion of them) six hours after the appointment had begun. On the way home, we went through the pharmacy drive-thru and picked up prescriptions and my kids confused this with the bank drive-thru where they give lollipops. My 78-year-old mother and my kids were chanting, "We want lollipops! We want lollipops!" and my mom and I were laughing hysterically.

Stress factor:	Examples:
Perceived ineffectiveness	Trying to get a child to do something important when they are resistant (homework, practicing, chores)
Stacked demands	Engaging in the family balancing act: any mixture of work, meals, rides, schedules, school, extra-curricular activities, fighting children, begging children, big messes—especially during already busy times (when caring for a newborn, during the holidays, prior to the arrival of guests)
Fragility	Having to function and interact with others through times of sickness, tiredness, hunger, or recent emotional injury (in ourselves and/or others)
Irreconcilability	Wanting two conflicting things; feeling pressure to decide; working to corral uncooperative children in the context of a strict time commitment; facing competing needs

I recall one evening feeling exasperated as my children ran riotously about, despite many initially kind reminders. One child, in his jumping and playing, jarred the ground sufficiently to knock a wooden statue off the piano and break it. The sight of the statue—a mother holding her young son, both figures now decapitated—seemed to be a sad symbol for my desperate feelings at the time. I saw that I needed to repair the moment as much as the statue, and other similar moments, where small frustrations had escalated to crowd out true perspectives.

Finding deliverance

In times of difficulty, God often helps us either by modifying the situation or providing added strength. Occasionally, burdens are entirely lifted, but more often they are reduced or we are strengthened "just enough." This load reduction may come by a mere shift in perspective, inspired solutions leading to revised methods, or by help from others. Obtaining deliverance often requires action on our part, such as viewing a situation differently, making specific personal or collective efforts, asking for help, or letting go.

Gaining perspective. Coming to expect, focus on, and eventually embrace necessary demands better enables us to meet them. It is only natural that as we have become "responsible" adults, our responsibility has become greater. The "balance point" of all we manage has moved farther from ourselves and has come to include many people and things. Recently I was shopping for a violin bow with my son and learned about "balance points." While beginning players often do better with bows that have a balance point close to the "frog" (the end held by the hand) because they feel lighter, more advanced players gain greater versatility—the option to do more elaborate or nuanced bowing styles—with a balance point farther out from themselves. Sometimes it seems like I'm not getting any better, but in reality, as the days go by I'm handling more and more and thereby becoming equipped to handle more and more.

Selective focus—either narrowed or expanded to acknowledge the "bigger" picture— helps us accomplish needed tasks. Recently, the kids and I went to the Science Museum and saw the movie *Hubble*. It told of an astronaut needing to do fine repairs on the orbiting spacecraft despite all his bulky gear. He had to take out 36 tiny screws wearing gloves like oven mitts. He described using the "Zen" approach: he only focused on the screw he was turning at the moment—not the one before, not the one after—as if the others did not exist. Perhaps we as mothers would better meet our challenges if we didn't lump them and face them as a running list, but one by one. Alternatively, we may take courage from *grand* views, by connecting to our ultimate purposes. I imagine the astronauts on the Hubble mission also took courage by looking into the vastness of space or at the grandeur of the swirled earth below.

Acknowledging the goals and purposes behind our actions naturally fuels our stamina. I know of a woman who dedicated each mile of her first marathon to a unique individual who had been instrumental in her life. This optimized her efforts and endurance. Similarly, when we dedicate our efforts to those we love—particularly God Himself—suddenly those efforts increase in value and meaning. Difficulties or "bumps in the road" do not seem so jarring, and our errand becomes simplified, yet more effective. Instead of working to please everyone, we work to please One. In any task, willingness makes all the difference; the scriptural injunction, "whosoever shall compel thee to go a mile, go with him twain" (Matthew 5:41), illustrates how, through willingness, one transforms from slave to benefactor.

Exerting personal effort. In addition to reframing, some situations call for reform—merely thinking differently may not be enough. For example, the summer my sister and I took on the task of clearing out my mother's home of forty years, we had a literal mountain to move. Having faith to move it (see Matthew 17:20) consisted not of a mere pronouncement followed by an effortless glide, but rather persistently lifting and carrying it, armload by armload. The exertions involved in such overhauls purify our desires, build our strength, and necessitate reliance on that God who grants us "breath that [we] may live and move and do according to [our] will" (Mosiah 2:21).

In our efforts, pacing and rest will be required. There is a direct correlation between rest and resilience; when we are running on little sleep, everything seems much more dramatic and difficult. During a recent backyard picnic, my three-year old quite uncharacteristically went around kicking and hitting people, despite several reminders. Then he walked over and poked a big hole in my sandwich. I took him inside to his room, which he cried about. When I returned after two minutes, he had fallen asleep on the wood floor. Tiredness can play such a large role in our mood and functioning! Mosiah 4:27 states, "And see that all these things are done in wisdom and order; for it is not requisite that a man should run faster than he has strength. And again, it is expedient that he should be diligent, that thereby he might win the prize; therefore, all things must be done in order."

Fortunately, small inspired changes often bring about large results. My junior high cross-country coach taught us that passing an opponent often was a matter of just a few steps of added effort. He'd always say, "Three quick steps!" In life we are not competing with others, but we are on a specific course and need to focus and push ahead at certain times. Even in the complexity of our families, real solutions may be a matter of small but significant adjustments. The scriptures tell us, "By small and simple things are great things brought to pass; and small means in many instances doth confound the wise" (Alma 37:6).

Receiving help. Asking for help feels risky because it may be refused, expose our weaknesses or fallibility, or partly relinquish our control of a situation. While we may need to be selective about who we ask, how we ask, and what we ask, our burdens can be lightened and our experience enriched as we accept help from others. Our circles of support may include family, friends, neighbors, or even kind strangers. At times professional help may also be needed, particularly when unresolved past or present issues affect functioning or wellbeing.

Circles of support benefit both givers and receivers. Once I received a surprising phone call from another mother—a very capable, accomplished woman—who was crying and beside herself. Her kids were driving her crazy, multiple things were going wrong, she didn't know what to do, and she felt hopeless and desperate. I listened and before long we were both laughing. Talking together completely reversed her outlook and made us both feel less alone. The fact that she would call made me feel I had a true friend. Another time I felt alone and desperate and called her. Then, when her washing machine broke, she let me do her laundry at my house. I have never been so happy folding clothes.

Being a caregiver for my mother has provided certain bittersweet lessons that also pertain to mothering. *The Caregiver Helpbook*, despite being written for those taking care of elderly family members, has been particularly applicable. It addresses communication issues, taking care of oneself as caregiver, and how to ask for and receive help. Sometimes we *feel* like we are asking for help, when in reality we are not being clear. We wish others would merely perceive it—and yes, perhaps if they were more inspired or more sensitive or thoughtful, they would. Lines from a poem by Stevie Smith capture a tragic miscommunication: "I was much further out than you thought/And not waving but drowning."[25] When feeling overwhelmed with everything, we often don't have the presence of mind to even identify or characterize the specific tasks at hand. Particularly at times when outside help is needed or anticipated, the *Caregiver* book suggests listing all necessary tasks, identifying ones with which we'd feel comfortable receiving help, and then letting people select from several options the ways they'd like to help. This also avoids awkward or hurt feelings when people sincerely seem to want to help, but always seem unable to do what we happen to ask. Even the exercise itself can be therapeutic—it shows us how much we really *are* accomplishing and which tasks we truly "own" or choose to own.

When my husband was out of town with my older boys at a scout camp, my mom got sick and needed to be hospitalized. When the time came to bring her home, I knew she physically could not climb into our larger car that fit all the car seats, so I would need to find someone to watch the younger kids while I picked her up from the hospital. The first person I called was not available. Though they expressed a wish to help and a genuine concern, I felt embarrassed for asking and also desperate and stuck. As I thought and prayed about it, however, I realized that I just needed to keep asking until someone said yes and not take it personally if they said no—my problem was real and I just needed to persist to find the right help to solve it. In this case, though I had to make ten calls before finding help and I ended up having to go two hours later than I would have wished, I did find help to accomplish the needed task. As it has been said, "God does notice us, and he watches over us. But it is usually through another person that he meets our needs."[26] Usually people genuinely enjoy and benefit from helping and will help if they can. Those who can but don't are missing out on a wonderful opportunity, and in general, I'd rather not have help from an unwilling party anyway.

In our own families, because certain work needs to be done and certain training needs to occur, sometimes we need to rally even the less-than-willing helpers. Just after my sixth baby was born, family was visiting and I was inadvertently left to host rather than be helped. Somehow I had been left with nine kids to supervise, dinner needing to be made, toys and luggage strewn everywhere, and a screaming baby needing to nurse. I started to feel resentful of the situation, but it suddenly dawned on me: *I have at least six able-bodied helpers who are sitting around playing.* Of course, I would have rather had someone else to "rally the troops," but right then it had to be me. I said, "I need to nurse the baby right now, so I'll need everyone's help getting things ready for dinner. I need you to work on dishes, you to clean the entryway, you to set the table, (etc.). . ." By the time the other adults returned, everything was calm and under control, but they were very apologetic to learn how overwhelmed I'd initially felt.

Letting go. In contrast to all we wisely embrace, much of the work of motherhood is the act of letting go—allowing the less essential to drop away, adjusting plans and expectations, giving way to growth and change,

75

accepting what is and what must be. Letting go may occur outwardly in a physical sense or inwardly in a spiritual sense and may last a long or short season.

Mormon handcart pioneers traveled westward with their most basic necessities and prized possessions limited to a few square feet. Still, particularly in crossing rugged and steep terrain, more unloading and lightening became necessary to complete the journey. Henry David Thoreau, writer and naturalist who self-subsisted for two years in the woods by Walden Pond, said, "I am convinced, both by faith and experience, that to maintain one's self on this earth is not a hardship but a pastime, if we will live simply and wisely."[27] More simplicity is called for in certain seasons of life than others. Nature teaches us this. In cold conditions, trees drop their leaves, animals migrate or hibernate, and plant roots go dormant. As we endure struggle or transition, we cannot expect to maintain our usual pace or productivity.

Certain things we can do nothing about. We can, however, choose to let go of our tensions around these issues in favor of a more relaxed approach. At one church Halloween party, seeing all the elaborate and creative homemade costumes on other people's children, I felt mildly mortified by my own family's slapdash appearance. I had thrown together a costume for my two-year-old that was cute (mostly because he was) but he wouldn't wear it; my seven-year-old wanted to be a mummy, so wrapped himself in toilet paper, which ended up strewn around the gym— a paper trail of all the inadequacies I felt. When he got tired of the toilet paper trail, he put on his winter jacket and told people he was dressed as an Eskimo. I wondered why I felt so devastated by this silly Halloween party—somehow it had become a metaphor for all my unmet ideals. Of course, it would have been a nice touch to work for days on six costumes, but I had chosen other things instead and in retrospect, still would. My husband listened sympathetically to my summary of the event, but then laughed until I couldn't help laughing with him. He helped me look at the experience as an opportunity for the kids to be resourceful and creative. And in fact, they had had a wonderful time.

For a few years my most difficult day of the week was Tuesday, because it entailed packing all the kids in the car to drive downtown and waiting while my older boys had music lessons. One particular Tuesday, I succeeded in getting the two younger boys into the van, but while I went to round up everyone else, they pushed a random array of buttons and locked the steering wheel. Everyone was loaded, but I couldn't unlock the steering. The minutes ticked by until travel time equaled remaining lesson time, so we all filed back into the house. I was beyond frustrated! I had my oldest son call the teacher and leave a message to apologize for the no-show, and then I started ordering everyone around like a drill sergeant to sweep, scrub, and organize. About fifteen minutes later, an electronic voice came from the phone that said, "Thank you. Goodbye." Then there was a dial tone. My son said, "Oops. I forgot to hang up the speaker phone." All week I chose to assume his teacher had simply stopped listening at the end of the main message and not overheard my ranting. The next week she acknowledged she had received the call, but commented simply, "That was a very long message." It took me at least another week to be able to laugh about that one. Sometimes all you can do is laugh—it purges the soul like tears.

The ultimate letting go entails personal consecration, the complete giving ourselves over to God and trusting in His care. This type of letting go exists only in the context of full personal effort and full faith in God's goodness, wisdom, and power. It is one of the great gospel paradoxes (like the servant is master or the last is first); we save ourselves by losing ourselves. We let go, but it is not an indefinite freefall. We are instead "caught up" in the complete safety and rescue of God's embrace—and in being so caught, we find ourselves not empty-handed, but successfully carrying all that is needful.

Reflect or discuss:

1) What demands do you currently face? How frequently and to what degree do you feel overwhelmed?

2) What help could you receive? Who do you currently consider to be part of your support circle? How could you build such a circle?

3) What continued or additional efforts are required? What tasks or commitments are unnecessary?

12~ Enduring weakness, loss, and lost perspective

At the park with my two youngest sons on a brisk autumn morning, we witnessed what we termed "leaf storms." Suddenly, red leaves showered down from a tree across the street, then the same thing happened to a neighboring yellow-leafed tree, then brown leaves showered down from the tree whose branches hung directly over us. The silently traveling gust moved through, disturbing any weakly bound stems. Similarly in our lives, during calm, unstressed times, a pervading smoothness of operations allows us to briefly forget our weaknesses. But then comes the wind, and multiple evidences of our weakness fall before us, gathering at our feet.

As mothers, we are often burdened with intense regret for times we have been anything less than an ideal influence to our children. Why? We are afraid of "ruining" them. There is some truth to our fear—they are impressionable and our weaknesses may rub off on them with some consequence. Seeing our own negative habits trickle through to our children awakens an urgency for reform, but there is much relearning and rethinking to be done. In the meantime, when their weaknesses mirror ours, we feel implicated, despite knowing we cannot entirely own the weaknesses of another person, no matter how close they may be. We feel frustrated with ourselves particularly for patterned weaknesses—familiar ones that keep cropping up despite repeated inward resolve (see Romans 7:18-19). Perhaps we have not sufficiently understood, desired, or worked for change in these areas. Or perhaps overcoming certain weaknesses will require more than inward resolve.

Overcoming weakness through grace

Several years ago, toward the end of a long car trip, I suddenly lost my composure with the kids. The last straw had been their failure to listen and stay with me at yet another gas station bathroom. I felt utterly overwhelmed to have these rambunctious, energetic, intelligent but devious, disregarding children under my care. Despite sleep deprivation, days in the car, and multiple settings in which supervision of small children was demanding and stressful, I had held it together; I'd tried to be patient for so long, but suddenly I was saying all sorts of things I'd been trying not to say or even feel—lots of "you always," "you never," and "why-can't-you-justs"—and then I felt awful, like all my good parenting efforts up to that point had been erased by a failure in the end. The kids just sort of looked at me with wide eyes, piled back in the car, and we merged back onto the highway. They soon resumed their previous reading, joking, and haggling; I sat in the passenger seat and silently cried. A minivan felt like very tight quarters with all that emotion; I wished I could be dropped off to live the rest of my days at the next Flying-J.

My husband drove on but reached out to take my hand. I quietly told him, "I ruined everything. . . . I don't know how to fix this." He said, "Mary, I think you do." I started by offering a silent prayer to tell Heavenly Father I was sorry. Then I apologized to my kids for how I had reacted, though I emphasized that they should have been obedient and that I was just trying to take care of them and keep them safe. At that point, something miraculous happened. As deeply and as suddenly as it had come, the tension and despair melted away. Later I came across a scripture that captured the wonderful transformative power I had experienced: "Who is like unto the Lord our God, who dwelleth on high, who humbleth himself to behold the things that are in heaven, and in the earth! He raiseth up the poor out of the dust, and lifteth the needy out of the dunghill; that he may set him with the princes, even with the princes of his people. He maketh the barren woman to keep house, and to be a joyful mother of children" (Psalms 113:5-9). I had felt as low as a dunghill and had been restored to joy. More than mere comfort, this was God's miraculous grace at work: I was changed, and my error had been swept away.

There is always a difference between what we theoretically "know" and what feels accessible, useful and renewing at the time of true struggle. Yet we are never too far gone—never a "lost cause." Seeing our weaknesses, if we have a mind to do something about them, is divine opportunity. Ether 12:27 states, "If men come unto me I will show unto them their weakness. I give unto men weakness that they may be humble; and my grace is sufficient for all men that humble themselves before me; for if they humble themselves before me, and have faith in me, then will I make weak things become strong unto them." Our shortcomings, however disappointing to us personally, position us to grow and to rely on God. As much as we would wish it otherwise, our weaknesses also afford similar opportunities to those around us. LDS Church leader Elder Maxwell taught, "Your lives . . . your marriages, your families . . . currently constitute the sample of humanity which God has given you. We are each other's clinical material."[28]

Though in our lives we frequently fall and struggle to get back up, there is always hope and opportunity for positive change. Trying again is a hopeful and holy act.[29] It has been emphasized that the "re" in "repent" signifies the need to repeat and practice new behavior: "You have to backtrack to the point where you went off track and go forward, free from the challenges that were with you then. The atonement is the mighty healer."[30] It is fitting then that Christ's earthly vocation was that of a carpenter. With the poet we ask,

> O Carpenter of Nazareth,
> This heart, that's broken past repair,
> This life, that's shattered nigh to death,
> Oh can you mend them, Carpenter?[31]

The New Testament tells of a woman with a longstanding infirmity gaining miraculous healing by reaching out and touching the border of Christ's robe (Luke 8:43-44). Though she had sought healing for years in other ways, it was her faithful, simple reaching for the Savior that accessed it. Similarly, with even one small, positive faithful action on our part, repair starts happening right away—any hopeful effort will result in power flowing to us, with some immediate benefit. Perhaps that faithful action is a simple prayer or stopping ourselves amid a negative cascade of behavior. Alma 34:31 states, "I would that ye would come forth and harden not your hearts any longer; for behold, now is the time and the day of your salvation; and therefore, if ye will repent and harden not your hearts, *immediately* shall the great plan of redemption be brought about unto you."[32] The Lord promises, "Return unto me, and I will return unto you" (Malachi 3:7).

The idea of redemption is very much operational in Jewish as well as Christian faith. The Jewish "High Holy Days" span both Rosh Hashanah, the celebration of creation, and Yom Kippur, the "Day of Atonement," occurring ten days later. The time between the two is a merciful "space" where one can become pure before the symbolic sealing of the "Book of Life" before the end of the year. The Sabbath between the two holidays is called *Shabbat Shuvah,* Hebrew for "the Sabbath of turning." The most holy day, Yom Kippur, considered to be the "Sabbath of Sabbaths," is one of introspection, repentance and correction of wrongs. Those physically able fast for twenty-four hours and inwardly acknowledge personal weakness and sin and absolute reliance on God. Some Yom Kippur services end with a Torah reading from Deuteronomy 29 and 30, ending with the phrase, "I have put before you this day life and death, blessing and curse. Choose life."[33]

Enduring loss by developing acceptance, gratitude, and empathy

Motherhood opens the way to many joys, but also leaves us vulnerable to deep sorrows. Paradoxically, it is the most universal transitions—birth and death, endings and beginnings—that carry the most personal and profound meaning. Beyond these are the unique extremes of experience through which some must pass, about which one cannot productively generalize. Writer Edith Hamilton has said, "Pain is the most individualizing thing on earth. It is true that it is the great common bond as well, but that realization comes only when it is over. To suffer is to be alone. To watch another suffer is to know the barrier that shuts each of us away by himself. Only individuals can suffer."[34]

Some sorrows come outside the context of motherhood, yet everything we experience falls back again into that central context and affects our functioning. While all family members may understand this on a cognitive level, loss brings a certain rawness or sensitivity that may increase both our tendency and susceptibility to hurt. A quote displayed on our living room wall, embroidered and framed by my mother-in-law, reminds us, "Family is a gift that lasts forever." But one day I walked by it and saw a dart suction-cupped to the center of its glass. The dart was a mark of living reality atop an ideal. Sometimes life gets a bit more complicated and crazy than we expected, yet there we bravely stand, despite the crossfire![35]

Difficult situations that cannot be changed have the greatest potential to change *us*. Anne Morrow Lindbergh stated, however, "I do not believe that sheer suffering teaches. If suffering alone taught, all the world would be wise, since everyone suffers. To suffering must be added mourning, understanding, patience, love, openness, and the willingness to remain vulnerable."[36] How can we acknowledge and maintain ideals without becoming over-serious or miserable in imperfect situations? How can we feel reconciled to a God who may allow our suffering for our growth?

While we often define our well-being by the perceived smoothness of our way, this misses the very purpose of our earthly existence: to prove faithful.[37] When I begin to feel resentful for certain difficulties or robbed

81

because of certain losses, I look at the people around me—particularly my patients. Recently in clinic, I saw a toddler with a wound infection after brain surgery for repair of a rare vascular abnormality diagnosed after she had a stroke. There was also a preschooler brought by her adoptive mother because of a high fever—she had a rare genetic abnormality that affected her vision and development. She was the most loving and polite patient of the day; she asked me to put down my laptop so she could give me a hug at the end of the visit. During my residency, I remember a little six-month-old boy in the pediatric intensive care unit with a head injury and how everyone cheered when he cried again for the first time. Going home from that I could not complain about late nights rocking a fussing baby—I was thankful to have a baby that *could* cry. Seeing cancer patients weak from chemotherapy made me thankful for a toddler strong enough to throw a tantrum. Seeing children born with developmental problems made me thankful for children with cognitive function enough to think up mischievous plans. Witnessing such significant challenges being handled so gracefully makes it seem ridiculous and presumptuous to ever ask "why." A more proper question for any of us would perhaps be, "why not?" The Apostle Peter advised, "Think it not strange concerning the fiery trial which is to try you, as though some strange thing happened unto you" (1 Peter 4:12). Looking at examples of those who have honorably endured difficulty may prompt us to wisely revise our expectations for only slight disruptions to ease and pleasantness, and instead anticipate greater amplitude in the vicissitudes of our lives.

President Spencer Kimball of the LDS Church, who himself endured multiple health challenges, said,

> If all the sick for whom we pray were healed, if all the righteous
> were protected and the wicked destroyed, the whole program of
> the Father would be annulled. . . . No man would have to live
> by faith. Should all prayers be immediately answered according
> to our selfish desires and our limited understanding, then there
> would be little or no suffering, sorrow, disappointment, or even
> death, and if these were not, there would also be no joy,
> success, resurrection, nor eternal life. . . . Being human, we
> would expel from our lives physical pain and mental anguish
> and assure ourselves of continual ease and comfort, but if we
> were to close the doors upon sorrow and distress, we might be
> excluding our greatest friends and benefactors. Suffering can

make saints of people as they learn patience, long-suffering, and self-mastery.[38]

If formulaic deliverance was always granted and blessings were always outward and immediate, God would have charlatans and opportunists for disciples, not faithful followers. No matter where we align ourselves, we will have our share of both struggle and providence.*

Despite difficulty, there are always blessings. I remember one day driving into the city feeling particularly burdened, tense, and frustrated. I didn't know what to do but pray. I desperately needed to transform my mood, so I began to thank God for everything I could think of, big and small. By the time I reached my destination, I was at peace. Gratitude is not an exercise in self-delusion, it is a balanced and true perspective that may take effort to maintain. I Thessalonians 5:21 says, "Hold fast to that which is good." Similarly, the Book of Mormon teaches that we must, "always retain in remembrance, the greatness of God . . . and his goodness and longsuffering" (Mosiah 4:11). Refusing to allow hardships to blind us to blessings requires conscious choice. The mourner's kaddish (prayer) in Judaism, rather than acknowledging sorrow, is purely an iteration of praise: "May His great name be blessed forever and to all eternity."

An awareness of God's personal care can bring great solace and comfort. Specific experiences that demonstrate His involvement in our own lives are at least part of the "tender mercies" spoken of scripturally.[39] Once I was up late at night going through a book of hymns. As I sang through one line of a certain hymn, the words were highlighted to my heart so powerfully that I knew God was assuring the truth of them to me personally. On that particular night, I needed desperately to know: "As thy days may demand, so thy succor shall be" (from Hymn # 85, "How Firm a Foundation").[40]

If it is true that "to suffer is to be alone," the corollary is also true: the moment we find we are *not* completely alone, our suffering is at least partially, but often profoundly, alleviated. The scriptures tell us that Christ experienced mortality and suffering, "that his bowels may be filled with mercy . . . that he may know according to the flesh how to succor his people according to their infirmities" (Alma 7:12). Christ offers not mere

---

* This being said, there is always greater peace in following the path informed by conscience, whereas disregarding it will always erode peace (See Isaiah 48:18-22). Also, in "drawing near" to God, we are inviting His full blessings (D&C 88:63).

sympathy, but true empathy. Only those with genuine understanding can effectively bring comfort to those that mourn—or more fittingly "*mourn with* those that mourn . . . and comfort those that stand in need of comfort" (Mosiah 18:8-9, italics added).

As we pass through our own struggles, we too will learn more wisely how to succor those around us. Elder Neal Maxwell stated, "Rather than simply passing through these things [trials], they must pass through us and do so in ways which sanctify these experiences for our good. Thereby, our empathy, too, is enriched and everlasting."[41] With growing insight, we can even begin to anticipate possible feelings in others and respond proactively, particularly with our children, who may need help processing loss and change.

Even with our attempted explanations, especially very young children often interpret situations in surprising ways. Just after the first frost of the year, I was outside with my four-year-old. I said, "Look at the sparkly coating on the grass and plants. Water collected on them in the coolness of the night and then it got *so* cool that the water froze and made frost—that sparkly coating is frost. Now all the plants in the garden will die." He scraped some frost onto his glove and licked it. He said, "Mmmm. I like this frost!" But then he quickly asked, "Will I die like the plants since I ate some?" Since even very young children recognize strong emotional undercurrent, it is vital to help them make sense of emotionally difficult times for the family. Openly discussing significant losses or stresses in a developmentally appropriate way can replace confusion, fear, or self-blame with accurate meaning.

Regaining perspective by remembering

When we have the luxury to have no true tragedy or crisis on our hands, we often dwell on smaller struggles enough to make us convinced that we do. Some of our suffering is tied to meaningful losses, but much of it rooted merely in lost perspective.

One day I felt angry because I was trying to hurry and load the kids in the car to bring back an overdue library book and they weren't cooperating. I felt like a failure for losing my patience *and* for getting yet another library fine when we didn't have any money to spare. The amount of the fine? Five cents. I was selling my happiness for five cents. After I realized the ridiculousness of this, I cheered up. At times of discouragement, disappointment, or embarrassment, it can be easy to

84

forget where our main loyalties lie. But it is not to onlookers, receptionists, store clerks, or other random people that we must ultimately answer; it is to God and those we love most.

Another morning, I picked up a bill from the kitchen table and realized it was late. Then the phone rang and I learned that my kids had been exposed to lice. While I was pondering that, my three-year-old spilled a 20-ounce bottle of bubble solution over the keys of our piano. Because of the bill I felt forgetful and wasteful; because of the lice I felt like shaving my head and screaming; and because of the bubble solution I felt that nothing I cared about was ever safe and that I couldn't properly supervise my children. How could I be cheerful in that moment? Why would I be? And that was only part of the story; these were just additions to the ongoing stresses, demands, disappointments and trials of my current life. But it was also only part of the story because of my underlying blessings: life, health, a kind and hardworking husband, nice kids, a home to live in, and food to eat.

The scriptures contain an account of Jesus healing a man "blind from his birth." The disciples ask, "Who did sin, this man, or his parents, that he was born blind?" (John 9:1-2). Though Jesus answers that neither did, sometimes our chosen perspective—what we choose to see or not see— is a sort of self-inflicted blindness. Regardless of root causes, if blind, the next needed act is healing.

It is the act of remembering truth that counteracts blindness. Truth is knowledge in full context.[42] Certain seeming "trials," when judged truly, have little significance.* For instance, my kids tend to complain about hot cereal in the mornings—we most often have oatmeal, but also cracked wheat cereal, "cornmeal mush," and occasionally eggs or pancakes. In contrast, one pioneer woman, Druscilla Dorris Hendricks, spoke of going weeks and weeks with only water and cornmeal to make small "cakes" for her family. Other times they had nothing. She writes in her memoirs, "Hunger makes sweet, cakes without sugar"[43] Sometimes in our abundance we come to expect certain delicacies and elaborations and wish for more; nothing seems "sweet" enough. Sadness, disappointment or

---

* Some "trials" may even be hidden blessings. Soon after commenting that I never seemed to be able to sit down for more than five minutes, I saw a headline about a study showing that getting up frequently during the day can add years to your life! (See article "Sedentary Behavior and Life-Expectancy in the USA" by Peter Katzmarzyk and I-Min Lee in *British Medical Journal Open* 2012;2:e000828)

irritation in such contexts may simply be ingratitude, and we could choose differently.

After hearing stories of extreme hardship or faith, how can we gather our new, emboldened resolve? How can we apply all the pity, inspiration, and gratitude engendered to triumph in the here and now? Does remembering really make a difference?

In 2007, an initiative to reduce paper waste was introduced involving stickers posted on paper towel dispensers with one simple reminder: "These come from trees." Follow-up studies showed that every sticker posted decreased paper towel usage by an average of 100 lbs. per year.[44] Even keeping simple truths in mind can inspire us to modify our actions.

The LDS sacramental prayer indicates that partaking the sacrament signifies a covenant to "always remember Him [Jesus Christ]" (D&C 20:77, 79). "Remembering" is not just an obligation or requirement to qualify for the other blessings of the atonement, but also one of the main parts of the blessing itself. "Remembering" distills the best in us and informs our actions. Mosiah 4:11-16 states that if we "always retain in remembrance the greatness of God," then it will naturally follow that we will: "always rejoice," "be filled with the love of God," "retain a remission of [our] sins," "grow in the knowledge of [truth]," "live peaceably and [fairly]" with those around us, not neglect our children but "teach them to walk in the ways of truth and . . . to love one another and to serve one another," and we will "succor those that stand in need of [our] succor."[45]

One of the best ways to remember truth is to have it continually before us, as we "walk by the way, lie down, and rise up . . . as frontlets between our eyes" (see Deuteronomy 6:6-9). In the tree of life allegory spoken of earlier (chapter 8), the only way the travelers reached the tree despite the obscuring "mists of darkness" was to hold to the "rod of iron," representing "the word of God" (1 Nephi 11:25, 12:17; see also 1 Nephi 15:23-24).

Many times I have found guidance and comfort in the scriptures. One representative example relates to an insight I gained that significantly helped me in caring for my mother. At times she would become agitated when I needed to bathe her. It was a physically challenging task already, but when she would cry through the bath, it became very emotionally difficult for me as well. I knew I had to bathe her, but felt so sorry that it was such an upsetting experience for her. One morning, I opened the scriptures to read the Sunday School reading assignment and found the

86

story of Jehoshaphat, King of Judah, and how he and his people won a battle by singing (2 Chronicles 20). I recognized this was an inspired solution applicable to my own situation. The next time I bathed my mother, I sang to her and she sat peacefully and listened while I washed her. Everything had changed. Opening the scriptures is like opening a window—because on that particular day I spent "some time in the scriptures,"[46] it let some light in.

Reflect or discuss:

1) Which weaknesses are you currently working to overcome? What have you done so far? What more could be done? Have you prayed for help?

2) Think about or list at least ten things you are grateful for. Repeat this exercise regularly. Is there anyone you know to be struggling who you could reach out to and help or encourage?

3) What helps you maintain perspective? Do you study the scriptures regularly? If not, try doing so for two to four weeks and noting your experience.

Summary table for chapters 11-13

Triggers	*Helps*
Negative and destructive thought patterns	Discernment and discipline
Overwhelming demands	Perspective and deliverance
Weakness, losses, and lost perspective	Receiving grace Finding acceptance, gratitude, and empathy Remembering

13~ THE MOMENT IS VAST

"The present moment is everything. The moment is vast."[47] Despite the constant passage of time, the present moment is a discreet, measurable entity that takes up space and significance. It is vast because of the scope and potential it holds; it is vast because it can be stretched for the purpose of choosing, savoring, and bridging; it is vast if we stop to notice. Ultimately, learning how to deal well in moments will help us teach our children how; it will enable us to live without regret. As the 19th century writer Maria Edgeworth stated, "If we take care of the moments, the years will take care of themselves."[48] Poet Emily Dickinson also reminds us, "Forever is composed of Nows."[49]

We take care of moments by responding appropriately to them— meeting the true needs they present within the context of our values. To avoid regret, we must uphold certain standards of behavior regardless of circumstance, rather than "lose [our] own soul[s]" (Mark 8:35) by acting outside of our value systems and the value systems we're trying to teach or emulate. Yelling, contending, or physically enforcing outwardly desired behavior only undermines our goals and fosters rebellion and resentment.* Our response to specific situations affects how we feel and how we make others feel—our ultimate experience and theirs. We may ask ourselves, "What will achieve the desired outcome, teach the desired lesson, or bring about the desired way of *being* over time?" Often the fitting or best response is not the reflexive or natural one. As acknowledged by Stephen Covey in his book *Seven Habits of Highly Effective Families*, "Between stimulus and response, there is a space."[50] Our choices in this space can override our initial tendencies. Through repentance and apology, we can in a sense "redo time" and go back and fix even poorly fitted responses. My friend has taught this to her four-year-old daughter, who sometimes says, "Mom, could we start over?" They literally retrace their steps and try again.

During times of greatest difficulty, soothing (bringing comfort, expressing love for and belief in) often brings better results than admonishment, criticism, or contention. We take care of moments by taking care of people—ourselves and those we love. Soothing measures for me include doing things I love, listening to music, singing, reading from

---

* See "Christian Courage: The Price of Discipleship" by Robert D. Hales. *Ensign,* Nov 2008. Consider applications to parenting.

inspirational sources, walking in nature, talking with someone who cares about me, and following simple personalized preferences. If we pay attention, we can learn specifically how to care for those around us—they will teach us. And we can help them know how to care for us, too.

One night my then two-year-old son Malachi woke up crying. I was holding him and rocking him by his crib. He was looking up at me and suddenly said, "Mommy, say 'Nice Malachi'" I often had whispered that over and over as I rocked or held him, and now I knew this repeated phrase was a specific comfort to him. Though just a toddler, he was able to recognize and then articulate the "right" soothing conditions for himself. Attunement and love can enable us to perceive and meet needs even without request. Once my sister gave me a pocket composition notebook she had made with inspiring quotes and pictures she selected specifically for me. The first page said, "I love you so much!" Other pages had words to a song we had learned as children, inspiring scriptures, pictures she had drawn, truths we had discussed in conversation. She left part of the book blank for me to continue to fill in. Opening this book at various discouraging times has helped me "come to myself"[51] and regain perspective; it helps me feel loved and known.

Distinctive moments span across change like a suspension bridge. On his children's show, Mister Rogers insisted on taking network time to change his shoes and sweater to send a message to kids of settling in to be fully present for the duration of the program. He thought it unfortunate that we adults tend "to hurry through transitions and to try to hurry our children through them as well. We may feel these transitions are 'nowhere at all' compared to what's gone before or what we anticipate is next to come,"[52] but honoring transition periods soften them and promote better acceptance.

As I referred to in a previous chapter, when my husband and older sons were out of town for an outdoor camp, my mom was hospitalized for an infection that had substantially weakened her. At the time of her discharge, because I had four young children at home, I initially thought of arranging to have her transported to the turnaround area so I could more easily pick her up. Instead, I found a friend to watch the kids so I could go in to help her dress and gather her things, which better communicated that I was again taking over her care. After we arrived home, we sensed other changes. We sat together at the breakfast table listening to some of her favorite music, the Mormon Tabernacle Choir, while I fed her spoonfuls of cereal and tears streamed down our cheeks. Simultaneously, other transitions were emerging. After spending that week with teenagers and adult leaders at scout camp, my second son laughed in both delight and astonishment to see his younger brothers. Upon returning he proclaimed, "You all look so small!" He later told me, "Mom, I feel happy and sad. It seems like home changed while we were gone." But I knew it was mostly that he had.

In Jewish tradition, there is a special Hebrew word used to mark transitional times while acknowledging God's hand in them: *shehechiyanu* or "you have kept us alive." The whole blessing, recited at Rosh Hashanah (the New Year celebration) and at Bar or Bat Mitzvahs (the ceremony which marks one's transition from child to adult member of the religious community), says, "Blessed are You, Ruler of the Universe, You have kept us alive and sustained us, and enabled us to reach this moment." *Shehechiyanu* is a prayer of thanks in a single word. It can mark any "first": the first flower of spring, the first time a child says a certain word, the first day of school, the first time child demonstrates maturity in a certain way.[53]

In order to mark or even perceive special moments, we must pause—just long enough. I love to watch the peaceful yet powerful movement of clouds in the sky, but often such movements remain imperceptible except to those who will stand still.

Cherishing moments stretches them; it increases our joy and effectiveness in relationships. In his book *The Seven Habits of Highly Effective Families*, Stephen Covey reminds us that "when [working] with your family, 'slow' is 'fast' and 'fast' is 'slow.'"[54] Forcing and rushing often lead to standstill, whereas standing still leads to a rush of insight and appreciation and often facilitates cooperative effort. Of his time at Walden Pond Thoreau writes, "There were times when I could not afford to sacrifice the bloom of the present moment to any work. . . I love a broad margin to my life. Sometimes . . . I sat in my sunny doorway from sunrise till noon, rapt in a revery, amidst the pines and hickories and sumachs, in undisturbed solitude and stillness . . . until by the sun falling in at my west window . . . I was reminded of the lapse of time. I grew in those seasons like corn in the night, and they were far better than any work of the hands would have been. They were not time subtracted from my life, but so much over and above my usual allowance [*sic*]."[55]

Watching a child sleep, rocking a baby, holding a hand, hearing the ring of laughter. These moments bloom into vastness.

A few days after finishing my first full draft of this section, on a Thursday at 2:52 pm, my son Ezra was born. Shehechiyanu.

Reflect or discuss:

1) What are the hardest times for you? What are the contributing factors? What leads up to them? When do things feel "too far gone"?

2) For each of the above scenarios, answer the following: Could any intervention/rescue be made to interrupt, prevent, or soften such moments? What could make these moments not happen/happen less frequently/be better endured?

3) Each time a significantly negative moment happens, process it. Processing can be done personally (pondering or journaling), with a trusted friend or family member (keeping productive purposes in mind, not bad-mouthing, not breaking confidences/loyalties except in cases of emergency), or through prayer.

4) How can you better "mark" or cherish the most special, meaningful moments? If any significant events have passed that still feel fresh enough to record, take time to write some of these down. Establish a system for regularly recording special moments, even journaling just weekly or monthly.

IV. STAYING POWER

On accessibility and loyalty

14~ THE PARABLE OF THE WORKING MOTHER

A novel written in the early 1900's by Berthold Auerbach entitled, *To the Heights* tells the story of a poor, young country girl named Walpurga. She and her husband are having their first precious days with their newly born child when a royal carriage comes and requests her to be wet-nurse for the queen. Among women in the kingdom who have recently given birth, she is particularly sought after because of her purity and simplicity. She at first refuses adamantly, but as various arguments are presented to her, she at last agrees. She suppresses all her natural feelings and leaves her child and husband for one year, seeing it as a sacrifice that will secure future comforts for her family. There is much talk around her of the honor and compensations promised, but her ultimate decision rests on the question of whether her presence or something else will be of greatest benefit to her child.

The entire novel emerges from this conflict and explores the ramifications of her choice. She enters into the world of the court and in some ways it changes her—she maintains her integrity, but not her simplicity. She and her husband are faced with challenges and temptations they otherwise would not have faced, others must step into her role to fill her place, and when she returns, her child initially treats her as a stranger. There is the question through the whole book of whether this sacrifice was noble and "worth it" or not. For me, it reflects the modern conflict of working women.

In what areas are we irreplaceable as mothers? What do we give up (or gain) when we choose other pursuits that take us away from home? What is ultimately worth this trade? In the above story, when Walpurga returns home after fulfilling her yearlong obligation to the king, she has secured wealth and position for her family and has performed what she and others consider an honorable work, yet naturally (or unnaturally), her child does not know her. My hours in pediatric residency were never so long as to render me unrecognizable to my children, but perhaps I too gave away connections by degrees, even if temporarily. Certain days I returned from school or work to find a sick child who I could have been home to hold. Returning another day, I came upon a pile of muddy kid clothes on the porch and went in to hear of an outdoor adventure the kids had with their dad—I was happy for them, but knew I missed out on something spontaneous and special.

Even though I made an effort to minimize my time away during my medical training, it was still significant. I was able to space out my clinical years in medical school by taking 4-6 weeks off every few rotations to be home with my first baby. Between medical school and residency I had an 8-month break to stay home with my then two kids. In residency, I chose to just push through and get it done. I had my third son in the middle of residency and my fourth as residency was ending. My husband knew my goal from when we started dating and (unlike some who never asked me out again after finding out I was "pre-med" and actually serious about it) he agreed to help me reach my goal. He finished his degrees around my medical school schedule, so one of us was always home with the boys. He took a three-year break in his schooling during my residency to stay home with the kids. Despite my efforts to make the process as "family-friendly" as possible, it was grueling and emotionally difficult. For about 5 years (the clinical years of medical school plus residency), aside from my scheduled-in breaks, I was gone all day every day except weekends that I was not "on-call." Every third or fourth night, I was "on-call," which meant I'd have to stay at the hospital overnight for a 30-32 hour shift, getting little or no sleep. Since finishing residency, I have been very blessed to find positions that fit around my family (very limited hours, schedules I can choose) but it's hard to have times I ever *have* to walk out the door. I went into medical school planning to be a stay-at-home mom, and that's what I consider myself to be. Luckily (or rather, very intentionally), I choose to be primarily at home so I miss very little now.

As one who has fulfilled the intense professional training of medical school and residency, I have been intimately aware of what is potentially lost, but yet feel I have averted much of it by choosing to work only very little once my training was complete. I have worked very hard and accomplished a hard thing—but I deserve no more kudos than the mothers who could have gone to medical school (or pursued any other dream) but chose not to. That too is a hard and noble thing.

Some of my female colleagues have said, "I could never stay at home!" They give varied reasons, from predicted boredom, to lack of modeling from their mothers ("I just don't know how to *be* at home with my kids— what do you do with them all day?"), to assumptions that they themselves are not patient enough. It is true that the professional world contrasts the

95

world of family—they are different systems to operate in. Between the professionalism of career and intimacy of family, one needs to change "currency," as if traveling to a new land. It can feel extremely frustrating for the goal-oriented, highly motivated person who always in their personal past has been able to "make things happen" to suddenly have to work with the unwilling and the untrained—not just at a surface level, but to the most intimate detail. And not just for a workday, but everyday.

For me, being at home with the kids *does* seem to place me more "face to face" with my personal limitations of patience, long-suffering and other attributes I seek to develop, but I wouldn't trade the opportunity for any amount of money, position, or accomplishment. Some have said, "There is just no way we could live off one salary anymore—we've grown accustom to two." With my husband in graduate school and six kids at the time, we got by with me working only very little because we made it a priority. In our family, we don't have the newest technological gadgets, we rarely eat out, for many years we shared one car (my husband biked to school and work even through MN winters), we have decorated with salvaged, fixed-up furniture, we do most home projects ourselves, we buy most clothes at thrift stores, we go on creative but simple outings and dates—and yet life feels abundant.

It is a disciplined choice to keep wants simple; as is stated in I Timothy, "Having food and raiment let us be therewith content" (6:7-11). Once the basic needs of our children are met, there are no guarantees that "more is better" in terms of wealth and meaningful outcomes. A neighbor once asked, "Why don't you just work more so you can get a bigger house or remodel to make more space for your kids?" But I know our shared time has been more worthwhile than open space.

Reflect or discuss:

1) How does the story of Walpurga relate to your life or experiences? What seems to call you away from family responsibilities or relationships?

2) What balance have you found between family time and outside pursuits? What has led you to choose what you have chosen? Do you feel peaceful and settled with the way things are?

15~ THE GIFT OF PRESENCE

It is not that women who are at home "full time" automatically nurture, or that women who work more than a certain number of hours automatically don't, but nurturing always requires time, dedication and commitment. I believe we'd all want to look back and say, "I was home to the degree I needed to be; I did not follow pursuits at the expense of my family; I did not miss or give away too much." We need to be careful about our choices so the people we love best don't get shortchanged.

Women have always worked, whether in their home or out if it. Historically, financially well-off women have had hired help with housework and childcare, while less well-off women have been that help. Before women entered the workforce in a more official sense, they were still main players in the family economy. My grandfather was foreman in a small Wyoming coal-mining town and my grandmother, remembered for her loving attentiveness toward her family, also kept the books and oversaw the post office. My Jewish grandmother cooked meals and washed clothes for her husband and twelve children before automatic washers, dryers, or microwave ovens. So it seems that *working* is not the primary issue, but where one's focus and devotion lies.

Many tasks traditionally performed by women have been lightened by technology and culture, but new possibilities compete for any salvaged energy: the building of career, enrichment opportunities for ourselves and our children, and then a myriad of potential time-wasters. We are civilized yet isolated, liberated yet lost.

My kids and I walk through our neighborhood on a sunny afternoon past empty houses, empty yards, and empty parks. Most adults are gone at work, most children in daycare. A woman and child come to the park where we are playing and I say, "Hello, how are you? How old is your baby?" She says, "He's 11 months, but he's not mine—I'm the nanny." She talks on her cell phone while he sifts through the sand.

Presence communicates care. It is not that we as mothers should never step away or pursue anything exacting that requires focus, but that we should choose carefully so our pursuits honor our true priorities. Though certain moments may be more important to share than others, one often cannot predict which these will be. Presence may be particularly vital and valued at transitions, crossroads (daily comings and goings), and landmark moments of triumph or difficulty, but sharing any experience elevates it with added meaning. I notice how my two-year-old's enjoyment in certain activities is enhanced by having an appreciative audience: for example, he'll go down the slide over and over when I'm there smiling and ready to catch him at the bottom. He also loves singing songs together especially when we clap together at the end.

For older children, "giving audience" may include attending performances or games that mark cumulative efforts or just listening when thoughts or ideas are shared. My four-year-old is in a stage where he tells me stories of things that "happened"—a crazy string-of-events that he's really just making up, but through it he gains practice creating a narrative line. My boys like to tell me about funny or strange dreams they have had, inventions they want to make, ideas they are writing about, and goals they have. When these listening opportunities arise, I'm often in the middle of something else, but I try to stop and listen or have them come along and talk to me while I continue with my work.

Though sometimes children don't acknowledge or may even resist a mother's presence, it still offers a background comfort and care. I remember my mom holding a cool cloth against my forehead when I had the stomach flu and how the soft pressure, the coolness, and her presence brought comfort though I still felt miserable and probably didn't appear comforted.

Even when unable to be physically present, there are ways a mother can make her influence felt. For example, a child who comes home left to himself in an empty house is in much different position than one who knows parental expectation of how the solitary time is to be spent, who finds meals or snacks prepared ahead, who receives a note of greeting, and who will have an opportunity to report on the day when parents return. Without concern expressed or accountability required, low supervision may be subconsciously interpreted as a broken contract leading to less inclination for future obedience or connection. Consequently, the erosion of parental influence affects even future times of parental presence. When we are preoccupied or mentally not present, children are also left to themselves in a different way. While focused tasks directly related to a child's care (preparing meals, organizing the house, etc.) may cause less disconnect than unrelated pursuits, distracted interactions of any kind carry less binding power than focused ones.

Though the role of an earthly parent does not exactly parallel that of a divine parent, examining God's qualities as a parent can be instructive. First, God is "there."* He is sheltering but not over-protective. He is continually aware of us and prepared to provide any needed or merited blessing that cannot be individually secured. He blesses, assures, and encourages in all the right ways. He is always accessible through prayer. He rescues and delivers as needed—not always correlating in timing and method with our wishes or expectations, but always according to the greatest wisdom.

Unlike God's, our presence is not perfect—we may accidentally hover, or wait too long to step in; we may be impatient, hasty, annoying, unwise—but still, in merely being there, we communicate love and dedication in a powerful way. The ability to step in at the right moments requires the acute awareness and connection only afforded by involvement and presence.

Being accessible

What is the difference between my rounding at the hospital for a few hours and someone else working on their self-selected project, like sewing a quilt or reading a book? In some ways, they are no different—time away physically or mentally is time away. Yet at the hospital, mine is a contracted commitment that I can't opt out of at a moment's notice based on surfacing needs. Having flexibility to respond to the needs of others requires not only willingness, but availability. A line from a hymn says, "The errand of angels is given to women," but how can we take on this errand—often spontaneously arising—if we have another appointment? Too many fixed, external commitments can pull us away from doing what's most needed in our primary stewardships. We must take care not to trade responsiveness in spheres where we are irreplaceable for involvement in spheres where we are replaceable.

Working in the hospital, I have "scheduled in" time to be helpful to a select group in need, however, I keep my days off less structured so I can be available for and responsive to the needs of my family. Emily Dickinson writes,

> They might not need me—yet they might—
> I'll let my Heart be just in sight—

---

* See Moses 7:24, 28-30.

A smile so small as mine might be
Precisely their necessity.[1]

I want to be home enough and in tune enough to ensure I am ready to respond when true needs arise.

More is happening than just being physically "there"

In a collection of professional essays, mother and anthropologist Dorothy Lee, acknowledges the intangible, unmeasurable value of shared experiences. She writes,

> When my first child was two or three, I used to shell peas with her. Nowadays I buy my peas already shelled and packaged. This saves me time; the peas are probably even fresher than they were when I used to shell them; and I get good and efficient nutrition. But was this all that happened when I shelled peas with my daughter? Did I merely get a dish of peas? If so, the package of frozen peas is more than an adequate replacement. Yet it was more than this. It was a total process; and if I am going to see to it that the totality of the important aspects of it are retained, I shall have to find out what these were and then find media through which they can continue to be expressed.[2]

Shared time and shared process provide many benefits to relationships. They bestow a common history that connects individuals. The choice to share time also communicates value and acceptance to those we share it with; it forges loyalties.* It provides an interface during which lessons can be transmitted. As stated earlier, opportune moments for teaching, spontaneous sharing, and fun often cannot be predicted. Useful skills and ideas can be informally but profoundly taught as we work and interact side by side. Just as family members often share certain inflections, phrases, mannerisms, deeper character traits are also transmitted by close association.

Longitudinal observation during time together affords a special attuned awareness. It provides intimate knowledge of a person—their

---

* See I John 4:19: "We love him, because he first loved us." Though choosing significant time away from family can have the opposite effect, it all depends on purpose—single mothers who must work, fathers who need to go far distances to provide for family necessities communicate devotion rather than neglect.

preferences, weaknesses, strengths, and tendencies. All this gathered data allows decoding of behavior and language. For example, being home with my kids allows me to recognize their early speech patterns that could have easily have been passed over as babbling: one of my sons said "mah" for mom, "mau" for mouse, and "muh" for mountain. Sharing time also keeps our hearts right. Not only do we focus on what we value, but we tend to value what we have focused on; "For where your treasure is, there will your heart be also" (3 Nephi 13:21, Matt 6:21).*

Presence is not a promise of perfection

A friend once marveled that I could stay home with my children; she commented, "I've found I do much better as a mother when I only see my son a couple hours a day." If we define "doing well" as maintaining a constant freshness or composed attentiveness for a 24-hour daily shift, none of us would be up to the challenge. Whether or not other individuals or institutions offer more specific skill or polish, they cannot adequately take our place. Though my husband tends to keep the house tidier than I do, though daycare centers offer more flashy crafts and consistent schedules than I do, though hired teachers (who have "off-duty" time) may better sustain their composure and enthusiasm for a day's duration than I do, it is *me* that the kids cry for. They display a special sense of well-being when I am around.

Though sometimes we may misjudge the best way to be involved or fall short, our efforts make a difference. Recently, my oldest son expressed interest in attending a performance at his school the following day. He mentioned he'd need a little money and a dinner packed and I agreed to help. The next morning, having been up late with the baby, I overslept and he was gone before I awoke. I felt bad to have not followed through and drove to his school to bring the money and the dinner. I had him called down to the office to meet me, but when he came he smiled and said, "Mom, I took care of it." Despite having to leave before six a.m., he had packed a dinner and scrounged up the money. I was proud of his self-reliance and knew he appreciated my attempts to support him.

We will not be perfectly kind, perfectly loving, perfectly wise, nor perfectly accessible (even having additional children challenges this

---

* Perhaps God's omniscience and love are more qualities of his character, more products of his involvement and concern than metaphysical powers; see Ps 139:1-7.

possibility), but we can *generally* be these things and perfectly "rise up" at certain crucial moments. Our imperfect presence also models the perfecting *process*, which is also vital; our children witness as we acknowledge mistakes and continually try to improve.[3] If we realize we have been choosing other things over family, peace will be found in making changes. Seeking fulfillment, rest, or relief always *outside* of the family system reflects a blind spot to the blessings right before our eyes. As a children's book states, "All the places to love are right here."[4]

Competing philosophies and demands

It can be difficult to discern which possibilities are inspired opportunities and which are distractions. Not every good thing is the best thing. Building gifts and talents is good. Education is good. Breaks or variety in activities can be healthy and refreshing. Employable skills are useful. Still, finding personal and family balance and avoiding future regrets requires a candid sorting through of details. Added learning does not bring wisdom if we begin to "hearken not unto the counsel of God [and] set it aside."[5] We can discern God's will for us by studying and praying about various choices. When all is said and done, even in a given day, I do not want to find my energies expended before I get to what matters most.

Some consider the vocation of motherhood menial and family responsibilities a burden; some claim that fulfillment comes only when pursuing personal interests and enrichments to the furthest extent possible; many seem to believe that interacting with family at only the edges of the day is sufficient. On these personal matters, there is no shortage of public opinion.

I have gotten all sorts of remarks[6] in elevators, grocery stores, or deeper conversation about having more than the average two-point-two children. As I walk to the park in a ponytail and sweats with a double-wide stroller and kids running ahead and trailing behind, I realize that to the outside observer it may seem that I am wearing myself out and losing out on a promising career unnecessarily. But this is the vocation I have chosen; I consider children a gift and the parenting relationship to be a treasured, ongoing bond—not a strained eighteen-year "accommodation." As I have had each additional child, I have prayed to be "made enough" to care for and love them well. Upon learning I had so many boys, one woman exclaimed, "You must be a saint!" But just *having* children doesn't automatically turn anyone into a saint. The lifelong process of giving our lives over to God and to care for others, however, just may.

Despite a few naysayers, I maintain that motherhood is my most important work, that building a strong family takes time and focus, and that no external enrichment program can substitute for good family teaching and love. No matter what "studies show," spiritual things cannot be measured on the world's scales (see 1 Corinthians 2:14).

Reflect or discuss:

1) Can you recall a treasured moment at home you were grateful not to have missed?

2) To what degree do you feel personal conviction and peace for the time balance you have found? Are you in agreement with those around you, or do you feel judged or pressured?

16~ LIABILITIES AND TRADE-INS

What are the gains and losses in having high career focus even during childrearing years? Benefits may include practical skills and enrichment through education, achievement modeling, satisfaction through more public contribution, and preparedness to financially provide for the family as needed. Losses may include divided energy and attention, diminished shared time, and conflicting messages sent about our priorities. Since the louder societal voices currently emphasize benefits, here I further explore losses.

As mothers, our energy is a limited commodity. Though some variation in activities brings renewal, taking significant amounts of time and focus away from family may diminish our feelings of success and fulfillment there. We may think that by sheer force of will or by giving up sleep or other personal needs, we can successful shoulder more, but if no reserve exists, the balance becomes quite precarious. Though we may have allotted a certain percent of ourselves to a given cause, it invariably takes more.

As a moonlighting physician I have freedom to choose my hours, which seems very family-friendly, yet when I'm trying to leave for a shift that may have outwardly fit into our calendar, it often turns out to be interruptive at the moment. Perhaps we are sharing a meaningful time as a family, or someone is sick and wants me, or things are left undone, and yet I still just have to walk out the door. Feeling divided takes emotional energy. Then there are the non-calculated "side" requirements like paperwork, recertification, and continuing education that all have their own deadlines. Still more, there is the distracted, self-focused preparation time required to get ready to leave the house—the subtle change in background air that settles in, even hours ahead, from knowing you need to be somewhere. For these reasons, though I love my work as a pediatrician, I feel grateful I can keep my hours limited during this season of my life. Though I could accept a significant but temporary imbalance for education (medical school and residency), my currently chosen balance allows my focus to be at home.

Since each mother has unique demands and unique reserves, which may vary over time, each will find a unique balance. According to data from the Bureau of Labor Statistics, 70.5% of all women with children under eighteen participated in the workforce in 2012 and approximately 40% of mothers with preschool-aged children or younger were employed full-time.[7] Even the 40-hour workweek, much less than is typical in certain high-demand professions, separates mothers from their children for nearly half of the 98-or-so shared waking hours per week—particularly when commuting time is figured in. Some choose full-time work to maintain professional involvement or a certain lifestyle, some simply have not known or considered another way, some have unique situations necessitating it.

Since moments of a child's need and moments of shared magic are unpredictable, more time away means more potential moments missed. Though interactions may seem smoother when fewer occur, less interface time decreases a mother and child's opportunity to improve character and relationship in the intimate context of family. I remember when residency ended, the days together which had previously been so automatically magical, like a holiday—were now an "everyday." I suddenly had the luxury and the challenge of jumping in with four children at once, asking myself, "How do I want our days to go?" Because I felt I hadn't yet mastered this transition, when a neighbor marveled and exclaimed, "This is so amazing—you must be so happy. You are done! This is what you have been working for all these years!" I went inside and cried. Still, I wouldn't exchange my time at home for greater prestige, recognition, wealth, upgrades, or opportunities. G.K. Chesterton wrote, "How can it be a large career to tell other people's children about the Rule of Three, and a small career to tell one's own children about the universe? How can it be broad to be the same thing to everyone, and narrow to be everything to someone? No, a woman's function is laborious; but because it is gigantic, not because it is minute."[8]

To give up more shared time than one's family can happily afford makes for an unfortunate trade. With significant time apart, even time together is changed. Though perhaps more appreciated, the shared time is also higher pressure. Parents, trying to keep things pleasant, may tend toward over-leniency or overindulgence. Kids feeling more in need of parental affection may paradoxically show this through disobedience, testing or pushing away. Since the main part of the day has been dictated externally and hasn't been established *within* the family, parent and child may feel out of step or rhythm with each other. Both may more easily experience disappointment or hurt because of greater expectations.

Choices of time and priority—these are high-stake choices. Ultimately, we would want our actions to send our children the message "you are important to me." We would want our children's definition of comfort and home to include *us*. We would want to teach and model that family relationships are more important than a powerhouse of credentials, that people are more important than things.

In Matthew 16:26, Jesus asks his disciples, "What is a man profited if he shall gain the whole world and lose his own soul [or the soul of his child]? What shall a man give in exchange for his soul?" As has been wisely said, "No success can compensate for failure in the home."[9] Giving up chances for one type of success does not guarantee another: I could give up a more comfortable lifestyle and personal dreams, only to be grumpy and distracted by *other* things, like housework, cooking, and the PTA. But choosing to put my greatest efforts into this important work of mothering increases the probability of the best possible outcomes. I do not want to be like the short-sighted Esau, who trades his inheritance for superficial satisfaction—"bread and a pottage of lentils" (Genesis 25:34). "Children are an heritage of the Lord" (Psalms 127:3); they are an inheritance too valuable to trade or risk.

Reflect or discuss:

1) Can you recall a time when an outside pursuit came at too high a cost?

2) What criteria do you use in deciding whether an external commitment is worthwhile? Is it always possible to know ahead of time?

17~ MULTIPLICITY AND MIRACLES

God is a multiplier—a God of miracles. Because of this, with divine help we can navigate creative paths that allow more to be accomplished than seemingly possible. My bible dictionary states, "Miracles are a response to faith and its best encouragement," they are "manifestations of God's power" and "instructive…of divine truths," they come in the context of prayer, a perceived need, and faith.[10] When people find out that I have eight children, that I am a pediatrician, and that I pursue additional personal interests, they look at me like I'm a math problem that doesn't add up. But I have learned that there are ways to hold onto dreams and ways to be "made enough" for the challenges that arise. As mothers, we do not operate in a void or vacuum; not every minute is filled or dictated. For this reason, we do not need to cancel every dream or passion, but rather pursue these judiciously. Meaningful productivity renews us; despite the busyness of motherhood, we can often find individualized ways to continue learning, creating, and contributing.

Women in my family have left a legacy that includes a love of learning. One grandmother attended Weber academy when few women pursued college degrees. My other grandmother immigrated to the U.S. from East Central Europe at age nine and never attended college. Yet, her children tell how she would take any free moment to sit and read on the porch, holding a dictionary in one hand and a book or newspaper in the other. My own mother wanted to attend school so badly that as a three or four-year-old, she'd sneak after her siblings to the town's one-room school. She was finally allowed to start early (after promising no more escapes) and ended up finishing high school and starting nursing school by age fifteen.

Growing up in the Church of Jesus Christ of Latter-day Saints, I have been taught to pursue learning "out of the best books . . . by study and also by faith" (D&C 88:118). Speaking to the women of the church, former LDS Church leader President Hinckley stated,

> Educate your hands and your minds . . . get all the education you can. Train yourselves to make a contribution to the society in which you will live. There is an essence of the divine in the improvement of the mind. "The glory of God is intelligence, or, in other words, light and truth" (D&C 93:36). . . . whether it is applied to earning a living or not, education is an investment

that never ceases to pay dividends of one kind or another. In the process of educating your minds, stir within yourselves a greater sensitivity to the beautiful, the artistic, and the cultivation of the talent you possess, be it large or small.[11]

In an earlier address, another former LDS Church leader President Kimball called for the women in the church to be scriptorians; he stated,

I stress again the deep need each woman has to study the scriptures. . . . As you become more and more familiar with the truths of the scriptures, you will be more and more effective in keeping the second great commandment, to love your neighbor as yourself. Become scholars of the scriptures—not to put others down, but to lift them up! After all, who has any greater need to "treasure up" the truths of the gospel (on which they may call in their moments of need) than do women and mothers who do so much nurturing and teaching?[12]

He goes on to encourage women to "seek excellence in all [our] righteous endeavors, and in all aspects of [our] lives," reinforcing the need to be careful, prayerful, and wise as we seek to build education, talents, and skills in order to make the most effective contribution to our families, communities, and humankind.

Worthy pursuits exemplify those characteristics praised in Proverbs 31 and taught in the parable of the talents: "Who can find a virtuous woman?. . . [she] worketh willingly with her hands . . . she openeth her mouth with wisdom . . . she looketh well to the ways of her household, and eateth not the bread of idleness" (Prov 31: 10-31) . . . "and [s]he that had received five talents came and brought other five talents, saying, Lord, thou deliverest unto me five talents: behold, I have gained beside them five talents more." (Matthew 25:21). God does not delight in shriveling stagnancy, but delights in our growth and productivity. We are enabled when doing God's will; he "prepare[s] a way" (1 Ne 3:7) but does not require us to "run faster than [we have] strength" (Mosiah 4:27). Such promises apply to pursuit of gifts, having children, and caring for others.

In cases of large need but few resources, faith brings divine help. The book of Matthew tells of Christ feeding a crowd of 5,000 people with five loaves and two fishes and later, a crowd of 4,000 with seven loaves and a few fishes. He does not only scantily provide, but in each case, there are even baskets to spare (Matthew 14:20, 15:37). The miracle occurred not only externally with the physical provisions, but also within Jesus himself, as he was able to attend to the needs around him despite the heavy personal burden of just having learned of his cousin John's death (Matthew 14:10-14).

During the first few weeks of pediatric residency, I became so exhausted I felt like I was walking in a fog. I wondered how I could endure three years of a schedule requiring little or no sleep every 3-4 nights, especially since I wanted to interact with my family when I returned home rather than just disappear to sleep. Also, as a member of the LDS church, I do not drink coffee or use caffeine-containing or other stimulant products. I prayed for natural stamina. My residency miracle was that the fog lifted. I was able to glean the small amounts of sleep possible during call nights, come home post-call and stay awake with my family until bedtime, and still feel functional and relatively rested. When tired, I felt giddy rather than crabby. In Mosiah 24:14-15, the Lord says, "I will . . . ease the burdens which are put upon your shoulders, that even you cannot feel them upon your backs, even while you are in bondage; and this will I do that ye may stand as a witness for me hereafter, and that ye may know of a surety that I, the Lord God, do visit my people in their afflictions." After residency was over I tried a few times to stay up late for personal projects, but as the true need for it had expired, the miracle was over.

Even when we feel we are missing out on things to care for our children, God provides compensatory blessings. For many years, a group of LDS congregations in the Minneapolis area had the annual tradition of "Women's Day," where women would gather for inspiring classes and then share in a delicious lunch, often donated and catered by a local LDS restaurant owner. I had to miss the conference for my three years of residency, but looked forward to attending the next year. My husband had a work commitment so could not stay home with the kids, so I arranged a babysitter. The night before the conference, however, all the kids got the stomach flu. At first I felt angry and cheated, but then decided to make the best of it—I spent a quiet day with the kids reading stories, holding them, comforting them, cleaning up after them, eating soda crackers and drinking ginger ale. I read the scriptures some on my own. That day several pure insights came to my mind and I was taught and uplifted, perhaps in a more personal way than I would have been at the conference. As writer Anne Campbell wrote of her children, "You are the trip I did not take, you

109

are the pearls I could not buy, you are my blue Italian lake, you are my piece of foreign sky."[13]

Besides physical accessibility, presence is about dedication: loyalty in word and deed, endurance through hard times, forgiveness. In families, it includes husbands and wives upholding and clinging to one another. To stay, to persist, to love—these are commitments made once, but affirmed again and again. C.S. Lewis wrote, "A promise must be about things I can do, about actions: no one can promise to go on feeling a certain way. [One] might as well promise never to have a headache or always to feel hungry. . . . [Love] is a deep unity, maintained by the will and deliberately strengthened by habit."[14] Especially at times when we have little to give, when we wish to be cared for but instead are providing the care, or when we extend love despite a lack of reciprocation or appreciation, "staying" means more. If marriage and motherhood were like a perpetual spa resort, we could never prove true commitment to ourselves or others.

I believe in poetic justice, but also poetic mercy. On a particularly hard morning of little cooperation, a burnt breakfast with associated complaints, and other assorted mounting frustrations, I said to my husband and kids, "I'm leaving. You can take care of yourselves today." I walked out the front door and down the road for several blocks, discretely wiping angry tears from my cheeks with bare fingers. Cars passed with anonymous drivers and houses lined the streets, but I felt utterly alone. After going about a mile and breathing the fresh air, I stopped by a wooded creek and stood under a tree that still held most of its vibrantly yellow leaves. I had never just walked away because of frustration before. I stayed by the creek to pray and to try to make further sense of my feelings. After a time, I was ready to turn around and head back home. My older boys had already left on the bus for school. My husband and younger boys welcomed me home and then the day went on like most others. I took time to write in my journal, and noticed the significance of the date: 11/02/2011—a perfect palindrome that mirrored my departure and return.*

---

* Note that this discouraging day happened when I was over halfway through my writing process. Focusing on ideals doesn't suddenly make everything ideal or preclude problems. Unless we maintain patience for processes, we can actually become more intolerant of or devastated by mistakes and imperfections in ourselves and others.

110

More important than counting our hours at home (though every hour counts), will be ensuring that our *hearts* are at home, "For where thy treasure is, there will your heart be also" (Luke 12: 33-34). Rather than becoming distracted with other matters and allowing our influence and connectedness to decrease, let us hold onto our children—our truest treasures. The scriptures record the lament of a destroyed civilization: "O that we had remembered the Lord our God in the day that he gave us our riches, and then they would not have become slippery that we should lose them; for behold our riches are gone from us. . . Yea, we have hid up our treasures and they have slipped away from us."[15] Instead, let us be diligent and engaged in our responsibilities toward our children—to "use all [our] endeavors to preserve them . . . [that] they should be protected."[16] "Let us cheerfully do all things that lie in our power; and then may we stand still, with the utmost assurance, to see the salvation of God, and for his arm to be revealed" (D&C 123:17).

Reflect or discuss:

1) In what ways do you currently demonstrate dedication to your family?

2) When was a time you felt God's enabling power helping you do what needed to be done?

V. FRUIT
On nurturing family and self

18~ NURTURING: THE CENTRAL WORK OF MOTHERING

Each spring our family plants some type of backyard garden. At minimum we plant tomatoes and zucchini, but usually the crop includes winter squash, Swiss chard, beets, radishes, peas, green beans, cilantro, and basil. Then there are the raspberries, black caps, and strawberries that return each year. My husband and older boys do the tilling and then line up string between two sticks to make straight rows. The younger boys hold a handful of seeds and plant them each a small fist-width apart. One of the delights of summer is watching the boys pick fresh produce to snack on while they play or to supplement dinner.

In the layered roles afforded by family life, we have opportunity to be simultaneously soil, gardener and plant—receiving and fostering the growth of others, and yet ourselves also growing. In the New Testament's familiar parable of the sower, the various soil types can instructively be compared to nurturing ground. The wayside parallels a neglectful or threatening environment; the stony ground conveys one of low support where parental enthusiasm and commitment fade quickly at any moment of hardship; the thorny ground portrays a distracted, detached context where outside attentions choke out parental responsiveness; and the good ground, bearing the best fruit, symbolizes a nurturing environment where needs are well met. Though as parents, we move through these categories to some degree, we continually work to cultivate the good ground. Children physically grow with the passage of time and even minimal care, but optimal conditions can help them truly thrive.

Adam and Eve, after choosing to seek greater knowledge (in part, naively so), were by necessity cast out of the Garden of Eden, where all had been provided for them. They went from a beautiful haven to a wilder place of greater possibilities—a place allowing an increased breadth of experience but also requiring more of them. This stepping-out into a world of thorns and thistles where bread is earned by sweat indeed is how family life often proceeds. But there is beauty in the wilderness. I've learned this truth by experience, but I also remember my mom telling it to me one day as we sat together in an LDS temple service in Salt Lake City, UT. Along the wall was a painted mural of the post-Eden wilderness with dry grass and a wild lion feasting on its prey; she leaned and whispered to me, "But it's *still* beautiful." She also sees beauty in sagebrush and the dry, dusty mountains of the West, aflame in spring with clusters of Indian Paintbrush.

The central work of mothering is nurturing—providing the right kind of care at all stages to foster healthy growth so the intended fruits may come in the end. With children, providing optimal growing conditions increases the likelihood of specific fruits but never guarantees them; since these seeds have independent will, we can only ever say that the fruits "may come." What are optimal growing conditions for a child? This largely depends on which child you are growing, or which you are trying to grow (which may or may not be the same thing).

After having raised a garden with my family for several years, I can identify most common seeds—some show obvious resemblance to what they will become, like the dry wrinkly pea seed; other seeds initially look deceptively similar to one another, like beets and radishes. The seed packages show pictures of end products and provide instruction: "Requires full sun. Plant 1/4 inch deep, 1 inch apart." With each child, unlike packaged seeds, only over time do we come to discover what we have planted. Though we know some conditions that are universally needed—the sun, water and soil of parenting—the other specifics we must learn uniquely with each child. We experiment with our best efforts, observe results, and adjust as necessary. As with seeds, which naturally become fruit-bearing plants or even large trees, our children also contain the built-in capacity for growth with a few simple conditions met. Growth in the natural world creates a fitting analogy for parenting because in both, as stated in Alma 37:6, "By small and simple things are great things brought to pass."

Reflect or discuss:

1) What does "nurturing" mean to you?

2) Do any particular scenarios come to mind where you've been able to provide a nurturing influence to your children or others?

115

19~ FIVE PRINCIPLES OF GROWTH

To nurture is to promote growth. Certain straightforward principles relating to environment, effort, patience, nourishment, and initiative govern growth processes.

1. Optimal growth comes in a nurturing environment.

When I was little, my Dad sliced apples for me and we sat together and ate. It was not ordinary in any way, but an elevated ritual of care. My Dad was a connoisseur of apples and fruit in general. At the grocery store, he'd pass over the bulk, packaged apples and instead would select his fruits individually. He'd lift each apple, smell it, and gently test its firmness before placing it in the bag. He would tell us how certain varieties were better than others and why. Our favorite was McIntosh: sweet and tart, soft but not mushy or pithy. Perhaps one of the best parts of this apple-cutting ritual was that it often occurred when I was supposed to be asleep in bed. My dad was a musician and often stayed up late practicing, but he'd stop and cut an apple for me if I woke up feeling hungry or scared. So to me it felt like an indulgence, despite its healthfulness. My dad called healthy food "real food," and though he didn't forbid other treats, offering and encouraging the "real food" was my first lesson that some things offer true nourishment, while others do not.

The scriptures call the fruit from the Tree of Life the "most precious above all other fruits"[1]; it represents the best gifts God gives, stemming from his love. This is the most "real" food of all. A nurturing environment is a loving environment. Though children may at times resist parental teaching, in the long run, they internalize instruction most easily from those who have demonstrated great care for them. Growth cannot be forced or imposed; "Nothing is so much calculated to lead people [to goodness] as to take them by the hand, and watch over them with tenderness."[2] Relating to our children in a "warm and loving"[3] manner will enable them to feel known and valued—a foundation to help them become their best selves.

A loving environment emphasizes strengths over weaknesses. Choosing to see our children's strengths helps them blossom. Nearly all weaknesses have inherent strengths attached (like when picking up a stick, we can't help but get both ends of it). For example, a child with seeming

116

oblivion to social graces and expectation may embarrass parents at a dinner party, but will likely bear a near-immunity to peer-pressure. A painfully perfectionistic child is likely also very conscientious and dependable. An energetic, talkative or even occasionally obnoxious child is often enthusiastic and fun. As we emphasize and give our children opportunity to utilize their strengths, these will become more prominent. Often situations of mutual benefit (symbiosis) can be found. For example, my elderly mom with limited ability to get around was able to sit with my son and help him with his spelling and poem memorization. In his need for help, he was able to spend time with his grandmother, who also benefited from the companionship.

2. Growth often is uncomfortable and requires effort.

Growth of a seed involves pushing through, breaking the system that is trying to contain it so it can become something bigger. Children also must challenge the status quo to move on to the next stage. The Gesell Institute of Human Development studied thousands of children to characterize patterns of development. One theme researchers noted was that children seemed to alternate between stages of "equilibrium" and "disequilibrium" roughly every other year.[4] Periods of disequilibrium, during which a child attempts to apply new awareness or ability, may feel less comfortable or smooth to both children and families.

Further, it takes honing to find the strength that underlies any weakness. For example, a child perceived as stubborn will likely shine with determination, a child perceived as emotional will likely have a gift for empathy, a child perceived as incessantly active or loud will likely come to lead others with energetic enthusiasm. Trimming and pruning may be required to enhance future harvests. However, before trying to stamp out these growing but presently less-than-convenient qualities, we must proceed with caution; these inherent qualities may be vital to our children's future survival or their ability to fulfill their life's role.

Nourishing a child's growth is not an easy work. As mothers, we experience simultaneous satisfaction and pain to see our children grow. Just as they grew out of the safety of our wombs, they eventually grow out of every containment system we properly create for them. We must adjust to ever-evolving needs and changing optimal growth conditions. Then there are the weeds. Raising a child is never a closed system—other influences and forces operate that we must continually weigh and determine whether to allow or to uproot. Then there is the dailiness—the unrelenting call-to-attention: we meet needs (both universal and unique) on a consistent basis. Systems of patterned nurturing often arise based on observations of typical need; for example, traditional mealtimes arise from the fact that people tend to get hungry every 4-5 hours when awake. More personalized nurturing occurs when specific needs are observed or predicted and then met based on intimate knowledge of an individual. This is the "milk" and "honey" of motherhood: the nourishment (meeting basic needs) and the sweetness (individualized serving, sharing and cherishing).[5] We "nourish *with great care*"[6] and await the fruits to come.

3. Growth requires patience, because it involves time and process.

Sometimes I feel impatient with my kids as they gain abilities, impatient with my mom as she loses certain abilities, and impatient with myself for being impatient. As mothers, we also are learning and growing—we must mercifully allow this process within ourselves as we do in our children.

While occasionally growth occurs in bursts and sudden breakthroughs, usually it emerges gradually and cannot be forced. As parents we make efforts, then we wait, "let[ting] patience have her perfect work" (James 1:4). My sister-in-law has this quote on her wall: "Sow. Weed. Water. Wait." Hope can be difficult to maintain when no immediate results are evident. If we demonstrate "patient continuance in well doing" (Romans 2:7), fruits will come.[*]

My friend planted blueberry bushes in her garden two years ago. She explained how they require special cages, special mulch, special trimming, and special soil pH—yet often no fruit comes until the 3rd or 4th year. I stick to simpler crops, like tomato and zucchini, but even these teach patience and contain certain surprises. At the end of the season, we picked a crate of green tomatoes for frying and canning as relish. Though we thought the time to enjoy the preferred red garden tomatoes had passed, by the time I got around to the project, a quarter of them had actually become red. The scriptures teach that, "Much ...lieth in futurity"[7] (in other words, many results and outcomes are not immediately apparent). As mothers, we deal mostly in seeds whose dormancy only later springs forth. Emily Dickinson writes,

---

[*] See also 1 Thessalonians 1:3 and Hebrews 6:12.

To venerate the simple days
Which lead the seasons by . . .
Needs but to remember
That the acorn there
Is the egg of forests
For the upper air![8]

The "simple days" of nurturing and waiting are what make up the greater part of seasons, years, and eventually, the totality of our lives.

Though we hope for certain outcomes, we must recognize that progress appears differently at different stages, and learn to value more than just end products. Tim Gallwey stated,

> When we plant a rose seed in the earth, we notice that it is small, but we do not criticize it as "rootless and stemless." We treat it as a seed, giving it the water and nourishment required of a seed. When it first shoots up out of the earth, we don't condemn it as immature and underdeveloped; nor do we criticize the buds for not being open when they appear. We stand in wonder at the process taking place and give the plant care it needs at each stage of development. The rose is a rose from the time it is a seed to the time it dies. Within it, at all times, it contains its whole potential. It seems to be constantly in the process of change; yet at each state, at each moment, it is perfectly all right as it is.[9]

Growth comes in stages. Just as we cannot tell our children to be two inches taller than they are, we cannot expect them to achieve instant mastery or maturity.

Nurturing at many levels goes on simultaneously and growth proceeds at different rates in different areas, never before an individual is ready. Emerson states, "No man can learn what he has not preparation for learning, however near to his eyes the object. A chemist may tell his most precious secrets to a carpenter, and he shall be never the wiser. . . God screens us evermore from premature ideas. Our eyes are holden that we cannot see things that stare us in the face, until the hour arrives when the mind is ripened."[10] Growth usually comes incrementally, though sometimes leaps in maturity seem to occur—a sudden ripeness. I have gone out into our backyard garden only to find a fully formed zucchini that didn't seem to be there the previous day, or soft, red tomatoes that were firm and green only a day earlier. Rather than this growth coming out of nowhere, it was proceeding quietly and unnoticed all along in the underbrush.

4. A lack of nourishment limits growth.

If we fail to notice growth "trying" to happen, we may accidentally hinder it. One of my sons often needed coaxing to come in for meals and would seemingly rather play or attend to personal projects than eat. When he did come, he would often take only a few bites before declaring himself finished. When he began asking for more food—a whole rather than a half-sandwich, a more generous helping of dinner—at first I caught myself saying, "No, you never eat that much. I don't want the food to be wasted." I quickly realized he was trying to grow, and I was inadvertently preventing him.

Sometimes we think certain feats of growth impossible only because we haven't tried them under the conditions of proper support and nourishment. My husband likes to run trail marathons, whereas I am happy running 2-3 miles at a time. I was telling him, "I was a sprinter in high school, never a distance runner—I don't think I'm made to run longer distances. After about 45 minutes, I always start to feel sick." Then he asked, "Do you drink enough water? Do you bring food along the way?" As I thought of it, I never brought food or water and likely began my runs in a depleted state, often exercising in the early morning with my last intake being the night before. It amazed me that all along I had operated with the assumption that I was not cut out for distance running, when in reality I did not nourish myself sufficiently for it. Though I still prefer shorter jogs, that Fall I trained for and successfully completed a trail half-marathon.

Sometimes I'm annoyed at myself for how much I "need" daily scripture study, daily prayer, and other meditative, centering activities. One afternoon, a few days after coming home from the hospital with a new baby, I was feeling tearful and frustrated with my older kids. I told my husband, "I'm doing better this time at not trying to do too much, but I'm feeling so mad at the other kids for not following directions. I don't even care so much that the tasks I've requested aren't getting done—I'm just mad they're not listening. I don't want to feel angry and march around barking orders at people. Do you have any advice for me?" He wisely said he didn't, but proceeded to step in and help. Then he asked, "Have you prayed and read from the scriptures yet today?" I took a few minutes to step away and pray and read a few scriptural verses and did feel much more

120

equipped to handle the challenges of the day. At times of turmoil or transition, taking time to nourish ourselves can be particularly difficult—yet just as we accept and comply with our perpetual physical need for food and water, we must humbly accept our need for constant nourishment also in spirit. Nourishing ourselves enables us to nourish others, therefore enhancing growth at multiple levels. Our nurturing occurs by simple persistence; it is the daily manna.

5. We can take initiative by seeking growth rather than just waiting for it to happen.

Often we say we want to grow in certain ways, but have truly not paid the price. The price may include focus, study, work, disciplined choice, and sacrifice. We must want the change *more* than we want the current situation, and all its attendant characteristics. A few years ago I decided I wanted to develop greater patience. I began by studying all the scriptures I could find about the topic and reading from other inspiring sources. I prayed for increased patience. Because patience was on my mind, this became a lens through which I measured my responses and interactions. My focused study tuned me into lessons offered by my daily long-term challenges. I realized that I could approach growth in any desired area by this same process.

In order to grow, we can seek nourishment in universal and personal ways: we can choose to foster our health; we can seek inspired answers from inspired sources; we can set up the particular conditions that we uniquely require to function optimally. We have little control over some circumstances and can pray for help in these areas. For example, though I consider myself a social person with a good network of support, there was a time when I felt particularly lonely. My family and closest friends were far away. Fostering new friendships was difficult as a mom of young children—there was little time for it and it was hard to find others who had a rhythm that matched mine (non-conflicting nap times, the constraints of specific leaving and coming home times for older children, the same degree of spontaneity, dependability, and flexibility). I decided to pray to find a good friend. My first realization was that relationships with my own family—my kids and my husband—were the most important ones to foster, but also, over the next few months I found two wonderful friends. One was a mother of boys with ages similar to mine, the other became my running partner for a year or so. Both are faithful, dedicated mothers and inspiring friends who I consider to have been hand-picked by God just for me in answer to prayer.

Reflect or discuss:

1) For each of the most important individuals in your life, what specifically constitutes a nourishing environment?

2) How have you been able to demonstrate patience for the growth process in yourself or others? Have you ever been happily surprised by sudden evidence of new growth?

3) Is there a time when you have actively sought growth in a particular area? What did you do?

20~ THE ART OF NURTURING

Nurturing is itself a garden that can be cultivated, an art that can be studied and grown. Just as an artist makes a careful study of his or her subject and with a series of small decisions—a line here and open space there—creates its likeness, we too help our children become who they need to be. Nurturing occurs in the details of interaction—the small daily choices of how we handle various situations. It involves intervention informed by careful observation.

Observing

We observe our children to know them. This involves continual finding out, since our children are growing and changing. Before I had a baby, my sister told me being a mom was like opening a present over and over again, and I've found that to be true. First you find out whether you are having a boy or a girl, then they are born and you get to meet them, after a few months you can tell what color their eyes will be, and on and on. Besides being delightful, observing our children becomes very useful and relevant to nurturing them. Just the act of paying attention both builds and communicates love. We also learn about their current state of development and readiness for new growth.

Intervening (or not)

Nurturing honors the principles of natural growth and involves understanding how to selectively "make grow" certain aspects— encouraging certain qualities and discouraging others. It involves taking the right kind of initiative at the right time to enable growth rather than attempting to force it. Certain interventions are unnecessary, some are vital, and others are detrimental.

Arnold Lobel's *Frog and Toad* series contains a story entitled "The Garden" that shows the irony of expending unnecessary energy to rush growth that was naturally occurring anyway. Toad sees Frog's wonderful garden and wishes to have one like it, so Frog gives him some seeds and tells him to plant them and wait for them to grow. Toad is very impatient with the process and bends near the ground and in escalating tones yells, "Now seeds . . . START GROWING!" Frog says, "You are shouting too much. These poor seeds are afraid to grow." So Toad rethinks things and returns to his seeds to sit with them in the dark, play music, and recite poetry to them. He is so tired after all this that he dozes off. When he wakes up, the seeds have sprouted.[11] All along, the seeds had what they *really* needed to grow in the sunshine, water, and passage of time; given certain simple conditions, the growth was programmed within them to occur naturally.

Similarly with children, some growth is developmentally determined, yet parents spend energy worrying, speculating, and attempting to orchestrate it. For example, the milestone of learning to walk primarily depends on timing of nerve myelination; regardless of parental intervention, babies typically start walking at or near twelve months of age. Underlying developmental problems or a deprived environment may delay it (in which cases extra interventions would help), but in most cases, the process cannot be significantly accelerated. Neuroscientist Steve Petersen says, "Development really wants to happen. It takes very impoverished environments to interfere with development."[12] We must be willing to trust natural processes, but also to contribute all supplemental investment that is required. As parents, therefore, we need to put our limited energy into nurturing the most relevant aspects, in effectual ways.

Like plants, our children are living, changing entities requiring different types of care over time. In gardening, certain acts like watering are always applicable: water to a plant is like love to a child. Other acts are fitting at certain stages and unhealthy at others: you bury a seed (like strict protection of an infant), but such an act would be damaging to a leafing plant (over-control of a growing, exploring child). Developmentally appropriate responses require knowledge of typical development. Parental misinterpretations of the meaning in a child's action may lead to an inappropriate response. For example, a mother who interprets infant crying as her own personal failure to comfort or the baby's willful rejection of it, limits her effectiveness at providing calm comfort; a mother who interprets the imaginative embellishments of a preschool child as willful lying or misrepresentation, may shame rather than gently correct accuracy and therefore interfere with the natural experimentation with narrative and magical thinking of this age; a mother who interprets a teenager's distinct but innocent preferences as pre-rebellion rather than healthy individuation, may in her resistance foster true rebellion. Practical application of child development data requires discernment, because unique variations and timetables exist within the realm of healthy growth.

Unlike plants, our children are self-willed. Some of that will is a deep self-knowledge or awareness which give clues to emerging identity. In our families, as neither seed nor crop come with labels or identifying markers, we must observe and come to learn (from their likes, dislikes, and dreams) who our children are. We must give space for our children to manifest themselves. If we involve ourselves in every situation, we cannot accurately assess how our children would function without us. For example, if I constantly stand over my kids to ensure that they complete their chores, I can learn nothing of their growing ability to work independently. Applied observation can even be more affirming than praise. Harvard psychologist Richard Weissbourd wisely observed, "The self becomes stronger and more mature less by being praised than by being *known*."[13] To first honor the intimate knowledge we gain of our children—their unique package of evolving strengths and weaknesses—increases the relevance of any subsequent intervention.

Nurturing involves providing wise encouragement and feedback. Utilizing current abilities fosters further growth. For example, my friend ingeniously labels her toy bins with pictures, which allows her toddler and preschool children to clean up more independently and develop greater responsibility. Supporting our children's healthy interests and inclinations also guides growth. Providing foundational, wholesome experiences will "feed" their good desires; whereas overindulgence will promote (rather than satiate) unwise appetites. Because of financial constraints in our family, some years at Christmas we have exchanged only small or homemade gifts. One would think the kids would feel cheated or perhaps greedy for presents, but the opposite has been the case. They have happily drawn pictures, decorated blocks, sewn mittens, and even wrapped their own prized possessions to give to their brothers.

A story is told of a Cherokee elder teaching his grandson; he says, "A fight is going on inside me. It is a terrible fight between two wolves. [One] is anger, envy, sorrow, regret, greed, arrogance, self-pity, guilt resentment, inferiority, lies, false pride, superiority, and ego. [The other] is joy, peace, love, hope, serenity, humility, kindness, benevolence, empathy, generosity, truth, compassion, and faith. The same fight is going on inside you—and inside every other person too." His grandson asks, "Which wolf will win?" He replies, "The one you feed."[14] It has been my experience that the more I eat sweets the more I want them, the more regularly I exercise, the more I want to exercise regularly, the more I practice singing, the more I want

125

to practice. A relationship is being built thorough experience; if it's positive and successful, I want more. Certain experiences can be like poison—the optimal "dose" of certain things is *none* (addictive substances, injurious or destructive behaviors). In other cases, there is no cap on the optimal "dose"—as long as balanced with other needful things, the more the better (like water, fruits and vegetables, studying good books, serving others, developing talents).

Our methods of giving guidance and correction can either dissolve or compound resistance (more on this in chapter 37). In contrast to a barrage of non-specific reprimands ("Stop that," "Cut it out," "Don't"), effective requests and directions possess purpose and clarity both for the giver and receiver. We increase clarity as we consider and communicate specifics to basic questions such as what, why, who, how, and when:

	Parent	Child
What?	Identifies and communicates the desired behavior.	Understands the behavioral expectation.
Why?	Communicates the desired underlying outcome for child or family (as developmentally and situationally appropriate).	As possible, shares understanding of purpose.
Who?	Takes into account strengths, weaknesses, and special circumstances of all involved.	Feels free to voice or clarify current personal circumstances (such as goals, intentions, preferences, mood).

When?	If possible, selects optimal timing to make requests; communicates expected timeline (which may be "now").	Understands timeline for expectation.
How?	Uses neutral tones. Uses "I" statements ("I need you to…," I expect….," "I feel. . ."). Acknowledges and allows choices within constraints. Holds children accountable. Remains available to offer step-by-step guidance when needed.	Respectfully receives and applies the direction given; seeks additional guidance as needed.

Though interventions do not always proceed according to the ideal, effectiveness can improve as the ideal is taken into account. As with pruning, small, early interventions are better received than major trimming, but both have their place in promoting growth and survival.

Optimal nurturing, however, does not always mean intervening, handling, or providing. More is not always better: sun scorches, water drowns, soil suffocates. If we consider nurturing to be only those things that promote healthy growth, then by definition we could not nurture too much—once we cross a line where caregiving actions turn detrimental (however unintentionally), this would cease to be nurturing. However, we often mistakenly consider embellished provisions superior to basic provisions. Is a fancier meal—one that delights in addition to nourishing—better than a basic one? Are extras—gadgets, toys, wishes granted—better than bare necessity?

We need not prohibit ourselves from embellishing in ways that we or our children particularly enjoy, that do not produce evidence of growing entitlement, and that do not detract from other essential areas, however, if providing an "upgraded" nurturing proves detrimental to our overall mood or functioning, it is not worth the intended benefits. Basic needs simply but consistently met likely provide more security than the combination of wishes and whims granted but basic needs only sporadically met. Meeting generalized, predictable needs and situational, personalized needs takes effort and experience. Though we may overdo and underdo while finding the perfect level of involvement, we must not foster helplessness or demandingness. If a child has become dissatisfied with our every effort to help, it may be time for *them* to invest more in the problem-solving process. Our ultimate goal in mothering is different from gardening—our seeds grow not just into plants, but into gardeners themselves.

Our own family "gardens" have more than one crop. Nurturing *all* family members, including one's spouse, indirectly nurtures each child; our nurturing will be more easily received and trusted by our children if they see us similarly nurturing others they care deeply about.

Reflect or discuss:

1) In thinking of yourself or a particular child, what are some demonstrated strengths you'd like to help grow? What are some weaknesses you'd like to deemphasize?

2) Have you witnessed multiple family members benefit when you have actively nurturing an individual?

3) How have you balanced your attention when a certain family member needed extra help?

21 ~ NURTURING BY LISTENING

Listening is a powerful nurturing tool. It validates the speaker and sends the message "you are worthy to be heard." It models respect and teachability.[*] As mothers we have the opportunity to listen at many levels—to God, to our family members, to ourselves. Mark 4:24 states, "Unto you that hear shall more be given." When we hear or "hearken," allowing information gained to be integrated or put to use, more instruction will be given—more divine instruction, more trusted sharing from our kids, more self-understanding. The Book of Amos refers to a "famine of hearing" (8:11)—sometimes when our relationships suffer and feel stressed and weak, it is because it has been too long since any of us has felt truly heard or understood. In such a case, listening can be like opening a door to share a nourishing feast: "Behold, I stand at the door, and knock: if any man hear my voice, and open the door, I will come in to him, and will sup with him, and he with me" (Rev 3:20).

We sacrifice many things to provide for our children—we spend time, effort, and preparation so their outward needs are met. But after all this, feeling we have nothing more to offer, we may fail to listen to them when that is what they would have wanted most. In the Old Testament, Saul mistakenly assumes the Lord would prefer sacrificial offerings above being carefully listened to, but he is chastened and told, "To hearken [is better] than the fat of rams" (I Sam 15:22).

Parent educator Glenn Latham has said, "Parental attention is the most powerful force in shaping children's behavior."[15] Listening, one way of giving attention, influences whether certain ideas flower or drop away. Like a plant reaches for sunlight, children tend to emphasize behaviors that earn attention. Listening does not necessarily imply agreement or sanction of an idea—paradoxically, allowing expression even of undesirable feelings may allow them to naturally extinguish. As stated earlier, "Strong feelings do not vanish by being banished; they do diminish in intensity and lose their sharp edges when the listener accepts them with sympathy and understanding."[16] Still, certain ideas do deserve immediate rejection and others careful consideration.

---

[*] See James 1:22 "Be ye doers of the word, and not hearers only."

The practice of listening includes both suspension and engagement. A wise teacher once pointed out that the letters in the word "listen" when rearranged spell "silent." Psychologist Michael Nichols acknowledges, "We may be interested but too concerned with controlling or instructing or reforming the other person to truly be open to his or her point of view. Parents have trouble hearing their children as long as they can't suspend their urgent need to set them straight. . . .Unfortunately, most people aren't eager to be changed by someone who doesn't take time to understand them."[17] Note that Nichols advocates we *suspend* (hold off on) our desire to "set straight," not abandon it entirely. Only after sincere listening can we truly know if anything *needs* correction. Also, children are much more likely to hear if they have been heard. Sometimes our children's actual "hearkening" only comes later, at which time "that which they had not heard, shall they consider" (Isaiah 52:15).

Effective parental listening is active, therapeutic, and selective. *Active listening* involves giving attention and offering proof of that attention: making eye contact, occasionally restating or rephrasing to verify understanding, encouraging the speaker to continue with verbal or non-verbal cues (saying "mm-hmm," nodding), and remembering the important details that have been shared. Active listening may also involve making comments or giving input, but only when the speaker is ready (perhaps signaled by a pause, sigh, or visible release of tension).

Therapeutic listening means hearing the message behind the message— listening to what your children are *really* saying, not to what they have actually said or what you want them to have said, but to their hearts. For example, a toddler laying on the floor screaming may in reality be saying, "I'm hungry. I'm tired. I feel desperate." A grumpy teenager may be saying, "My friend hurt my feelings today" or inwardly asking, "Am I pretty enough? Smart enough? Good enough?" Perhaps a child comes home and says, "I hate school!" If you negate or discount them, this reinforces their need to defend their position. But if you try to wisely translate the comment, you may reply, "Did you have a hard day? Tell me about it." Though our initial translation may require some correction, as mothers we often do have the gift to hear the message of the heart. Sometimes getting the hidden message requires *not* getting too caught up in delivery (the "extra packing"). Being able to recognize or surmise unstated needs will allow us to meet these needs rather than neglect them, distracted by emotional escalation and defensiveness.

Selective listening acknowledges that certain expressions deserve more or less attention than others because of intent, content, or delivery. Though we must be *able* to ignore delivery (when focusing on it would detract from a more important task at hand—perhaps that of connecting or teaching despite it), sometimes the task *is* to teach about delivery and guide content. As parents we are the ones to set boundaries that teach acceptable behaviors in the realm of communication. We must work to discern whether escalating emotions mean a child is approaching the heart of a matter *or* getting "stuck" in unproductive circles. In general, paying more attention to ideas or behaviors we want to encourage and less to those we don't "selects out" these more positive ideas and behaviors.* God models this to some degree—though he extends his mercies to all ("He maketh his sun to rise on the evil and on the good, and sendeth rain on the just and on the unjust" (Matthew 5:45)), he listens preferentially to those who merit it.[18] As mothers, we likely will be able to sense which direction a discussion is heading and respond appropriately.

Some of the most important listening occurs not in formal sit down sessions, but as we note passing comments. We must listen especially well during the sharing of deep feelings, fears, hopes, dreams—but even how we hear casual, less vital statements builds trust. At times, effective listening requires a more ordered, structured setup. To prevent utter chaos as I have had more children, it has become necessary for the kids to learn to take turns speaking or even to wait in line to talk to me; to prevent oversights, sometimes I mentally schedule time to talk with each child so I don't neglect interacting with any certain individual.

The scriptures direct, "Let not all be spokesman at once; but let one speak at a time, and let all listen unto his sayings, that when all have spoken that all may be edified of all" (D&C 88:122). Though listening should take high priority, in a busy household, some points cannot be heard *yet* or heard to completion in one sitting. For example, if one child is telling me something and another brother has a sudden need, I stop, assess, and prioritize. If the problem can wait, I stay to hear the story through; if the

---

* Of course, negative communication or behavior cannot be ignored when it truly threatens safety. Sometimes this means that even small statements need to be discussed because they imply an unhealthy perspective. In contrast, other seeming alarming acts or statements do not even deserve the slightest attention or response, just a sort of detached supervision. For example, calm dismissal of inappropriate, experimental "shock" talk will likely extinguish it faster than overemphasizing it.

problem cannot wait, I excuse myself and attend to it (in which case I make mental note to come back to request the rest of the conversation or story). Unfortunately, sometimes the moment cannot be recaptured; sometimes I forget and they remember; sometimes we both forget and that fragment of conversation is left unfinished. For these I must forgive myself. If we realize we have not listened well, all is not lost—we might say, "I don't feel like I took the time to really understand you yesterday." Often, doors can be reopened; often, plants can revive.

By listening, we come to know our children better, we participate in a worthwhile and meaningful exchange, we gather valuable information that helps our counsel be more wise and pertinent, and we ourselves are more likely to be heard. If we are "swift to hear, slow to speak" (James 1:19), we will "save [ourselves] *and* them that hear" (I Tim 4:6, italics added) by avoiding saying superfluous or hurtful things.

Reflect or discuss:

1) Has there been a time where stopping to listen and understand gave you important information you otherwise would not have had?

2) What one change could you make to improve the quality of your listening? How will you implement this change and measure your progress?

22~ Nurturing in hope

Why should we as mothers nurture with hope? It is a true, foundational principle that tends to be self-fulfilling. A wonderful law of physics applicable to parenting is the law of conservation of energy, which states that energy invested doesn't just disappear. All reasonable effort pays off, whether directly or indirectly, if nothing else by demonstrating care and engagement.

It has been said, "Hope is one leg of a three-legged stool, together with faith and charity. These three stabilize our lives regardless of the rough or uneven circumstances we may encounter at the time . . . Faith, hope, and charity complement each other, and as one increases, the others grow as well."[19] I like to think of the stool having a fourth leg—one of agency or will, because faith, hope, and charity require concerted choice. The scriptures state, "Wherefore, ye must *press forward* with a steadfastness in Christ [faith], having a perfect brightness of hope, and a love of God and of all men [charity]" (2 Nephi 31:20, emphasis added).

When my son was six, he announced that he wanted to build a stool. My husband said, "Draw up your plans and I will help you build it." Together they built a four-legged rectangular stool and painted it purple. Similarly, if we go to our Heavenly Father with detailed, worthwhile visions for our family relationships, he will help us build them—with faith, hope, and charity and our own resolve as the foundation. Just as the scriptures state that "if [we] have not faith, hope, and charity, [we] can do nothing," with them we can do just about anything (see D&C 18:19, Phil 4:13).

Maintaining hope as a parent entails choosing to see our children not only as they currently are, but as they can or will be. When we give a child feedback, we are aiming towards his or her potential self, not attacking the current child as "target." To proceed with hope we can:

·**A**sk about motives or intent with true curiosity and openness toward the answer, avoiding labels* and negative assumptions.

---

* When I hear my boys labeling each other—saying things like, "You're mean!"—I say, "Tell him how you'd like him to behave, rather than telling him he already IS the way you don't want him to be." When teachers or other adults have try to label my children, I redirect the conversation away from generalizations and toward specifics. Our language can be a powerful force in helping others become like we'd hope them to be.

·**I**ndividualize the feedback, by giving it privately, respectfully, and in context of deep regard for the person.

·Stick to the **m**ain message or teaching point (limit the amount or scope of feedback so as not to overwhelm).

Hopeful communication is respectful communication and is thereby more easily received. "A courteous tone makes your words, not your behavior, worth remembering."[20] All our positive interaction builds a reserve that makes our children more able to accept correction when needed. We "plow in hope" and "[thresh] in hope," acting as "servant unto all . . . that [we] might gain them" (1 Corinthians 9:10, 19, 21). "For in due season we shall reap, if we faint not" (Galatians 6:9). As visionary mothers, we proceed with "the *patience* of hope and the labor of love" (1 Thessalonians 1:3 emphasis added)[21]—not in discouraged, frustrated waiting. This will be a choice and a labor. The only risk in hoping for the best in our children is we might be wrong, despite having done everything possible to improve the odds of being right.

Nurturing "despite"

As mothers we nurture our children despite perceived weaknesses (in us and them), despite non-ideal conditions, despite a frequent lack of perceptible effect, despite occasional antagonism or rejection, and despite a lack of guaranteed outcomes. The text to a hymn acknowledges such challenges, but also the helps available and the fruits to come:

> We are sowing, daily sowing
> Countless seeds of good and ill,
> Scattered on the level lowland,
> Cast upon the windy hill;
> Seeds that sink in rich, brown furrows,
> Soft with heaven's gracious rain;
> Seeds that rest upon the surface
> Of the dry unyielding plain. . . .
> By a whisper sow we blessings;
> By a breath we scatter strife.
> In our words and thoughts and actions
> Lie the seeds of death and life.
> Thou who knowest all our weakness,
> Leave us not to sow alone!
> Bid thine angels guard the furrows

Where the precious grain is sown,
Till the fields are crown'd with glory,
Filled with mellow, ripened ears,
Filled with fruit of life eternal
From the seed we sowed in tears.[22]

In Matthew 9:11-13, the Pharisees criticize Jesus for eating with the publicans and sinners; Jesus explains, "the whole need no physician . . . go ye and learn what that meaneth." Our children are not whole or complete in their development and we as parents, though imperfect, must instruct and nurture them; our parenting is "learning what that means"—to minister among the imperfect while being imperfect ourselves.

Even though we cannot create, maintain or guarantee perfect growth conditions for our children (one child needs "full sun," the other "shade;" one crowds out another; or perhaps it is a time of drought)—in all this, the Master Gardener has a way of making our best parenting efforts sufficient to bring many good fruits (see Jacob 5:21-22). Even the naturally occurring gaps and omissions promote heartiness in our children. And, because our parenting efforts must proceed against resistance or backlash, *we* gain resilience too. Our nurturing ground is a wilderness; no matter how diligent and intentional our cultivating attempts, there is always a certain wildness there. Some unwanted things and some beautiful things just crop up. Growth happens because of us, independent of us, and in spite of us. The "wilderness factor" of our lives—the reality that without our effort and care, things would fall to ruin—calls forth our best. Though we have to suffer pain and peril, each generation, in the very process of being nurtured and then nurturing and sheltering the next, learns to grow and be hearty. It turns us and our children, by necessity, into gardeners.

A tree or fountain "in you"

The words of another hymn come to mind: "Oh refresh us, oh refresh us, traveling through this wilderness . . ."[23] The scriptures say that from a wilderness, God can make "Eden" (Isaiah 51:3, 41:18), that we can become "like a watered garden, and like a spring of water, whose waters fail not" (Isaiah 58:11, see also Jeremiah 31:12). If only we, as mothers, could obtain and bestow even a portion of such nourishment! The rich scriptural symbols of the "tree of life" and "living water" illustrate how such a hope could be realized.

135

The Book of Mormon refers to the tree of life in its infancy—that culminating tree with fruit delicious and pure "above all"—starting from a mere seed that we nourish:

> We will compare the word unto a seed. Now, if ye give place that a seed may be planted in your heart, behold if it be a true seed, or a good seed, if ye do not cast it out . . . it will begin to swell within [you]. . . . As the seed swelleth and sprouteth, and beginneth to grow, then you must needs say that the seed is good . . . for every seed bringeth forth its own likeness. . . . And behold, as the tree beginneth to grow, ye will say: Let us nourish it with great care, that it may get root, that it may grow up, and bring forth fruit unto us. And now behold, if ye nourish it with much care it will get root, and grow up, and bring forth fruit. . . . And because of your diligence and your faith and your patience with the word in nourishing it, that it may take root *in you*, behold, by and by ye shall pluck the fruit thereof, which is most precious, which is sweet above all that is sweet, and which is white above all that is white, yea, and pure above all that is pure; and ye shall feast upon this fruit even until ye are filled, that ye hunger not, neither shall ye thirst. Then, my brethren, ye shall reap the rewards of your faith, and your diligence, and patience, and long-suffering, waiting for the tree to bring fruit unto you" (Alma 32: 28-43, excerpts, emphasis added, see also Proverbs 11:30).

Through our choices and God's grace, this prized seed grows and swells, slated to be a "tree of life"—not in a distant field or garden—but *in us*, in our children! This type of nurturing, beginning with good seeds and progressing with great care, reaches not just the outer person, but the "fleshy tables of the heart" (2 Corinthians 3:3).

Another symbol of divine sustenance is Christ's "living water." He offers the Samaritan woman at the well a distinct type of water that satisfies in a lasting and complete way. He says, "Whosoever drinketh of the water that I shall give him shall never thirst; but the water that I shall give him shall be *in him* a well of water springing up into everlasting life" (John 4:14 emphasis added). This, again, is an ultimate gift of nourishment—to have received a pure fountain that springs forth from within!

What does all this mean? 1 Nephi 11:25 teaches that "the fountain of living waters" and "the tree of life" are both "a representation of the love of God." To receive and share this love: here is the key to nurturing.

Reflect or discuss:

1) What has helped you maintain steady diligence and trust in God even when results are hard to see?

2) How do you maintain hope in others' potential despite current mistakes or poor choices?

23~ NURTURING GOODNESS

In the Bible, Matthew records the account of one who comes to Jesus, calling him "Good Master," and asks what he needs to do to gain eternal life—the ultimate reward and seal of goodness. Jesus replies, "Why callest thou me good? There is none good but one, that is, God" (Matt 19:17). This somewhat startling response gives light unto the question of how we find and point others toward goodness: it is by pointing them to God. As mothers we do this by precept and example, and ultimately, by inviting them to experience for themselves God's goodness. Truly pointing our children to God means taking care to avoid inadvertently pointing them some other way.

Though wishing to nurture our children's goodness, we may inadvertently emphasize other things instead, such as their personal fulfillment, comfort, compliance, or outward success. Stephen Covey has stated, "Let us never forget that primary greatness is character; secondary greatness is popularity, prestige, and 'success.' Relatively few people have both. I know you want the children you are raising or teaching to have both, but of course, primary greatness is and should be first and foremost."[24]

A prominent speaker once said, "Parents have the duty to be what they would have their children become in regard to courtesy, sincerity, temperance, and courage to do right at all times. Example is far more important than precept."[25] The surprising (or not-so-surprising) conclusion that naturally follows is that as parents too, our goodness or "primary greatness" should also be foremost—ahead of to-do lists and ahead of outward success for us or our children. If we allow ourselves to behave poorly in efforts to gain our children's compliance or insist upon their performance, we have sacrificed providing an example of goodness for something else.

Richard Weissbourd, Harvard child psychologist and author of the book, *The Parents We Mean to Be*, acknowledges that what most parents want is not only happy children, but *good* children and that true innate goodness is ultimately what brings happiness. He states that, despite the many factors at play, "*We* [parents] are the primary influence on children's moral lives."[26] According to Weissbourd, our ability to inspire goodness in our children will rely as much upon the day-to-day details of relationship as it will upon specific instruction.[27] As is stated in the title of Dorothy Law Nolte's famous poem, "Children learn what they live,"[28] not merely what is told to them.

Part of nurturing anything is the ability to see what's already there—to nurture it for what it is, to recognize all good in its earliest stages in order to preserve and foster it. Since children possess inherent goodness and an innate ability to tell right from wrong,[29] our task is not to *instill* goodness but through guidance and instruction to nurture it. Though adults may have greater sophistication or experience in moral decision-making than children, the scriptures remind us that in many ways, *we* are to be more like *them* (Matthew 18:3-4).

Social science research indicates that moral development occurs in a predictable, stepwise way that parallels cognitive ability for abstraction and "perspective-taking."[30] Despite all our parental angst over it, moral maturity (often in part defined as the capacity to consider others' feelings) tends to improve naturally with development.

While younger children tend to be concrete and self-focused, they at times display high reasoning and selflessness that behavioral literature does not capture. Their capacity to comprehend, to feel compassion, and to act according to a high inward sense for right occurs in brilliant flashes even at the earliest ages. I remember one evening when I was sick with a cough. I tiredly sat on the stairs, gathering my energy to get the kids to bed. My two-year old looked at me, disappeared for a moment, and returned with a large teetering cup of water for me (which he could have only obtained through careful climbing and balancing). He sat next to me on the step insisting I keep drinking until I drank it all up. No scientific paper could convince me that young children are incapable of true empathy.

Notwithstanding the preexisting goodness of our children, we have a parental obligation to give further instruction. Formally and informally, we set forth a curriculum of goodness—we teach them about God, help them establish righteous habits, and expose them to uplifting influences. We teach by both precept and example, thereby providing both the theoretical, intellectual understanding as well as the applied demonstration. Ideally, our instruction would include and foster respectful communication, productive processing of emotions, self-reflection, and compassion.

In all this, we would afford our children time to meaningfully reflect upon their experiences, rather than dictating or filling every minute with activities or allowing large quantities of time spent in mind-numbing

139

distractions. We would direct them to take initiative, to ask questions and seek answers themselves, personally appealing to God through prayer and study. We would create mind-expanding and heart-expanding opportunities for inspiration and service. Much like feeding physically, however, our role is to set before them a healthy plate—we can invite our children's to partake in goodness but cannot force them. As they accept, they will experience the attendant good fruit and develop the inherent desire to continue to foster it themselves. This is goodness taking root.

Just as one does not require a degree in botany to raise an effective garden, one does not need a degree in social science to have effective family relationships. Though trained observation and research may enhance our understanding of family systems, the practice of parenting exists in the layman's sphere; it confounds experts more in practice than in theory and may be mastered by the sincere and simple. One doesn't have to know all the science behind natural laws for them to be operative. In families, over time, we tend to reap what we sow. A good fountain bears pure water, a tree bears fruit after its kind. Seeds of contention, strife, retaliation, or seeds of peace, kindness, and wisdom, tend to bear the same. In contrast to worldly ways, "the wisdom that is from above is first pure, then peaceable, gentle, and easy to be entreated, full of mercy and good fruits, without partiality, and without hypocrisy. And the fruit of righteousness is sown in peace of them that make peace." (James 3:17-18).

We trust in our children's innate goodness, in their consciences "at work," in their naturally increasing capacity for empathy that comes with development; we put forth our best efforts at teaching, exemplifying, and inviting goodness; but most importantly, we trust God—that He watches over, guides, and blesses our children even beyond our awareness, that He shares the agenda to nourish the goodness that is in them. Thus, we do not sow, tend, or reap alone. In nurturing, we turn the soil and we turn our hearts—to our children and their hearts to us. Our efforts affect not just one crop or season, but the harvest through generations. We have this potential within us—to grow and to help grow. The innate capacity for development, like a seed sprouting spontaneously, is a divine endowment. Frances Hodgson Burnett, in her classic story *The Secret Garden*, even calls it "magic." Young Colin says,

> *The flowers are growing—the roots are stirring. That is the Magic. Being alive is the Magic—being strong is the Magic. The Magic is in me . . . It's in every one of us* [31]

140

Reflect or discuss:

1) What good qualities do your family members already have?

2) Are you able to regularly communicate appreciation for the good that you see?

VI. THE BEST GIFTS

On fostering talent and ability

24~ Recognizing and Understanding Gifts

We will best nurture our children as we gain insight into their special hopes, dreams, and abilities. Dreams can be fragile things, but also tenacious. When my boys start telling me about their nighttime dreams—bizarre, funny, interesting, or scary twists arising out of subconscious thought—I try to listen: "I dreamed I was hiding behind a chair and two witches came riding on ponies, then I fell into a whirlpool and my bed was at the bottom, and then I woke up." But dreams in wakefulness—secret discoveries, hopes and wishes—to these I listen even more carefully. Whether "uttered or unexpressed,"[1] dreams are visions of gifts fully enacted, of possibilities come to life.

Once my six-year-old son walked over to me with particular deliberateness and, as if confiding in me and informing me both, he said with emphasis, "Mom . . . I can float!" I could have discounted or made light of his claim, but I didn't. I asked him what he meant and he described the brief sensation of hanging in the air at the height of a jump. I marveled with him in his discovery and his ability to have noticed such detail. He reminded me of young Georgie from the book *The Fledgling* who is convinced she can fly: "'If only I could do it again,' she thought. Because she had done it. She had. She knew she had. She had waked up in the middle of the night. She had jumped down the stairs in two floating bounds. Unless it was only a dream. . . . But she didn't really think it had been a dream. It had been so bright! It had felt so lovely! She had flown! Like the swans!"[2] To Georgie's claim others respond with a combination of endeared amusement and worry. Her uncle says, "Poor Georgie. . . she is too young to know the limits of human possibility. For Georgie, anything is possible! She lives entirely in the pure ideal."[3] Children often do, and this is what makes them so wonderful.

My kids say things like, "I'm going to have a carnival in our backyard and all the neighbors will come." A wheelbarrow going down a plywood plank propped on a horizontal log is the 10-cent ride and ice cream cones will be a quarter. Or they want to go door-to-door selling homemade products, like crushed colored rocks or potions made from dissolved bars of soap. One of my sons spent days notating songs he'd picked out by ear and some newly composed songs too; he neatly wrote the names of the

144

notes: "C-C-C-F-C-B-A-G," but a few days later ripped out all the pages to use the notebook for something else. I felt like reprimanding him for disregarding his own painstaking work, but instead, appeased by tucking away a few of the discarded pages, let him happily go where his next bit of ingenuity carried him.

Early 20th century writer and teacher Brenda Ueland acknowledges how children naturally possess imaginative drive; they create elaborate projects and productions "working only for fun, for that glorious inner excitement." She continues,

> But this joyful, impassioned energy dies out of us very young. Why? Because we let dry obligations take its place. Because we don't respect it in ourselves and keep it alive by using it. And we don't keep it alive in others by *listening* to them. . . . [T]he only way to love a person is not, as the stereotyped Christian notion is, to coddle them and bring them soup when they are sick, but by listening to them and seeing and believing in the god, in the poet, in them. For by doing this, you keep the god and the poet alive and make it flourish.[4]

We help gifts flourish sometimes by standing back and observing, sometimes by stepping in and intervening, always by valuing and appreciating.

All human beings have gifts—unique endowments that can and do change the world in some way. The scriptures state, "For all have not every gift given unto them; for there are many gifts, and to every man is given a gift by the Spirit of God."[5] My friend Theresa has a gift for maintaining a beautifully organized home. When I went over for a visit, I laughed to notice that not only were the magnetic alphabet letters all off the floor (unlike in my kitchen), but they were in neat rows and displayed alphabetically. This is the kind of attention to detail she has—there is beauty and clarity in it. Certain natural characteristics or abilities like this we can't help but notice. Others are not yet developed but show up as deep or resurfacing interests whose evidences keep cropping up spontaneously like spring flowers that can't help themselves. When we see this, we must pay attention.

Besides each possessing inherent gifts, we are invited to develop these and seek more.* Shinichi Suzuki, founder of Suzuki education, tells of his striking realization that talent in a given area, rather than being categorically present or absent, could be fostered. His book *Nurtured by Love* begins with these words:

> Oh—why, Japanese children can all speak Japanese! The thought suddenly struck me with amazement. In fact, all children throughout the world speak their native tongues with the utmost fluency. . . . Does that not show a startling talent? How, by what means does this come about? I had to control an impulse to shout my joy over this discovery. . . . If a child cannot do his arithmetic, it is said that his intelligence is below average. Yet he can speak the difficult Japanese language—or his own native language—very well. Isn't this something to ponder and think about? In my opinion the child who cannot do arithmetic is not below average in intelligence . . . his ability or talent simply has not been developed properly.[6]

Even if children have different starting points in a given skill area, desire, effort, support, and opportunity all play a great role in what trajectory they follow. How does one develop an ability "properly," and what is a parent's role?

To wisely guide our children, we must understand about gifts ourselves—not only how to recognize and pursue them, but why. The scriptures direct, "Seek ye earnestly the best gifts, always remembering for what they are given. For verily I say unto you, they are given for the benefit of those who love me and keep all my commandments, and him that seeketh so to do . . . that all may be profited thereby."[7] Gifts help us through life and help others around us by enriching our experience overall and by fulfilling specific needs.

Singing hymns, art songs, or arias at the piano and capturing insights in my journal bring me joy, peace, and a greater love for life and those around me. As we exercise our gifts, we tap into these feelings—it is the language of the Spirit: "But the fruit of the Spirit is love, joy, peace,

---

* See 1 Cor 12:31 and Doctrine & Covenants 46:8. I acknowledge that it is a luxury to think of gifts and enrichments. Depending on context of time and place (war, poverty, extreme conditions of any kind), some mothers have had little opportunity to look much beyond necessities of life and survival.

longsuffering, gentleness, goodness, faith" (Gal 5:22). We experience a second layer of joy when we can share our gifts to benefit others—to bring comfort or rescue. In C.S. Lewis's allegorical *The Lion, the Witch, and the Wardrobe*, Father Christmas comes and gives Peter, the "son of Adam," a shield and a sword. To the "daughters of Eve," he gives Susan a bow with arrows and Lucy a dagger and a bottle of healing potion. He says, "These are your presents, and they are tools not toys. The time to use them is perhaps near at hand. Bear them well."[8]

Recognizing the purpose of gifts is recognizing the purpose of ourselves. Looking at the parable of the talents, one may incorrectly think God is interested only in productivity, not process, but surely he cares for the growth of a stewardship *because* of what it means about the growth of the steward. This growth can be collective rather than competitive. When we come to know that all people have gifts—gifts that can be improved upon with effort and guidance—it instills a sense of value, direction and appreciation. Such knowledge allows us to be inspired rather than defeated by others' contributions or accomplishments.

Some make beautiful music, create beautiful pieces of artwork, or demonstrate physical strength and agility. In his letter recorded in I Corinthians chapter 12, Paul names several spiritual gifts including wisdom, knowledge, faith, and healing. Other less visible gifts may include "the gift of listening . . . the gift of avoiding contention . . . the gift of seeking that which is righteous; the gift of not passing judgment; the gift of looking to God for guidance . . . the gift of caring for others; the gift of being able to ponder."[9] Whatever our particular ability, we are told, "This is thy gift; apply unto it."[10]

Gifts rightly pursued come not at the expense of character, but naturally enrich it. In the New Testament we are told, "[seek] earnestly the best gifts: and yet I shew unto you a more excellent way" (1 Cor 12:31). What follows in chapter 13 as the "more excellent way" is a sermon on charity, reminding us that no matter what our outward accomplishments, if we "have not charity, [we] become as sounding brass, or a tinkling cymbal . . . [we are] nothing." (1 Corinthians 13:1-2). Every great scholar or artist who remains devout has come to a point of decision: to choose God, not their study or art as Master. Artists too can be saints and servants; they sacrifice hours of leisure to achieve precision and give service in the aesthetic realm.

Shinichi Suzuki tells of how once a mother of his violin student asked him, "Will my boy amount to something?" He replied, "No. He will not become 'something.' He will become a noble person through his violin playing. Isn't that good enough? You should stop wanting your child to become a professional, a good money earner. . . . A person with a fine and pure heart will find happiness. The only concern for parents should be to bring up their children as noble human beings. That is sufficient."[11] As stated by Elder Richard G. Scott, "Righteous character is more valuable than any material object you own, any knowledge you gain through study, or any goals you have attained no matter how well lauded by mankind. In the next life, your righteous character will be evaluated to assess how well you used the privilege of mortality."[12] Development of virtues and the development of gifts go hand in hand; virtue brings God's Spirit, which is the medium of all inspiration and creative work.[13]

Reflect or discuss:

1) What special talents have you seen in each of your children? Have they consistently shown a particular love for or interest in any specific area?

2) Do your children clearly know you value and cherish them apart from their outward accomplishments? Do they have a vision of why talents are worth pursuing? Are they able to show initiative and find joy in this process?

25~ Encouraging our children

How many children this very minute are practicing their scales or reviewing their spelling at a mother's request? Why do mothers expend such effort? We want our children to experience the joy of doing quality work; we want to foster character traits such as discipline and perseverance that may be transferable to other areas; we want to prepare them to make a meaningful contribution. Parents who help children discover and develop gifts bestow a priceless, expanding inheritance. But how is it done?

Supporting Vision

Even as a young girl, my sister Laurie loved the violin. My mom recognized this and fostered her playing. She allowed family outings to be delayed two or three hours while my sister finished her practicing, which annoyed me. She let my sister bring her violin on car trips and practice in hotel rooms, which embarrassed me. One professional musician who was a friend of the family generously but foolishly volunteered to hear my sister play and tell us if she "had any future" as a professional musician. Wisely, my mother had no interest in this. She believed in my sister's dream and dedication alone; an outsider's pronouncements of "potential" meant little to her. Laurie is now a violin teacher at a music school near Chicago and has her own family of talented musicians.[14]

I read an article of another mother who many years previously had received a call from the Sunday school chorister requesting she tell her daughter not to sing above the other children. Wisely, she chose to ignore the suggestion. Now this daughter, Rachel Willis-Sørensen, performs leading operatic roles at the Royal Opera House at Covent Garden.[15]

How did my mom know to protect my sister's practicing time? How did Rachel Willis-Sørensen's mother know to disregard well-meaning advice? As mothers, we get inklings of who our children really are and who they can become. We gather and hold these—like Mary who "kept all these things, and pondered them in her heart" (Luke 2:19)—and then we believe in our children and support them, allowing even ourselves to be surprised observing the gifts and their applications unfold.

As mothers, we can pray to gain insight into our children's gifts and how best to encourage them. Once having glimpsed our children's potential, we can't just shoot them off according to *our* trajectory—we must help *them* "aim high."[16] We can foster gifts by encouraging experiences that inspire and spark the imagination in general or specific ways. I recall one particular night when our family drove to a state park to look through a powerful telescope at the moon. To personally see the detailed contours of the moon's surface infused new perspective and appreciation in each of us suddenly and naturally—more than any theoretical lecture or photograph could.

Another night several years ago, my son James told me excitedly in one sentence how he wanted to be a tap dancer, a professional violist "like grandpa," a scientist, and an inventor. This string of dreams came forth at 11 o'clock at night, after we had attended a Bobby McFerrin concert at Orchestra Hall. For some time, my son had been enamored with an album entitled *Hush,* a recorded collaboration of classical cellist Yo-Yo Ma and improvisational vocalist Bobby McFerrin. When I learned Bobby McFerrin would be performing at Orchestra Hall in Minneapolis, I arranged to get tickets. Early in the concert, Bobby McFerrin asked for a few audience members to come up and dance while he spontaneously composed and performed matching music. James stood as if personally called to the stage (which surprised me because he was only nine), but then hesitated. Soon the audience was told that enough volunteers had come up, so James sat down; he looked disappointed to have missed the opportunity. I whispered to him, "It's okay, James. But learn from it— next time there is something you really want, go after it right away."

A bit later in the program, Bobby McFerrin again asked for volunteers—this time to sing a song to which he would improvise a vocal accompaniment. To this invitation, James ran. When his turn came, James didn't even have a song in mind (unlike some participants who seemed to have volunteered for display and recognition, rather than for the pure experience). I sat in the audience and watched my son suddenly on a concert stage, looking small compared to the other mostly adult volunteers and bright under the lights. He started his own improvised pitches and rhythms and Bobby McFerrin joined in. They were like two kids jamming in the basement for pure fun, oblivious to a spying audience. Attending this concert—the whole experience of it, awakened such excitement in James as to come out in his string of dreams. Though his aspirations may have since changed, those early dreams became seeds for others.

The most fundamental vision to share with our children, however, is a general, rather than specific one: that they are worth investing in. To

150

illustrate, I refer to one man's account of his life-changing meeting with Einstein. He found himself sitting beside the iconic scientist at a dinner party and, just before the start of a performance of Bach chamber music, he confessed he was tone deaf. Einstein led him out to a room with a phonograph and began playing a familiar Bing Crosby tune, instructing him to sing it back. Einstein declared to him, "You see! You do have an ear! . . . This simple, charming little song is like simple addition or subtraction. You have mastered it. Now we go to something more complicated." Einstein went through a succession of pieces and eventually said, "Now, young man, we are ready for Bach." They walked back to the concert and the man recalls, "Without the effort he had poured out for a total stranger I would never have heard, as I did that night for the first time in my life, Bach's 'Sheep May Safely Graze.'"[17] Einstein built upon what was familiar and bridged to new possibilities. By teaching a simple lesson, he communicated that this man was worth his time and effort. If we can communicate one vital message—that our children are loved and valued by us independent of any particular dream or accomplishment, that their worth does not hinge upon anything—this vision alone will enable them to accomplish all that is necessary.

Advocating Work

Upon hearing that his preschool-aged brother wanted to harvest pet earthworms from the garden, my well-meaning older son got a shovel and soon had covered the bottom of a pail with writhing worms. "Here!" he said. Do you think the younger brother was pleased? No—he started to cry and dumped the worms back in the garden. No one is truly satisfied to have a treasure merely handed to him; there is satisfaction in the digging. Sometimes we are handed the beginnings of a treasure—the natural ability or aptitude for something—but if there is to be true pleasure derived from it and the best good accomplished, work will first be required. Anything worthwhile takes work. It's something even little children know. Despite this, work is also something we all (to some degree) try to avoid.

Who has the harder job, the parent who over and over and in multiple areas must teach needed but resisted lessons, or the child who must enact them? Often children lack the experience and foresight to spontaneously choose what is in their ultimate best interest. How much do we insist upon? How much is up to us and how much is up to them? While allowing ownership and fostering personal initiative, two reasonable paths seem

151

possible: either proving to our children the value of work, or trusting them to discover it for themselves over time. One may be a more direct course than the other, but some children may not tolerate the more efficient, accelerated lesson. Instead, they insist upon walking all the way down a dead end street before turning back.

Once I said to my teenaged son, "You can excel at anything you choose." He teasingly retorted, "What if I choose to excel at being a lump?" I replied, "I would not let you rest!" Parents have the uncomfortable task of not allowing their kids to get too comfortable when they are off track. Socrates' comparison of his role as a philosopher to that of a "gadfly," could appropriately apply to parenthood; he taught, "God has specially appointed me to this city as though the city were a large thoroughbred horse that because of its size is inclined to be lazy and in need of stimulation by some stinging fly. It seems to me that God has attached me to this city to perform the office of such a fly, and all day long I never cease to settle here, there, and everywhere, rousing, persuading, reproving every one of you."[18] Inspiring, enabling, or insisting upon the work involved in developing a gift or ability—the studying, practicing, enacting, utilizing—this is often the thankless job of a parent.

While our children ideally would work out of pure desire, realizing how work bridges between dreams and reality, they often do not spontaneously choose the greatest enrichments or see the steps required to reach their ultimate goals without guidance and intense support. We keep "rousing [and] persuading" because we believe that if our children could somehow experience the fruits of their work, this could instill lasting intrinsic motivation. Sometimes as parents we must sacrifice pleasantness and ease in our current relationship to ultimately teach this valuable lesson, thus forging bonds for a more meaningful enduring relationship. But the interchange of our rousing and their resisting does have its reasonable limits.

Even as a five or six-year-old, one of my sons would sit at the piano for long periods, delighting us and himself playing familiar songs by ear and composing others. When shortly thereafter he started piano lessons, he struggled with the uncomfortable transition from joyful, spontaneous, unschooled playing to reading notes and rhythms, where the joy and satisfaction tend to come after some disciplined work. He resisted lessons and practicing, but I dutifully persisted, knowing that a higher level of enjoyment would be possible for him once he gained mastery. His piano

152

teacher said, "Maybe he's too young—two of my kids resisted like this and it just wasn't worth it." I asked her, "Do they play now?" She admitted they had never gotten back to it. I vowed to keep insisting, but then a standoff began. Finally I conceded that, at least for right now, it had become not "worth it."

The specifics of what this means may vary by situation, but I have learned that when underlying relationship suffers, little else makes a given course right. Healthy parent-child relationships give the best overall leverage and allow the greatest global influence. Though perhaps not exactly well received, *our* efforts to optimize *their* efforts should be more like stabilizing a bloom than forcibly opening a bud. Or better yet, we'd attend to the roots—the underlying motivations. We'd help our children notice and enjoy small successes, we'd help them navigate challenges and setbacks, and we'd give them tools[19] to sift and weigh the many expectations placed upon them from within and without.

There has been a recent acknowledgement that the most highly skilled individuals often are those who have put in the most work over time. For example, James Allen's classic *As a Man Thinketh*, which expounds the scriptural aphorism, "As a man thinketh in his heart, so is he," has been rewritten by a contemporary author with a new emphasis: "As a man thinketh in his heart *and practices*, so is he."[20] Though practice naturally follows when a desire or wish is written in the heart, sometimes practice must precede the desire. Persistent practice brings mastery and skill, mastery and skill bring fulfillment and greater desire, desire leads to further practice: the "virtuous circle" of progress, along which insistent mothers guide their initially reluctant children.

Providing Mentorship

Recently one of my sons came home from Cub Scouts and told me, "I wish I wrote neatly like Jason. His mom works with him and has helped him have good handwriting." Another evening when my oldest son was practicing violin and I caught myself shouting from the next room, "Make those eighth notes even!" and "A little higher on that last note!" I wistfully remembered hearing of my college roommate's mom who sat beside each of several children for daily piano practice. Comparisons can bring both inspiration and angst. They leave me wondering, *Have I been dedicated enough in the most important ways to help my children optimize their potential? To what degree do my children's weaknesses reflect my own failings? Why do they resist my help,*

153

particularly in areas I have the most to offer—have I been too intense or didactic? For all sorts of reasons, I rarely manage to do all the mentoring I once imagined doing (regularly drilling my kids on their schoolwork, participating daily in their music practice, assuring that each writing assignment has gone through the process of editing and revision . . .). Because I love that shared process of learning, I want to be instrumental in every lesson, discovery, or incremental development. But fortunately for our children, perfect fulfillment of this lofty wish is barred from every mother, leaving our children room for independent growth and initiative.

Ideal mentorship is the perfect balance between availability and unavailability, between giving knowledge and giving the tools to find it, between insisting and inspiring, between correcting and encouraging. Feedback must be carefully dispensed, like a needed medicine: it must be given in the proper doses, at the proper time and may be more easily tolerated by some than others. Often children will self-correct and require no external feedback at all.

Whether we directly provide mentorship or arrange and enable it, observing and guiding an independently-willed or perhaps resistant child can require immense patience. Concerning the seeming arduous process of supporting a child in developing any gift, one Suzuki teacher recounted a realization that came to her while looking out an airplane window. She was surprised to see the winding, circuitous path of the Mississippi but noted that, despite all its meandering, "the Mississippi River does make it to the Gulf of Mexico."[21] Similarly, though development does not tend to proceed in a straight line, it does proceed. Though children ultimately possess jurisdiction over their own gifts, dedication of both parent and child will pay off over time

We may wonder how mentorship can be accomplished, particularly with multiple children at once. Often, children of several different ages present conflicting needs. With some in the "cuddle" years (when it's just as good or better to stay at home and foster a simple, consistent schedule), and others in the "productivity" years (when specific skill acquisition and involvement matter and, by necessity, require more set appointments), sometimes I feel caught in the middle. Despite the need for sharing and simplification, blessings have come. For example, I have witnessed lessons previously taught to older children naturally trickling down to younger siblings. Some of the most important mentorship we provide is in "germline" areas that go on to affect all areas. For example, helping our

154

children develop a love of learning bears more fruit than drilling specific facts; helping a child read enables them to instruct themselves.

Though at times we have chosen to sacrifice for or invest in select lessons, camps, or enrichment activities for our children, sometimes we have had to find creative alternatives. Not only has this spared us high costs and fragmenting busyness, but has provided happy, shared times. One year my sons begged to attend their school's spaghetti dinner and book fair, but I knew that at the time we could not afford tickets for the dinner or any new books. I proposed we hold our own book fair; I made spaghetti while the kids excitedly made posters saying, "Come to the Book Fair!" We made a display of books from our own shelves—some well-used favorites, some rediscovered, some new from the library. We ate spaghetti and then we sat together on the couch reading books.

Another time, inspired by their dad who had run a 50K trail marathon, the kids expressed interest in running a race. So we trained for a 5K together. A few times a week we jogged about a mile down the road and back, sometimes to a nearby creek—usually pushing 2 strollers, doing some walking, and stopping to catch frogs. Though initially we had planned to run in a community race, we decided to host our own race with some friends. My husband marked the course and I packed supplies for an "aid station" in the trunk of our car, which we parked at the turnaround point. Our eight-year-old led the pack much of the way and even our five-year-old hopped out of the jogger stroller and ran much of the way. I have learned that meaningful participation does not always necessitate a highly trained instructor or formal involvement, especially for young children. D&C 88:78 says, "Teach ye diligently and my grace shall attend you." Grace is God's enabling power that makes our best efforts sufficient.

Exemplifying

With much of our focus rightly funneling into our children's needs and development, we may forget the parallel importance of our own. We read in Ecclesiastes: "To every thing there is a season, and a time to every purpose under heaven" (3:1). While acknowledging that not all harvests come at once, this familiar verse does not relegate our children's summer into our winter—our gifts need not go fully dormant just because it is the season for theirs. Rather, attending to our gifts in addition to our children's both renews us and teaches them. Writer Brenda Ueland states,

[T]o teach, encourage, cheer up, console, amuse, stimulate, or advise a husband or children or friends, you have to be something yourself. And how to be something yourself? Only by working hard and with gumption at something you love and care for and think is important.

So if you want your children to be musicians, then work at music yourself, seriously and with all your intelligence. If you want them to be scholars, study hard yourself. If you want them to be honest, be honest yourself. And so it goes.[22]

Perhaps the art of mothering itself is that "something" we love and consider important, but even this depends upon our unique gifts. How do we find and build these gifts when caught up in basic tasks of mothering— the feeding, clothing, housing and transporting—to such a degree that it seems a rare luxury to participate or share in anything more? With every crumb of my energy expended in nurturing others or seemingly for mere survival, I wonder, will my children know me? Will they know what I love, what I think, what I most deeply want? Have I made my convictions known?

Reflect or discuss:

1) How do you inspire children and teach discipline without pushing too hard?

2) Have your children been able to watch you joyfully pursuing a gift?

26~ Pursuing our own gifts

Once in the children's play area of the Minneapolis Institute of Art (where children, after seeing untouchable creations of others, can come build their own), I overheard an interesting conversation between five-year-olds. Over a colorful, foam block tower my son (who had been contesting with me all day, rejecting every suggestion) said to another boy, "My mom is smart." The other boy said, "I didn't know moms *could* be smart." While I gained personal consolation in my son's words, I felt sad for misunderstood, underappreciated moms everywhere.

As any mother, I give up multiple personal opportunities in order to create opportunities for my children—a truth to which they, at least currently, are often oblivious. (And to some degree, rightly so; it is the way of childhood). I have books to write, songs to practice, medical journals to read—I am practically bursting to do these things—but instead spend my mornings insisting one son does his homework and the other practices and the other attends to his chores. It is my fair trade to make—a willing investment for the future of those I love. Yet, to never pursue anything (or to have nothing to pursue) seems an unhealthy and untrue lesson.

I notice how spending even twenty minutes nourishing my own gifts centers me with a sudden readiness to face any challenge and to absorb every joy. What we are trying to teach our children is also true for us: "Creation brings deep satisfaction and fulfillment. We develop ourselves and others when we take unorganized matter into our hands and mold it into something of beauty."[23] Honoring this truth is a faithful kindness to ourselves. By so doing, we model the happy pursuit of gifts—often a more effective alternative than a relentless pursuit (chasing down) of our resistant children. (Interestingly, while I've been working on this book, three of my sons have also started books of their own.)

We can approach the pursuit of our gifts in five main ways: completely abandoning the possibility, fitting it in around the "edges," involving our children, securing protected time, or pursuing gifts exclusively. Perhaps each of these has its place—though the first and last only rarely. I tend to favor utilizing edges of time or involving my children, though each possibility warrants discussion.

Abandoning the pursuit of gifts

Specific intense periods of nurturing occur universally, such as the time following the birth of a baby, when all else is rightly set aside. This is not abandonment, but a temporary "tucking away" of one love to make room for another. Certain seasons of life may necessitate revised focus and a pared down pursuit of a certain talent or gift. But the inclination to bury the whole of it—to resign entirely from any further attempts to build one's gift—may be a sign of unbalanced discouragement.

Though it doesn't seem so, free moments do arise in mothering; we do not operate in a vacuum. In an unpredicted, surfacing patch of free time, I occasionally have found myself settling upon mindless, time-wasting activities rather than choosing something deeply meaningful or renewing. For a while I was in the habit of eating a treat after putting the kids in bed. Sometimes I'd make a small fraction of a recipe to eat by myself. One of my favorite mini-batches was brownie batter, a recipe I thought I'd include and entitle "Recipe for a Discouraged Mother."* I quickly realized the double meaning in this ("for" as in "benefiting" *or* as in "bringing about") and thought it appropriate, because though sometimes eating brownie batter was a welcomed treat, other times it left me more discouraged than I had begun. It tasted good for the moment and the results were predictable (seemingly better guaranteed than my other efforts through the day), but it usually got me nowhere.

In contrast, when I stand ready to utilize any "extra" time to do something meaningful and productive, I truly progress. I have used driving time to talk to my kids, do vocal exercises, or to pray. I have utilized a ten-minute window of time to read my scriptures, write in my journal, or revise a few sentences in this book. My husband listens to books on tape when he runs. I know another father who decided to devote twenty minutes a day to learning the oboe. Unlike less meaningful pastimes, developing gifts enriches us *for* rather than distracting us *from* the tasks of parenting. Indeed, "wise time management is really the wise management of ourselves."[24]

Pursuing gifts at the "edges"

I do much of my writing before my kids wake up or after they are asleep ("in bed," at least). That this time exists and adds up gains proof by

---

* Melt/mix together in a small saucepan on med-low heat: 2 Tbsp. butter, 4 Tbsp. sugar, 1 ½ Tbsp. cocoa, 1 tsp. water, 2 Tbsp. flour (~300 calories).

the book in your hand; though specific ideas came to me in the midst of the work, play, and interaction of daytime hours, I never could have organized and synthesized it without some time of quiet concentration.

The description of the exemplary woman in Proverbs 31 acknowledges use of edge-time: "her candle goeth not out by night" (v. 18). Yet edge-time does have its practical limits—when I give into the temptation to prolong such time, cutting into needed sleep to widen its border, it jeopardizes my functioning for the next day or days. Also, edge-time may be unreliable, being frequently encroached upon by necessary tasks of the day. But when utilized consistently and with careful discipline, much can be cumulatively accomplished. This discipline to which I refer is more than a clock-watching kind of discipline, but an emotional discipline to accomplish things in pieces despite compromised efficiency, despite the wish to keep going, and despite inevitable interruptions. It is being satisfied with small tastes of self-directed progress.

Because I want to focus foremost on attending to the needs of my family, the sense of independent progression becomes less desirable than a collective, shared progress. Despite this edge-time being as a discovered treasure, it does not replace the greater treasures. Sometimes I wake up early for solitude but then the baby wakes earlier than usual and needs to be nursed, or my toddler has a bad dream and needs soothing and reassurance. To put aside or feel angered by these opportunities, just because I had other plans in mind, would be short-sighted. Often, a greater progression occurs in yielding to communion than fighting for solitude.

Involving children

We can involve our children while pursuing gifts either by inviting their participation or by finding ways to apply our gifts in the family context. My voice teacher once said, "Given your life currently, it will be hard, if not impossible to think you'll get uninterrupted time at the piano every day to practice. Do these things in 'real time'—while you do dishes, take a walk, or rock a baby."

Many times I have practiced singing with a toddler or baby on my lap at the piano. Sometimes I have had them press the key to give me my starting notes. This may be slightly less productive for me, and more difficult to enact, but has allowed me to practice on days when I otherwise wouldn't have. Rather than seeming to take away from my family, it has been a happy, shared time. My boys love to tease me about my vocal

159

exercises and have even made up some of their own: "Ho, ho, ho, I have a hairy toe . . ." (all on one note and then moving up the scale).

When I'm having a particularly enjoyable or productive practice, I do feel disappointed to be interrupted. Some boundaries for the interaction may be necessary to allow the activity to even take place, yet too much rigidity or tension surrounding it (especially if expectations are not age-appropriate) may cause negative associations. While I'm practicing, if one of my sons begins randomly banging on the piano, I have a choice to make—my response may depend on their age and intent. Part of putting a child "first" may include teaching him or her about focused effort and respectfulness; part may also include some playfulness and flexibility.

As a musician, my dad would often record himself playing specific passages on different violas using different bows and then would play it back to choose which combination sounded best for a given piece. I have a cassette tape where he is practicing and then a little voice starts humming along. He says, "Mary Elizabeth, I'm practicing, you shouldn't interrupt me." I say, "But *I* want to do it!" The tape stops and restarts and suddenly he's plucking "Mary Had a Little Lamb" and I'm singing along. Then we do "The Farmer in the Dell." The tape stops and restarts and he's back to his practicing again. Since my dad often practiced at night, I knew if I ever woke up thirsty or scared, I'd likely find him playing the viola in the basement. On several occasions, I remember him stopping his practice to give me a snack and sit with me. Yet, then he'd be back to practicing—or else I'd never have come to know and love his signature pieces, like Schubert's "Arpeggione."

In *Jo's Boys*, Louisa May Alcott's story of the grown up "Little Women," Amy develops her gift of sculpting by working alongside her daughter Bess:

> Amy had her protégés among ambitious young painters and sculptors, and found her own art double dear as her daughter grew old enough to share its labors and delights with her; for she was one of those who prove that women can be faithful wives and mothers without sacrificing the special gift bestowed on them for their own development and the good of others. Her sisters knew where to find her, and Jo went at once to the studio where mother and daughter worked together. Bess was busy with the bust of a little child, while her mother added the last touches to the fine head of her husband.[25]

160

Alcott's idealized scene depicts an endpoint—a gift successfully shared and together enjoyed, but this occurs over time, in graduated fashion.

Whether or not we pursue our gifts in any professional way, we can find homemade applications. Whatever we love, we can share: making music, enjoying literature, enjoying nature, becoming physically fit, gardening, organizing, decorating, communicating, creating scientific experiments, or studying in a specialized area. Our children may not choose these same things to pursue, but inviting their participation will have an impact; they will remember what it looks like to see another "working hard and with gumption at something [they] love and care for and think is important."[26]

At times our children resist our attempts to involve them (or to pursue anything not centered upon them); at times the nature of our activity or their stage of development precludes it. To what degree do we proceed anyway, and how?

Arranging protected time and space to build gifts

Because of the preciousness of the childrearing years and the blessings derived from attentive parental engagement with children, other pursuits must be chosen with care—timing, duration, and purpose all factor in when deciding their relative importance. Virginia Woolf argues, "A woman must have money and a room of her own if she is to write fiction." She alludes to women absent to their art, "for they are washing up the dishes and putting the children to bed."[27] Speaking to mothers who wish to write but never find time for it, writing instructor Brenda Ueland adds,

> If you would shut your door against the children for an hour a day and say: "Mother is working on her five-act tragedy in blank verse!" you would be surprised how they would respect you. They would probably all become playwrights.[28]

But these sentiments must be balanced with the truth that a mother, with doors *open* and attending actively to her children's needs, teaches another important lesson: that she values them beyond any outward pursuit, for their glory and remarkableness is inherent rather than acquired. By "opening our doors" to our children, at least primarily, we "shut our doors" to the secular notion that identity and worth come from outward accomplishment.

All this being said, I acknowledge that some talents cannot be realistically pursued with children in-tow; some fixed time away or otherwise focused may be warranted, necessitating established boundaries or outside help. A "room of [our] own," whether physical or figurative, may beneficially promise certain protections, providing a temporary refuge from the press of awaiting duties and unnecessary interruptions. From my own creative, intelligent mother I learned this simple lesson: that some things are more important than housework. Though household tasks can accumulate unpleasantly when ignored, such tasks will always be there—certain other opportunities will not.

We care for our children by attending well to "the ways of [our] household" (Proverbs 31:27), but the health and vitality there depend not only upon physical environment. There are times to choose blindness toward the dishes on the counter and allow dinner plans to wait; our inward to-do lists must incorporate the work of the heart. Sometimes I wish my mom had taught me how to keep a more consistently tidy house, but it is partly because she did not that I feel inward permission to walk away from a sink of dishes. In a chapter entitled, "Why Women Who Do Too Much Housework Should Neglect it for Their Writing," Brenda Ueland invites women to give time to their gifts; she says, "Menial work at the expense of all true, ardent, creative work is a sin against the Holy Ghost."[29]

Particularly at the height of a project, which may naturally involve intense feelings and require intense focus, structured help provided by a support person may be what enables us to more feasibly proceed through. Such arrangements safeguard needed conditions not only for us, but also for our children and our work; young children may not understand processes and can innocently disrupt, erase, or destroy the products of our efforts. Florence Nightingale writes, "Women are never supposed to have any occupation of sufficient importance not to be interrupted. . . . When shall we see a woman making a study of what she does?"[30] A "study" must be made to produce fruits of beauty, meaning, and value.

Pursuing gifts exclusively

Today I woke up at 5:30 a.m. to write. The baby started to fuss and my toddler awoke and called out to me. If I were to begrudge this or constantly have someone else acting in my stead, what would come of it? While balanced striving brings joyful fulfillment, over-striving may lead to burnout, angry impatience, and compromised relationships. When pursuing gifts, at every point we must discern to what degree.

Certain seasons of life may allow complete immersion in developing particular gifts, but allowing other pursuits to supersede family responsibilities jeopardizes happiness. As we strive to "neglect not the gift" within us (1 Tim 4:14), neither should we neglect the gift that *was* within us but is now running around and requiring our time and attention. For me, the "right" manner of pursuit involves faith, purpose, and high personal effort, but also acceptance and flexibility in areas I cannot control. When I have felt the effect of or the potential for imbalance, I have foregone opportunities or adjusted my commitments.

One summer I made it my goal to audition for the Minnesota Chorale, the symphonic choir that often collaborates with the Minnesota Orchestra (the orchestra in which my dad spent most of his career). I restarted voice lessons—once per month was all I could fit in—and practiced daily. I looked over audition specifications, reviewed music theory, and dug out sight-singing exercises. To cover my bases, I scheduled auditions for several local choirs. When I called to set up the audition for the Minnesota Chorale, I was crushed to learn that no new sopranos would be needed that year. I went ahead with the other auditions and made it into every choir. One particularly prestigious choir had weekly (and sometimes biweekly) rehearsals and multiple required performances; though I was honored by the opportunity, it was simply too much. I selected a smaller choir, which focused on international repertoire, with fewer rehearsals and performances. Over the course of that year, I had gained valuable experience singing under a very exacting director in over ten languages. The next year, Minnesota Chorale auditions were again opened to sopranos and I got in. As a member of this choir I have the exciting opportunity to perform symphonic and operatic masterworks, yet the flexibility to sign on for a fewer number of specific concerts. My participation energizes me—not only musically, but also for my work as a mother.

The need for balance always exists between sharing our gifts and the personal study and reflection time required in preparation to do so. This personal preparation time is also needed in the realm of parenting, but can be challenging to find. The scriptures evidence this duality even in the life of Jesus Christ, who himself was repeatedly interrupted when seeking to be alone. In Matthew 15:29-30, we read that Jesus "departed. . . . and went up into a mountain and sat down there. And great multitudes came unto him, having with them those that were lame, blind, dumb, maimed, and many others, and cast them down at Jesus' feet; and he healed them." His life's work was among the people—to serve, teach, and save them—yet he also required times to ponder, pray, and prepare. To be "like Him,"[31] we must follow the pattern of how accessible he made himself to others in their need, and also the conscientiousness with which he prepared. It may seem that our gifts are something separate from what we do all day, but ultimately and ideally, one will reflect the other.

Reflect or discuss:

1) Is there a creative outlet that has enriched your mothering, increased your joy, or infused you with energy?

2) In what contexts have you abandoned certain gifts, pursued gifts at the edges of your other responsibilities, involved your children, arranged for protected time, or exclusively pursued your gifts? What have been the results?

27~ THE RESULTS

Developing any gift is an exercise in faith. As with Sarah of the Old Testament, who saw promises "afar off, and [was] persuaded of them, and embraced them" (Hebrews 11:13), much will come of our faithful continuance. As we seek all that is "virtuous, lovely, or of good report, or praiseworthy,"[32] who can know the fruits? Some fruits will be ours to pluck down; others will be left to seed, an endless crop to come and come.

The poet Emily Dickinson once wrote to a mentor, "Are you too deeply occupied to say if my verse is alive? The mind is so near itself it cannot see distinctly, and I have none to ask."[33] Despite little public recognition during her lifetime, she wrote prolifically—over 1500 poems—on life, death, human interaction, God, and the natural world. She captured simple detail astutely in a voice of "gentle, wide-eyed astonishment."[34]

Early Mormon settler and artist Minerva Teichart said of herself, "I *must* paint." As a young woman she saved money to attend the Art Institute of Chicago. She once questioned an instructor for being harder on her than other students. He replied, "Miss Idaho, can it be possible you do not understand [?] . . . [T]hey will drop out, but you—oh there is no end."[35] A mentor from an art school in New York suggested she paint "the great Mormon story" and she considered herself personally commissioned. Teichart painted a mural in the LDS Temple in Manti, Utah and over forty large works illustrating both pioneer history and the events recorded in the Book of Mormon. Notwithstanding Teichart's passion for painting, her work received wide acclaim only after her death. During her life, she painted, raised children, nurtured grandchildren and served in her community.

Attending to day-to-day family needs and pressing forward despite life's challenges may seem like nothing flashy or special, but often it is exactly the contribution most needed. Whether pursuing or sharing our gifts visibly or more personally, we nonetheless can share our legacy— "[filling] the measure of [our] creation" (D&C 88:19).

Any pursuit becomes a metaphor for one's whole person. Within a single sphere, we learn lessons about our strengths and weaknesses that apply to other areas. This is how building even one gift promotes self-awareness and refinement. Also, the creative process builds on itself:

striving for excellence in one area teaches us a process applicable to all areas. The scriptures reference this compounding, spiraling progression: "For intelligence cleaveth unto intelligence; wisdom receiveth wisdom; truth embraceth truth; virtue loveth virtue; light cleaveth unto light . . . and that body which is filled with light comprehendeth all things."[36]

In his "Music and the Spoken Word," Lloyd Newell has stated, "One of God's most precious gifts to humankind is our opportunity to add our own beauty to that of the creator."[37] From the beauty of the sunrise, or a mountain, or a small flower, we see that God values quality work. The Book of Exodus tells of artisans being raised up to participate in building the temple: "And I have filled [them] with the spirit of God, in wisdom and in understanding, and in knowledge, and in all manner of workmanship. . . . Them hath he filled with wisdom of heart to work all manner of work, of the engraver, and of the cunning workman, and of the embroiderer, in blue, and in purple, in scarlet, and in fine linen, and of the weaver, even of them that do any work . . . even every one whose heart stirred him up to come unto the work to do it" (Exodus 31:3, 35:35, 36:2). As we follow the stirrings of our hearts to find and develop our gifts, we will be participating in God's work.

June 17, 2012

On Friday I once again had the amazing privilege to perform with the Minnesota Chorale for the Minnesota Orchestra's season finale concert, marking the last concert in Orchestra Hall before planned renovations. Singing with this chorus of over 120 voices is like being raised, buoyant amid beautifully spinning harmonies, and collectively transformed. But this night held more transcendence. Stanislaw Skrowaczewski, former conductor of the Orchestra, stepped to the podium to lead Bach's "Toccata and Fugue"—the same piece he had conducted for Orchestra Hall's opening in 1974. When the music began, with all its intricacy and power, the baby began to move relentlessly within me. From the brightness of the stage lights I could see to the seventh row where my mom sat in the audience. On this same stage where so often I had seen my father perform, it was now me—sitting, watching, listening, and feeling three generations connect between heaven and earth, sharing in this gift!

Reflect or discuss:

1) What gifts do you feel inspired to pursue?

2) What specific work has God prepared and positioned you to do with your unique set of gifts and experiences (either in addition to or within your role as a mother)?

VII. A TEMPLE HOUSE

On making home a sanctuary

28~ HISTORIC SITES, SACRED SITES

One way we nurture is through the environment we create for our children. A home becomes sacred because of what happens within it: moments comfortingly familiar or marking change, times of sickness and being nursed to health, acts of service given and received, opportunities to forgive and be forgiven. The atmosphere of a home, therefore, reflects the people living within it and the history that is being made within its walls. When religious devotion occurs within a home, it also becomes a sanctuary for God's spirit. My mom used to sing me a song that captures the dual nature of the sacredness of a home—that it is derived both from the specific people there and the religious practices that occur:

> I can see the lights of home
> Shining brightly o'er the foam.
> Beckon to me while I roam
> Away from lights of home.
> I can see somebody there,
> Glowing eyes and silver hair.
> I can see her kneel in prayer
> Beneath the lights of home.[1]

When my aging mother became increasingly dependent in daily activities, she moved in with us and her house sat vacant for an extended time. When it became clear that she could not return to her home, my sister and I embarked on the task of clearing it out for other purposes. We found blessing certificates, our grade school artwork, old letters that weaved together enlightening narratives about our past, concert programs, photographs capturing forgotten moments, half-used bottles of my mom's favorite perfume, a dress she had worn to the Symphony Ball, books we remembered reading as children, records we remembered listening to, articles clipped from the newspaper reflecting important events and interests, over one hundred neckties belonging to my father, my grandfather's banjo, and much more. We noted Hummel figurines, books on the shelf, and pictures on the wall—some we had made ourselves— that had held their position for decades. As sweet testaments of our past, each relic carried meaning.

My young son delightedly went through the house gathering pennies and dimes from drawers and open dishes. When it was time to leave he resisted. For days he repeatedly asked, "But why do you have to clear out grandma's house? When you take everything down, you can never put it back—it won't be the same." He wisely discerned the sacred history the house held and articulated our own inward longing to be children always in this home of our childhood, to escape the pull of time. Attempting to prepare my mother for coming transitions, I told her, "It will be a time of change." In a moment of clarity, and in her characteristic wise way, she comfortingly stated, "It is always a time of change—to live is to change." Still, we gather out treasures, physical mementos and memories, in attempts to preserve this sacred history.

My mom told me when I was a little girl that the wooden plaque displayed on our kitchen wall used to belong to my grandmother. It has the painted words, "As for me and my house, we will serve the Lord." Our Catholic neighbors posted within their home the saying, "Christ is the head of this house, the unseen guest at every meal, the silent listener to every conversation." Many of our Jewish neighbors displayed mezuzahs on their doorposts, small boxes containing words from the Torah. Though reflecting distinct beliefs, these evidenced families giving a priority to religious devotion.

Many in the Judeo-Christian tradition share the lofty thought that a home, the place a family gathers, eats, sleeps, and lives day to day can be a sacred space, even in the religious sense. In LDS tradition, the home is called "a temple"; in Catholicism, "the domestic church"; in Judaism, *mikdash ma'at* or the "little sanctuary."[2] Though I hope for my home to be a temple, at times it feels more like a zoo, a gym, a disaster area, or a battlefield.

In approximately 500 B.C., the people of Judah were commanded by the Lord to reconstruct the temple after it had been burned and destroyed by the armies of King Nebuchadnezzar. Though likely daunted at first, "the Lord stirred up [their] spirit[s]. . . and they came and did work in the house of the Lord" (Hag 1:14). The prophet Haggai acknowledged the largeness of the task, saying, "Who is left among you that saw this house in her first glory? And how do ye see it now? Is it not in your eyes in comparison as if it was nothing?" But the Lord tells the people, "Be strong . . . for I am with you. . . . The glory of this latter house shall be greater than of the former . . . and in this place will I give peace" (Haggai 2:3-4, 9).

171

Like the temple builders in Haggai's time, we do not work alone. The scriptures say, "Except the Lord build the house, they labour in vain that build it."[3] A temple house is built and maintained by revelation, "according to the instructions of the Lord."[4] When the Lord commanded Noah to build an ark for refuge and protection, he gave very specific instruction, down to the number of cubits (Genesis 6:14-16). The Lord told Noah, "With thee will I establish my covenant" (6:18). The Lord also gave directions to Moses for another "ark of the covenant"—a container to hold scripture within the tabernacle, the portable temple of the children of Israel: "And they shall make an ark of shittim wood: two cubits and a half shall be the length thereof, and a cubit and a half the breadth thereof, and a cubit and a half the height thereof. And thou shall overlay it with pure gold" (Exodus 25:10-1). The Lord tells Moses, "And let them make me a sanctuary; that I may dwell among them. According to all that I show thee . . . even so shall ye make it" (Exodus 25:8-9, see also v. 40). In Exodus 25-27, detailed specifications are given for the building of the tabernacle; in Exodus 36-38, successful completion of the plans is reported (see also D&C 88 & 109). 2 Chronicles 2-5 records building plans for another sacred edifice generations later "wherein Solomon was instructed for the building of the house of God." With divine guidance, we also can make our homes into sanctuaries where the Spirit of God can dwell.

It is fitting for a home to be a sanctuary, because "the family is sacred . . . and is the most important social unit in time and eternity."[5] The home is where we first learn gospel principles and then practice living them. Having helped bring our own children into this world, we also create a place "whereon these may dwell" (Abr 3:24). As we have such influence in determining this home environment—how it looks, how it feels, what functions it serves—"homemaking" is like creating the world.

Reflect or discuss:

1) Where are some places in the world that have been a sanctuary to you?

2) How is your home like a sanctuary? How could it be more so (for you and for *each* member of your family)?

29~ CHARACTERISTICS OF A TEMPLE HOUSE

The individualized characteristics that make a home comfortable and familiar vary depending on a family's unique characteristics. The characteristics that create an atmosphere of devotion, however, tend to be more universal. Certain scriptural references outline qualities to develop that invite God's spirit. Surrounding the construction of the first Latter-day Saint temple in 1836, for example, early church members were directed, "Organize yourselves; prepare every needful thing; and establish a house, even a house of prayer, a house of fasting, a house of faith, a house of learning, a house of glory, a house of order, a house of God" (D&C 88:119). Though this scripture originally referred to a literal temple, the suggested components also elevate a home.[6]

House of prayer

Parents who teach their children to pray unlock an otherwise unknown gate toward a rich inheritance: endless resources of wisdom, comfort, direction and divine relationship. Parents who pray for their children amplify their own efforts by invoking the powers of heaven. This is not to imply that prayer staves off all trouble or tragedy, but it is a companion through it. Though forms may vary among different religions, most prayers share important qualities. The act of prayer is undertaken with reverence, God is addressed, praise and thanks offered, help or blessings requested, and God's will sought. Some utilize established wording, some utilize specific tools (such as rosaries, shawls, or rugs), some pray according to specific schedules. But independent of such details, "The effectual fervent prayer of [the righteous] availeth much" (James 5:16). The scriptures extend this generous invitation: "Cry unto [God] for mercy; for he is mighty to save. . . Cry unto him when ye are in your fields, yea, over all your flocks. Cry unto him in your houses, yea, over all your household, both morning, mid-day, and evening. . . But this is not all; ye must pour out your souls in your closets, and your secret places, and in your wilderness. Yea, and when you do not cry unto the Lord, let your hearts be full, drawn out in prayer unto him continually for your welfare, and also for the welfare of those who are around you" (Alma 34:18-27).

In our family we kneel together at least once a day to pray, we pray together at mealtimes, and my husband and I encourage each child to have personal morning and evening prayers. When circumstances allow, I make bedtime rounds to say goodnight and chat for a minute and then help the youngest boys pray (sometimes directing their words or asking questions to prompt their thinking). For the older boys, sometimes I just remind them to pray as I'm leaving or ask if they'd like me to stay and kneel with them while they offer their silent prayers. When invited to stay, I utilize this quiet time to specifically pray for them, supplementing my own morning and evening prayers. I don't have bedside time as often as I'd wish, but one particular night after reinstating it once again, I remember sensing it was more important and meaningful than any recent scrambling or striving I had done. Admittedly, family prayer sometimes seems like a fiasco with poking, giggling, frustration and fighting rather than a sense of reverence and unity, but I trust that consistent efforts will pay off.

Regarding the worth of daily devotional practices in a family, Elder David Bednar states,

> In my office is a beautiful painting of a wheat field. The painting is a vast collection of individual brushstrokes—none of which in isolation is very interesting or impressive. In fact, if you stand close to the canvas, all you can see is a mass of seemingly unrelated and unattractive streaks of yellow and gold and brown paint. However, as you gradually move away from the canvas, all of the individual brushstrokes combine together and produce a magnificent landscape of a wheat field. Many ordinary, individual brushstrokes work together to create a captivating and beautiful painting. Each family prayer, each episode of family scripture study, and each family home evening is a brushstroke on the canvas of our souls. No one event may appear to be very impressive or memorable. But just as the yellow and gold and brown strokes of paint complement each other and produce an impressive masterpiece, so our consistency in doing seemingly small things can lead to significant spiritual results. "Wherefore, be not weary in well-doing, for ye are laying the foundation of a great work. And out of small things proceedeth that which is great" (D&C 64:33).[7]

At times I see glimpses of emerging landscapes. Once after walking to the park with my third grader, my preschooler, and my newborn, the sky got dark. I quickly packed our things and turned to my older son. He had stopped to sit on a park bench with his arms folded and head bowed; he told me he prayed that the rain would wait so his baby brother would not get wet. The full, gray clouds hung over us during the mile walk home, but only as we crossed the threshold of our house did the downpour begin. Another son once insisted on bringing his new Lego pirates on a walk to a creek, despite my concern he may lose them. After we played all up and down the muddy creek bed, he burst into tears because his toys were gone. I told him I thought it would be near impossible to find the small figurines in the long stretch of leaves, mud, and tall grasses, but suggested he try praying. We circled the area a bit and then he stopped to pray. After completing his prayer, he took a few steps and then shrieked with joy because his Lego guys were sitting in the mud at his feet. We stopped again to offer a prayer of thanks. These are preparatory lessons—future scenarios will hinge upon more than weather or lost toys.

Sometimes during our family prayer I peek at the boys all kneeling in a circle, even down to the two-year-old. We take turns offering the prayer from night to night and sometimes, in a particular shining moment, one of the boys prays like a patriarch—for each family member one by one, for a sick neighbor, for a struggling friend. All this is enough to keep me going. There is still much to do: the younger boys need to be freshly taught and the older boys need reminders or more advanced lessons (on how answers come, how answers can be recognized, and how to proceed when there seems to be no answer). I once taught a family night lesson about elements of prayer using a toy hamburger—the bun being the opening and closing, and the meat, lettuce, tomato and pickles being everything you can put in between. Right now my "everything" includes praying for wisdom as a mother, for love, for patience and praying that my boys will learn to pray.

House of fasting

In an interfaith publication examining fasting from different religious perspectives, professor Kevin Corn comments, "We know a lot about the purpose of food. What can we learn from each other about the purpose of hunger?"[8] The tradition of fasting, held by many religions despite varied definitions and practices, usually involves abstaining from food or other pleasures for a higher spiritual purpose. Jews fast for Yom Kippur (the "Day of Atonement") and avoid leavened bread products during Passover; Catholics and certain Protestants fast or give up items for Lent; Muslims fast during daylight hours for the month of Ramadan. Purposes for fasting may include fortifying, purifying, sanctifying, dedicating, amplifying, illuminating, commemorating, praising, pleading, unifying, communing, mourning, or rejoicing. It is a trading of carnal for spiritual, old for new. Often fasting is connected with charity or offering—dealing "bread to the hungry" (Isaiah 58:7). In the LDS Church, for example, members fast each month for two consecutive meals and contribute the money they would have spent for food (and more if possible) to assist the needy among the congregation or wider community.

Most religions specify that nursing or pregnant mothers, young children, those who are sick, or those who cannot safely fast for other reasons are not expected to do so. As children grow, the practice of fasting can be introduced gradually, in an age-appropriate way. In our family, we have chosen to invite our children to fast one meal once they have been baptized at age eight and the full two meals once they turn twelve. We direct them to pray at the beginning and end of their fast and to choose a spiritual purpose for it. Since as parents we are usually in the business of feeding and providing, we may feel uncomfortable seeing our children go without, but teaching them to fast will open doors to greater spiritual maturity, strength, and blessing. The 58th chapter of Isaiah lays out some of the promised blessings for which they will qualify: "Then shall thy light break forth as the morning, and thine health shall spring forth speedily: and thy righteousness shall go before thee; the glory of the Lord shall be thy rereward. Then shalt thou call, and the Lord shall answer; thou shalt cry, and he shall say, Here I am. . . . And the Lord shall guide thee continually, and satisfy thy soul in drought, and make fat thy bones: and thou shalt be like a watered garden, and like a spring of water, whose waters fail not" (vs. 8-11). In a house of fasting, a family shows willingness to give up the temporal for the spiritual—to trade brief hunger for a filling of the soul.

House of faith

Faith in God is a "sure foundation" upon which a family safely builds.[9] Faith undergirds everything and leads to purposeful action; it is "hope for things which are not seen, which are true" (Alma 32:21, see also Hebrews 11:1). Faith is gained through spiritual instruction and experience. Some parents withhold specific religious teaching from their children in order to "let them choose," but this leaves a void rather than a foundation. Parents have always had the charge to pass on the best truths they know.

Yet we cannot simply "hand over" our spiritual knowledge and convictions to our children. As Elder Bednar puts it, "The tuition of diligence and of learning by study and also by faith must be paid to obtain and personally 'own' such knowledge." He explains further, "Giving a man a fish feeds him for one meal. Teaching a man to fish feeds him for a lifetime. As parents and gospel instructors, you and I are not in the business of distributing fish; rather, our work is to help our children learn 'to fish' and to become spiritually steadfast. This vital objective is best accomplished as we encourage our children to act in accordance with correct principles—as we help them learn by doing."[10] We teach our children scriptural truths, provide a faithful example, and allow them to observe and experience the fruits.

When a seed of truth is found, one nourishes it by living according to it. In this way, faith closely ties to obedience. John 17:17 states, "If any man will do his will, he shall know of the doctrine, whether it be of God" (John 17:17). In the Book of Mormon, Alma calls this process an "experiment" in faith; he writes, "Now let us compare the word unto a seed. Now if ye give place that a seed may be planted in your heart, behold, if it be a true seed, or a good seed, if ye do not cast it out by your unbelief, that ye will resist the Spirit of the Lord, behold, it will begin to swell within your breasts; and when ye feel these swelling motions, ye will begin to say within yourselves—It must needs be that this is a good seed, or that the word is good, for it beginneth to enlarge my soul; yea it beginneth to enlighten my understanding, yea, it beginneth to be delicious to me" (Alma 32:28). As more seeds are found, planted, and nourished, the garden of faith flourishes. Though often not immediately discernable, this delicate process occurs within us and within our children day by day. We cannot force such processes, but diligently afford our children experiences where the Spirit of God is likely to be felt. We can bring them to church or synagogue, gather with family, visit holy sites, serve together, and regularly acknowledge God's blessings in our lives. As we define our family experiences within a context of faith, our children will learn to do the same.

One day my three-year-old asked, "Why does Jesus whisper so quietly? I can't hear him—only the big boys can." I told him I knew God and Jesus were real. I asked, "Have you ever felt happy inside after doing something kind for one of your brothers?" "Yes," he replied. I told him,

"That is the Holy Ghost telling you Jesus is happy with you." He thought for a moment, then said, "I *have* heard Jesus whisper!" and ran away happily to play.

During a time of financial struggle, my husband and I marveled with our children about various miracles that came. Just as our refrigerator began to have problems, a neighbor who was moving spontaneously offered us her relatively new one; a retiring couple in our congregation moved and apologetically asked if we'd have any use for their freezer items that they "just couldn't bear to see go to waste"; we needed to replace a bathroom sink at my mom's house and found one nearly identical to the one I planned to buy at the edge of a neighbor's lawn with a large "free" sign on it; my husband had additional opportunities for paid work. We could have called these events luck, but chose instead to see them as blessings.

As we nurture faith in ourselves and our children, we can acquire all the helps necessary to succeed in our most important endeavors and to endure the challenges of life. "For he that diligently seeketh shall find; and the mysteries of God shall be unfolded unto them, by the power of the Holy Ghost, as well in these times as in times of old" (1 Nephi 10:19). Faith can be an anchor to our souls and with it, we can be an anchor to our families.[11]

House of learning

A temple house fosters both spiritual and secular learning. Spiritual learning reminds us of a Godly perspective and positions us to qualify for His blessings; secular learning increases our capabilities and positions us to serve. These two need not conflict, and will not, if we learn "by study and also by faith" (D&C 88:118). The scriptures direct us to "seek out of the best books words of wisdom" (88:118), yet caution us against pride: "When they are learned they think they are wise, and they hearken not unto the counsel of God, for they set it aside, supposing they know of themselves, wherefore their wisdom is foolishness and it profiteth them not. . . but to be learned is good if they hearken unto the counsels of God." (2 Nephi 9:28-29).

Our homes can be places of "higher education," providing lessons that edify, enlighten and inspire. My husband and I have established several patterns in our family to help foster learning. Our home is filled with books, instruments, art projects, rock collections, and bug jars. We encourage our children in their schoolwork and also go on educational family outings to museums, concerts, and historic sites. We spend time outdoors enjoying the wonders of God's creation. We read the scriptures each day as a family and discuss their application in our lives.

One of our favorite places to go as a family is the public library. As each child turns about six or seven, getting a library card is like a rite of passage. Since our local library had a checkout limit of 100 books per card, I established my own limit by saying to the kids, "You can check out as many books as you can carry." One particular day we were hobbling out, each child with a towering stack. A concerned librarian said, "Do you need help out to your car?" I laughed and said we'd better say no—that our "all you can carry rule" had better not include the help library staff or other patrons!

Learning happens continually; important lessons arise in the everyday details of our lives. I take the opportunity to make up a bedtime story for the younger boys each night that often that address problems or issues from the day and reinforced intended lessons. For these few minutes each night, I have their mesmerized attention.

As directed in Deuteronomy, we can saturate our homes with truth "upon the posts of [our] houses, and on [our] gates" and teach it when we "sittest in [our] house, when [we] walkest by the way, and when [we] liest down, and when [we] risest up" (6:7-9). Home is where children best learn to build their own houses of God someday.

House of Glory

A home bears the spirit of those who live within it—that is the sad and happy truth. If we operate only by natural tendencies, our homes will be governed by entropy, no different than the untamed world outside. If we want a heavenly atmosphere in our homes, we must live by heavenly laws. The scriptures state, "For he who is not able to abide the law . . . cannot abide [the corresponding] glory . . . And unto every kingdom is given a law, and unto every law there are certain bounds and also conditions. All beings who abide not in those conditions are not justified. For intelligence cleaveth to intelligence; wisdom receiveth wisdom; truth embraceth truth; virtue loveth virtue; light cleaveth to light" (D&C 88:22, 38-40). The laws we choose to live by will determine the glory we choose to foster—both within ourselves and within our homes.

179

Glory is not a foreign quality to be pressed upon us from the outside—it is intrinsic because of whose children we are. In his "Ode on Intimations of Immortality from Reflections of Early Childhood," William Wordsworth writes:

Not in entire forgetfulness,
And not in utter nakedness,
But trailing clouds of glory do we come
From God, who is our home:
Heaven lies about us in our infancy!
Shades of the prison-house begin to close
Upon the growing Boy,
But he beholds the light, and whence it flows,
He sees it in his joy;
The Youth, who daily farther from the east
Must travel, still is Nature's priest,
And by the vision splendid
Is on his way attended;
At length the Man perceives it die away,
And fade into the light of common day.[12]

O, the glory in a newborn baby, who bears the aura of heaven! (Perhaps this is one reason pregnant mothers "glow.") Some of the most sacred days of my life have been those surrounding the birth of my children. As I have held, nursed, rocked, and sung to each new baby, the hospital room has felt like holy ground. The special insights and comforts of those precious early days with each son are still with me.

Preserving and recapturing such glory is the work of our lives, in order that we may comfortably return to it in the end. To counter its natural fading requires continual effort to "stand in holy places," where God's spirit can dwell—where His glory can shine upon us. When Moses returned to his people after speaking with God on Mount Sinai, "the skin of his face shone" so brightly that he had to cover it with a vail to address them (Exodus 34:28-35). Similarly, we are told, "If your eye be single to my glory, your whole bodies shall be filled with light, and there shall be no darkness in you" (D&C 88:67), and, "That which is of God is light; and he that receiveth light, and continueth in God, receiveth more light; and that light groweth brighter and brighter until the perfect day" (D&C 50:24). The glory of an individual (and her house) increases with every godly act— every prayer uttered, every mercy extended, every loving service, every commandment faithfully observed. If there be glory in a house, children will "go forth from this house armed with [God's] power . . .[with His] name upon them, [His] glory round about them, and [His] angels [having] charge over them" (D&C 109: 22).[13]

House of order

"Behold, mine house is a house of order, saith the Lord God, and not a house of confusion" (D&C 132:8). God himself was presented with a space "without form, and void" (Genesis 1:2) and His work was to organize it. Every declaration of "let there be," with its associated efforts, brought increased order to the earth, until God saw that "it was very good" (v. 31). Establishing a house of order encompasses more than physical order, though it is partly that. Required "points of order" are unique to each family and situation. At various times we notice things in our families "that ought not so to be" (James 3:10) and must begin a repair process. This frequent "housekeeping" takes work, but will serve as an invitation for God's spirit to fill the sanctuary.

In a family, we find order by establishing clear priorities, expectations, and routines and then doing our best to follow them. Every family experiences "off track" or less-than-ideal moments, but if these become pervasive, changes are likely needed. Even small course corrections but may lead to vastly improved outcomes for the future.[14] The prophet Haggai says to his people, "Consider your ways. Ye have sown much, and bring in little; ye eat, but have not enough; ye drink, but ye are not filled with drink; ye clothe you, but there is none warm; and he that earneth wages to put it in a bag with holes. Thus saith the Lord of hosts; Consider your ways" (1:5-8). He then directs them to restore their focus and rebuild their fallen temple.

At one point, after "considering my ways," I realized I needed to be stricter with the kids than I had been. I had recently read a parenting book that identified important components of obedience including timing, thoroughness, and attitude. My husband and I discussed these with our children, requesting they do better about obeying quickly, completely, and cheerfully. The next week we stopped at the downtown library that had new moving shelves and glass elevators. When I said it was time to go and one son protested, I reminded him of our obedience discussion. He immediately changed his tune and came along. When we got to our car the meter had just run out and a policeman was just finishing printing a ticket

181

for the car in the stall ahead of ours. That day, establishing greater order in our family saved us sixty dollars; over time, it will have even higher yields.

A house is in order when family relationships are attended to, when interactions are kind and respectful, when children honor their parents, when parents value their children, when practices match priorities, when God is not forgotten. A house comes to order with patient, diligent upkeep.

House of God

A family creates a "house of God" when they make a clear choice to worship God and serve Him. I was raised attending the Mormon Church with my mother, but gained exposure to Jewish faith and traditions through my father. I felt no conflict in this—I considered that Jews and Christians and other faithful people worshipped the same God, just from different angles.

The doorposts of Jewish homes often bear an encased *mezuzah*—a printed scriptural excerpt drawn from Deuteronomy called the *Shema* signifying that "God alone is worshipped."[*] The text begins,

> *Listen, Israel, Adonai the Eternal, Adonai is one.*
> *You shall love your God with all your heart, with all your soul, and with all your might. And these words, which I command you this day, shall be upon your heart.*[15]

As God's law is truly in our hearts we will have the desire to act upon it. Our lives will give evidence of our devotion to him. Various ordinances can also make our commitment to God more of a formal one. In ways afforded by our particular religious traditions, we and our children can pledge loyalty to God—through baptism, confirmation, sacrament, communion, or bar/bat mitzvah.

One enduring sign of dedication to God is Sabbath observance. In a world that increasingly does not recognize the Sabbath, keeping it may involve sacrifice. Our family has missed certain parties, sports and music opportunities, and chances for additional income, but the blessings of focusing on worship and service on the Sabbath surpass all we have gone without. Ezekiel 20:20 says, "And hallow my Sabbaths; and they shall be a sign between me and you, that ye may know I am the Lord your God." In

---

[*] Deuteronomy 6:4-9 & 11:13-21

Exodus 31 it is called "a perpetual covenant" (vs. 16-17) between God and his people. Essayist Ahad Ha-'Am wrote, "more than Israel has kept the Sabbath, it is the Sabbath that has kept Israel."[16] Keeping the Sabbath is more than getting to church or synagogue, being on time, or having well-behaved kids there—it is a whole day of dedicated devotion, a two-way gift.

Over time I have learned to step back further to guard the edges around the Sabbath day; its preservation requires advanced preparation, much like one would make anticipating the arrival of a "special, beloved guest."[17] We can think of preparing our homes, our clothing, our food, and our minds for the day, so nothing will distract us from being fully present to experience the Sabbath and dedicate it to God.

In Jewish tradition, it is the mother who brings in the Sabbath by lighting the Sabbath candles and reciting a blessing, which says (in part), "May the Sabbath light which illuminates our dwelling cause peace and happiness to shine in our home." The father blesses the children: "May God make thee as Ephraim and Manasseh," or for daughters, "as Sarah, Rebekah, Rachel, and Leah." "May the Lord bless and keep thee: May the Lord cause his countenance to shine upon thee, and be gracious unto thee. May the Lord lift up His countenance towards thee and give thee peace."[18] At the close of the Sabbath, the Havdalah blessing is recited—"Blessed are you, Lord, our God sovereign of the universe who separates between sacred and secular, between light and darkness."[19] This closing ritual involves smelling sweet spices, representing how the delight of the Sabbath can linger with us, even after it is over.

Indeed, worship is not a singular, one-in-seven day event. A "house of God" naturally emerges as its inhabitants develop greater godliness day by day. 2 Peter 1: 2-8 lays out the pathway for putting on the "divine nature," including developing attributes such as faith, virtue, and patience. Such a process often involves change and sacrifice. One humble convert in the scriptures prays, "O God, . . . I will give away all my sins to know thee" (Alma 22:18). To become acquainted with God, we must "give up all our sins, big or small. . . . We are to forget self-justifying stories, excuses, rationalizations. . . . We are to separate ourselves from all worldliness and take upon us the image of God in our countenances."[20] This is the necessary trade we make.

Reflect or discuss:

1) Have you taught your children to pray? Do you regularly pray as a family?

2) How does fasting fit into your religious tradition? Do your children have the opportunity to give anything up for a higher cause or to practice self-control rather than self-indulgence?

3) In what ways do you cultivate faith in your children? Have you shared with them details of your own spiritual journey? Do they know what you believe in and see you act in accordance with these beliefs?

4) How have you created a learning environment in your home?

5) Do you feel like your day-to-day life reflects your highest priorities?

6) How does your family currently observe the Sabbath day?

30~ ESTABLISHING A HOUSE OF PEACE

A classic children's book, *The Little Woman Wanted Noise* by Val Teal, tells of a woman who moves from the city to the country but finds it too quiet. She attempts to fill the void by getting chickens, pigs, and other animals, but only when she gets children, does she finally find what she is looking for: there is "no rest," but there is "peace of mind."[21] Being part of a lively household brings a certain comfort; we really wouldn't wish it any other way. As Emily Watts states in her book about parenting, "The years fly by, even though some of the days are mighty long."[22]

Mothers all know that a house that is too quiet means trouble. Occasionally I have overslept in the morning or fallen asleep while reading stories to my kids, then have awoken to find some interesting developments. Once, our kitchen cabinets had been conveniently labeled according to contents with a permanent marker. Another day, the younger boys had just begun eating chocolate muffins they had made *mostly* following a recipe—only substituting malt powder for oil, giving up on the flour because they couldn't get the lid off the bin, and baking them for a total of seven minutes.

At a recent lunch, my three-year-old and five-year-old repeated their typical banter. "I got more milk than you." "We're not having a contest." "Well, we are not having a *contest*, but we *are* having a race. And the race is who can finish first." "I'm done, so I won!" There is wrestling in the living room, Nerf darts on the fly, rhythms being beaten out on assorted surfaces, and objects preferentially thrown instead of placed or handed. A temple house is a house of peace, but a house with eight boys has a peace all its own.

Above such scuffle, noise, and movement, ultimate peace can still be found. Many factors contribute to peace: comfortable surroundings, adequate preparation, respectful communication, and faithful living. Other factors erode it. We perceive a comfortable and pleasant environment through the five senses—through touch, sights, sounds, smells and tastes; these tangible details ultimately shape our definition and memories of "home." But it is more than this. Much of the sense of peace in a home derives from feeling cherished or valued there. One children's song states, "Home is where the heart is, where warmth and love abound; home is where warm circling arms go all the way around."[23] My childhood home was not immaculate or showy, but a place where I knew I was loved. A grown cousin once came for Thanksgiving and said that, except at times in his own childhood, he'd never felt the warmth of home like he felt during his stay at our house. In a thank-you letter to my parents, he stated, "I must say that I never felt as comfortable and at ease in any home as I did in yours. . . . Being with you those four days restored to me the knowledge of family-living as the procurer of warmth, love, and security."[24]

Working for peace

Though peace may be associated with being "at ease," peace is not always easy to come by, but often requires resolve and work. The scriptures reinforce that it is "by *laboring* . . . [we] establish peace" (Words of Mormon 1:18, italics added; see also Mosiah 29:14). King David of the Old Testament disqualified himself from his original charge to build a temple (2 Samuel 7:13) because he had become a "man of war" (1 Chronicles 22:7-10, 28:3, 9-10). If we, in contrast, create within our homes a culture of peace, a temple-like environment becomes possible. The small degrees of peace preserved as family members choose to avoid an offense, settle an arguments, or offer sincere apology will incrementally increase the collective harmony. Though it may feel like the hundredth time we've appealed for it, family peace is still a worthy and winning cause.

Child psychologist Haim Ginott observes, "The peaceful home, like the hoped-for warless world, does not depend on a sudden benevolent change in human nature. It does depend on deliberate procedures that methodically reduce tensions before they lead to explosions."[25] With personal resolve, those same deep family bonds that sometimes rope us into escalating conflict can instead serve as securing, steadying connections that lift and anchor. Certain communication practices, like using "I" messages rather than "you" messages (i.e. "I feel hurt when you say that" instead of "You are being insensitive"), tend to create less defensiveness. Tone and content are also important. The scriptures remind us, "A soft answer turneth away wrath" (Proverbs 15:1) and that our communication is to be edifying (Ephesians 4:29) and congruent (James 3:9-10): "Therewith bless we God . . . [and] curse we men, which are made after the similitude of God. Out of the same mouth proceedeth blessing and cursing. . . . [T]hese things ought not so to be." Ideally, respectful communication reflects underlying respectful attitudes. In the spirit of

186

authenticity, sincere irritation may be preferential to pretended sweetness, however, when we truly seek to understand others, irritation often melts away.

Seeking to understand

For a string of mornings my kindergartener decided he was no longer interested in going to school. The first day he just dragged his feet. The next day he refused. After inquiring further and assuring myself that his resistance was not rooted in any worrisome issue, I informed him that school was an expectation and commitment to be met except in cases like sickness or extreme weather. He somewhat reluctantly got dressed and headed to the bus stop that second day, but the third day he said he was sick. I said I was sorry to hear it, especially since that would mean he'd have to miss his brother's pinewood derby race that night. His eyes lit up and he jumped out of bed, informing me he wasn't too sick after all—that he had just felt tired of learning math.

Only when we act from a bigger picture, from the context of understanding and empathy rather than from the conflict of the moment, can we effectively address the conflict. Founder of the "Aikido" style of martial arts (translated as "the art of peace"), Morihei Ueshiba taught, "If your heart is large enough to envelop your adversaries, you can see right through [them] and avoid their attacks. And once you envelop them, you will be able to guide them along a path indicated to you by heaven and earth."[26] These principles have also been adopted and applied as a communication strategy. "Aikido regards anyone who behaves aggressively as 'not balanced.' Based on this belief, the aikido style involves recognizing and understanding the other person's needs or motives. The goal in using aikido is to help the person regain balance by meeting some of his needs." To utilize aikido in relationships, we "align [try to imagine being in other person's place], agree [empathize], find areas of common ground, redirect energies, [and] resolve problems."[27] In the example of my son's school avoidance, I could see through his excuses. Though I did not initially know his motives, I sought to understand them. Instead of getting into a power struggle, I redirected his focus to positive future events that he could look forward to if he fulfilled his responsibilities. This was enough to prompt him to share his true motives, overcome his conflicting feelings, and move forward peacefully.

187

Creating a refuge

Our sense of peace relies partly on our sense of security. As mothers we can help create a refuge for our children—a place where they can experience emotional and spiritual safety, where they can come for rest and repair. Elder Scott states, "Many voices from the world in which we live tell us we should live at a frantic pace. There is always more to do and more to accomplish. Yet deep inside each of us is a need to have a place of refuge where peace and serenity prevail, a place where we can reset, regroup, and reenergize to prepare for future pressures. The ideal place for that peace is within the walls of our own homes."[28]

When our children walk back through our front door, we often have no idea what they have faced or surmounted; we often underestimate the refuge home provides. A few weeks into kindergarten, my son brought back a self-portrait he had been asked to draw on the first day. He drew himself with bloodshot eyes and wrote the caption underneath, "I miss Mommy." A few times I have welcomed back a very grouchy child, only later to learn the specific challenges they've encountered—if I had retaliated, I would have only added to the unseen injury.

Our homes can also provide a refuge from destructive, unhealthy influences. It is becoming increasingly difficult to honor and preserve the innocence of childhood. Julie Beck has said, "Women are like lionesses at the gate of the home. Whatever happens in the home and family happen because she cares about it and it matters to her. She guards that gate."[29] Beyond our vigilance, praying for our children adds another layer of protection. Security comes not in a void, but in a fullness; part of resisting negative influences is filling with the good. One tenet of the LDS Church states, "If there is anything virtuous, lovely, or of good report or praiseworthy, we seek after these things" (Article of Faith 13). We can teach our children to discern the difference between the "holy" and "profane" (see Ezekiel 44:23) and having "tasted" goodness, they will be more likely to "cleave" or return unto it (Psalms 34:8, Romans 12:9). Surrounding our children with an uplifting environment will provide peace and protection (see Ezekiel 43:10-11, D&C 88:34), so home can be "a place of refuge, and for a covert from storm and from rain" (Isaiah 4:5-6).

Receiving God's peace

Beyond all outward conditions, the ultimate bringer of peace is God's spirit.[30] One gospel scholar stated, "There is nothing as important as

188

having the companionship of the Holy Ghost. . . . There is no price too high, no labor too onerous, no struggle too severe, no sacrifice too great, if out of it all we receive and enjoy the gift of the Holy Ghost."[31] That "price" may include choosing humility over pride, forgiveness over retaliation, understanding over harsh judgment, and kind words over criticism. Peace propagates peace; it invites God's spirit, which in turn brings greater peace.[32] Fittingly, Isaiah compares such peace to a river, which flows on and on (48:18).

Jesus said to his disciples, "Peace I leave with you, my peace I give unto you: not as the world giveth, give I unto you (John 14:27). The peace God provides is distinct from a transitory absence of noise, worry, or conflict but can exist despite these things. Trusting in God's daily care, we can "let the peace of God rule in [our] hearts" and our homes (Colossians 3:15).

> *For the mountains shall depart, and the hills be removed; but my kindness shall not depart from thee, neither shall the covenant of my peace be removed, saith the Lord that hath mercy on thee. O thou afflicted, tossed with tempest, and not comforted, behold, I will lay thy stones with fair colours, and lay thy foundations with sapphires. And I will make thy windows of agates, and thy gates of carbuncles, and all thy borders of pleasant stones. And all thy children shall be taught of the Lord; and great shall be the peace of thy children* (Isaiah 54:10-13).

Reflect or discuss:

1) Read James 3 as a family. Invite family members to share their feelings about how words and tones affect the peace in your home.

2) How could you improve your physical environment so your surroundings promote peace?

3) What other changes could bring greater peace to your family?

31~ THE BLESSINGS OF A SANCTUARY

What will be the result of creating a sanctuary for our family? Having gone through the sustained effort, sacrifice, and disciplined focus to create such a home, we ourselves will be transformed. Still, this will be a perpetual work rather than a singular event.

Recently I attended the LDS temple in St. Paul, MN. It is very quiet and peaceful, as if an oasis from the cares of the world. The walls display inspiring art, the décor has a simple but ornate quality, the chandelier sparkles with soft, bright light. On this particular evening, members of our congregation had been asked to help clean the temple after the sessions of worship ended. I had never before taken much thought of how the temple always looked so pristine. As I scrubbed water spots off the mirrors and shined fixtures, I suddenly understood something: the temple did not cease to be a temple because upkeep was required. For us, like the people of ancient days, creating a temple will be an ongoing restoration project.

In LDS history, Church members worked for 40 years to build the Salt Lake Temple. After the grueling process of hauling large stone to build the foundation, it began to crack. Church leaders prayed to know what to do and concluded that the foundation had to be torn out and rebuilt with granite, stone-on-stone rather than with mortar, and so this was done. In this early period of the Church, many gave one day in ten to physically labor on temples or add provisions in some way for the workers. Some donated their prized china to be crushed to add sparkle to the temple walls. In the work of temple building, not only were edifices created, but also a dedicated, faithful people.

Focusing our lives on central matters will enliven and bring healing to hearts and relationships. The book of Ezekiel records a vision of a temple from which waters flow forth to heal the Dead Sea. "And, behold, waters issued out from under the threshold of the house . . . and everything shall live whither the river cometh" (Ez 47:1, 9). How often have our family's dedicated choices blessed or protected our children or others? This we may not yet fully know.

One year two neighbor boys occasionally stopped by after school to get a snack. They were polite and non-obtrusive; I liked that they often asked for fruit instead of packaged things. One day the older boy sat at the table talking to me while I sliced and spread honey on warm, homemade

190

bread. He openly reflected, "Your kids are lucky." I asked, "Why do you say that?" He replied, "Because their dad's not in jail and their mom cooks for them." By the next school year the boys had moved away, but I was glad I had welcomed them into our home.

Fostering family connections opens our doors to another guest—Elijah, the symbolically invited guest of the Passover seder. The spirit of Elijah "turn[s] the heart of the fathers to the children, and the heart of the children to their fathers" (Malachi 4:5-6). Reciprocal healing and rejuvenation comes of the intergenerational ties created.

One spring, after completing daily reading logs for school, my son had acquired a few prized coupons for free pizza. Instead of using these all himself, he invited his grandma to come along and treated her to a meal. She loved going on the outing and sharing in the treat. My son told his grandma about a neighborhood bully with whom he was having trouble. I had spoken to the boy's family and the school, but had perhaps been too judicious. In contrast, my mother spoke up in fierce loyalty and later went on to send my son encouraging postcards in the mail. In this brief outing, my son and his grandma served important roles for each other.

Though for several years my mom has not been able to care for me in the way some mothers of adult children do—watching the grandchildren or helping with decorating, organizing, or gardening projects—I so greatly value the prayers she has offered on my behalf. Before her strokes, she mentioned she was praying for me to finish this book—"that it would be to [my] satisfaction." As do all righteous practices, "The effectual fervent prayer of a righteous *mother* availeth much."[33] The blessings do not stop with one generation, but provide a perpetuating inheritance. As we establish houses of prayer, fasting, faith, learning, glory, order, godliness, and peace, the Lord's spirit will come: "And the name of our [dwelling place] shall be, The Lord is there" (see Ezekiel 48:35 and Malachi 3:1).

Reflect or discuss:

1) Have you ever been around someone who has a healing or uplifting presence? How do they live their life? Describe how you feel around them.

2) Have you ever been in a home that had a particularly peaceful feeling? Describe the things you noticed there that may have contributed to this quality.

3) What could you do in your home to elevate the feeling there? Brainstorm many ways and select a few initial action points.

VIII. SYSTEMS AND MEASURES

On matching outcomes and intentions

32~ THE ROLE OF SYSTEMS

When the scriptures refer to various inspired building projects like Noah's ark, the tabernacle, or Solomon's temple, detailed plans are set forth.[1] Even God doesn't accomplish his purposes out of the blue; He has a certain methodical way of doing things. Alma 37:7 reads, "And the Lord God doth work *by means* to bring about his great and eternal purposes; and by very small means the Lord doth confound the wise and bringeth about the salvation of many souls" (italics added). In seven "days" or creative periods, God set in motion self-sustaining systems based on natural laws: planets with orbits and rotations providing days and seasons, fruits bearing seeds of their own kind. Though changes continue to occur within the system, "creation" was a finite act and was accomplished. Just as God methodically creates systems to accomplish His work, as parents we can set plans and routines to help us accomplish ours.

Nurturing in a systematic way helps to ensure that important lessons will be taught and necessary tasks will be accomplished within our families. To consistently foster these key elements, we often naturally create shortcuts, or established methods to avoid having to reinvent the wheel. For example, we make chore charts, cycle through certain familiar meal choices, and establish set bedtimes. With a routine or system in place, we don't have to continually wonder what to do; logistics have been worked out, expectations have been set, and we move forward more automatically toward our goals.

Systems are the inner workings of our families that allow our vision to come about. Certain tasks are particularly central in making entire systems run smoothly. Sometimes the connectedness of everything feels overwhelming—one "cog" gets loose and seemingly everything falls apart—yet the ability to identify these central cogs, these hinge-point tasks or routines, is key to functionality. For example, our family has noticed that the single act of making dinner "on time" translates into more consistency in other important routines, like bedtime, finishing homework, and leaving on time the next morning. We can focus our energy on the most vital processes, and though they may not happen exactly on schedule (to the hour, day, week or month) or sometimes even at all, acknowledging them will increase the odds.

Systems allow for a sense of completion in an otherwise ongoing context. At our house, though the floor could use a good sweeping about five times a day, I trust it will be done after dinner as part of the chore rotation and can therefore ignore a few crumbs. Though the work of bath time can be undone in an instant, sometimes one good scrubbing in a day has to be enough. When the allotted work is done, we may rest.

Certain days defy all systems, which is no surprise. Systems are just tools for most days or many days—they do help streamline our lives, but certainly do not eliminate the ongoing work of motherhood. Implementing systems requires supervision and frequent revision. Systems are means to an end. I recall one morning feeling annoyed that the minute I sat down, hoping to read my scriptures, my boys handed me a pile of books to read them. I had created a system, or set plan, to read my scriptures each morning and it was being interrupted. I quickly remembered, however, that the "end" was not "reading the scriptures," but studying God's teachings to apply them in my life, particularly as a mother. Angrily or resentfully choosing either the scriptures or storybooks would violate my underlying purposes, whereas choosing wholeheartedly and communicating respectfully about either option would preserve these purposes.

Our children often do not fully appreciate all the considering, arranging, and effort that goes into running a successful day, let alone week, family event, family vacation, or school year—even we ourselves do not acknowledge or dwell upon it. Similarly, we do not fathom all the workings of God on our behalf and on behalf of our children. Every system we create exists within a greater context. In the Old Testament, the Lord converses with Job about this, saying, "Where wast thou when I laid the foundations of the earth? Declare, if thou hast understanding. Who hath laid the measures thereof, if thou knowest? . . . Or who hast shut up the sea with doors, when it break forth . . . and said, Hitherto thou shalt come, but no further: and here shall thy proud waves be stayed? Hast thou commanded the morning since thy days; and caused the dayspring to know his place?" (Job 38:4-12). Any implemented system established for good has God's grace, or enabling power, behind it. Notwithstanding our personal effort, we recognize that God's system—his vision, plan and mercy—extend beyond our own. As we "do all," we can "stand still" and watch the unfolding of events in grander ways than we have ourselves brought about (D&C 123:17).

195

Reflect or discuss:

1) What systems have you already created? Think of routines, patterns, and traditions.

2) Which have been most effective at creating the desired effect? How have these been successful?

3) What other areas could benefit from a system? What improvements to current systems could help vital things happen?

33~ IMPORTANT FOCUS AREAS

Only through inspiration can we select the most applicable routines to teach our children the most vital lessons. The systems we choose will grow out of our own unique situations. They will be simple and sustainable, and both reflect and foster our values. Over time we will discover them, continually revise them, and strive to make them work. We cannot expect to copy another family's system and have it automatically operational—reaping new benefit always takes fresh effort.

Designing systems that implement our family vision is part of the creative work of parenthood. Some focus areas to consider may include systems that build specific skills, teach work, instill values, and preserve family time. Such systems will bring order and efficiency into our current lives and set the pattern for our children's future.

A way to teach specific useful or meaningful skills

For what coming tasks and tests do we prepare our children? We cannot know all that lies ahead for them, but certain skills are universally needed and others universally helpful. For example, our children will all likely someday have to prepare a meal, wash clothes, clean a bathroom, and sew on a button; they will gain wide benefit from thoughtfully navigating challenges, establishing a love of learning, and building relationship skills. We cannot teach every lesson—some skills may be acquired later as the need arises—but we can teach many.

To foster general life skills, one simple approach is to involve our children in daily processes. In an age appropriate manner, children can participate in scheduling, budgeting, gardening (planting, tending and harvesting), cooking, repairing, and shopping (including talking through the decision-making process of what to buy)—not necessarily every time, but a least some of the time. This not only contributes to the functioning of a household, at least eventually, but teaches valuable lessons. It is a naturally occurring, daily apprenticeship.

Also very naturally, challenges will arise. As we help our children wisely navigate these, their insight and confidence will grow. One summer our family decided to train for a 5K together. One of my sons has asthma and would often stop jogging because of perceived shortness of breath. I wondered whether this was true airway reactivity due to asthma, or simply deconditioning. If it was tightness, he certainly should stop and address it (and perhaps we would have to change his preventative medications). Alternatively, if it was the physiologic increase in breathing depth and rate to support exercise, he certainly should push on to develop greater health and endurance. I ran alongside him and we talked about this. He decided he thought it was the latter. He pushed through on that day and subsequent days and, at the race at summer's end, was our family's top finisher.

Other skills to cultivate such as time management, organization, reading, writing, and arithmetic are also initially learned by family participation and later by more formal instruction. Too many parents feel unnecessarily pressured to "formalize" education too soon with drilling and assignments, when children placed in an educationally rich environment (like nature, the library, and other varied settings that stimulate the imagination) will naturally run to explore it in a self-directed manner. They will catch hold of some idea and make a study of it on their own accord, with little need for a task master—or even a school master, for they are their own school. Every day presents matter (space and time) to be organized in some way; every day holds issues and ideas to discuss; every meal, every shopping trip, every building project, every schedule is embedded with decisions and calculations.

Besides both the informal, experiential learning built into daily routines, and the more structured, assigned learning the kids experience at school, one system we have established in our family is a summer learning program called "Wilde University." Before school gets out each year, we select a few topics of focus and then rotate through them, spending about an hour each weekday doing an educational activity together. We have done science projects, inventions, book groups, sculpting, traveling, creative writing, math practice, cooking, sports, music, and more. Though degree of participation varies according to each child's age, development, and temperament, even those not fully participating learn something by watching older siblings and experiencing togetherness. Our kids sometimes grumble about it, but we have shared enriching experiences and have modeled the pursuit of ongoing learning. We also like to read together: *The Chronicles of Narnia*, *The Prince and the Pauper*, *Farmer Boy*, Emily Dickinson's poetry, and other classics. The kids write their own stories, write letters to family members, and write in their journals. They will not

198

become artisans, mathematicians, or novelists with these things alone, but it is the path's natural beginning.

Physicist Richard Feynman tells of how his father influenced him early on to ask questions and think deeply. Even before he was born, his father told his mother he would grow up to be a scientist. Later, his dad would set up small colorful bathroom tiles on his highchair, saying, "I want to show him what patterns are like and how interesting they are. It's a kind of elementary mathematics."[2] Of course children will need guidance along the way, and eventually the opportunity to connect with true masters or mentors, but it does not take a formal degree to lead children in the initial stages of critical thinking or through the process of discovery.

Children may not gravitate toward certain needed lessons, or may even strongly resist them. Why would they initiate or invest in what they do not know? Therefore, some teaching efforts proceed despite resistance, to facilitate at least a needed introduction. Being guided to a degree of mastery in a given area is often what translates later into actually liking it. The initial process, however, may not be comfortable.

Before one of my sons learned to read, he went through a stage of refusing help, yet finding himself unable to proceed without it. He stood stubbornly in front of the book, insisting he would read it himself, wanting to know what the words said, yet unable to independently decipher them. Similarly, our children often want to know how to do things, to have independence and responsibility, but resist any sort of direction in the matter. Being teachable allows one to get "unstuck." A child who experiences the process of being "taught through" the difficult, uncomfortable parts of learning to reach rewards on the other side of knowing, will become teachable. Parents may ask themselves, "How will I reach my child's heart?" For until a child will allow himself to be taught, he will not learn, and a parent who pushes an issue too hard may lose their child's heart. Yet a parent who abandons important lessons loses their child in another way. Endurance is required of both parent and child.

Preserving a love of learning, despite the occasional drudgery of it, requires a balance between instruction and discovery. For one school year, a friend and I created a "science school" curriculum for our preschool-aged boys. We gathered each week and covered a new topic; we studied the phases of the moon,, looked through microscopes, mixed chemistry potions, and discussed the laws of motion. Though we taught short lessons, much of the learning was hands-on. My boys still refer to lessons they learned in science school and consider their former classmates almost like brothers.

In addition to formal teaching, we must allow our children opportunities for self-directed study, questioning, and research based on true curiosity. Such initiative arises naturally in spontaneous play. In modern society, there is too little of this—even the seeming helps of scheduled play times, set playgrounds, and activities requiring purchase and enrollment betray the opportunity. Passive but engrossing entertainment such as TV shows, movies, and video games also encroach upon time for spontaneous play, experiential learning, and meaningful skill development. The common childhood complaint that "there is nothing to do" never is true. (Instead, as parents we know that *multiple* things are begging to be done!) Brief boredom often spurs ingenuity. Recently, my sons gathered old PVC pipes, a broken rain spout, bricks, a wheel barrow, two picnic benches and other various items to create an intricate, homemade "golf course" (a track to roll a golf ball down). I dispensed with my afternoon agenda for them, a small trade-off for the chance to see their enjoyment and to briefly talk physics at the dinner table.

Finally, more pertinent than laundry, piano playing, or physics, are relationship skills. While some children particularly struggle in this area and may need even more concrete instruction and practice to optimize their abilities, most every child could benefit from clearer guidance. The foundational system for learning about relationships is to participate in them. As parents, ideally we model healthy relationships: ones free from rudeness, roughness, or abuse; ones undergoing repair where mistakes have been made; ones full of kindness, service and care. Living in families and as part of neighborhoods and communities, we have many opportunities to mentor "in the moment," as occasions arise. Some specific relationship skills to consider may include: how to initiate a conversation or a friendship, how to choose friends, how to deescalate situations, how to (sincerely) apologize, how to forgive (and communicate that forgiveness), how to make a polite request, how to calm down, and how to show love. Some of these lessons our children will learn by trial and error, by discovering what works and what doesn't. They must learn that "effective" behavior, which gets them something they want, may unfortunately not equal "acceptable" behavior. At times I have coached two of my sons through an interaction, or given instruction and had them try again. Other times I wait and watch the situation play out and then

200

discuss it with each child privately, asking questions like, "How did you feel about that interaction? Why do you think your brother reacted that way? What could you each have done differently?" Instruction about relationships can occur in casual conversation or occasionally, more formally, in family meetings or discussions.

Skills and scholarship do offer their own rewards, but they are not an end in themselves. As we teach our children anything we recall that gifts are developed not to excel above others but for enjoyment and blessing, for the benefit of all (see chapter 24).

Reflect or discuss:

1) Which skills do I consider vital for each of my children to acquire? Which skills may be uniquely needed by a certain child?

2) What pertinent systems are already in place? What else may be needed?

A way to teach responsibility and work

Of all systems I have attempted to implement, it is the chore chart that has undergone the most revisions. One discarded system utilized a big laminated poster with pockets and rotating cards that even I, the plan administrator, couldn't keep up with. (It laid to rest behind my dresser for many years, because I worked too hard on it to throw it away). Only now that our oldest son is a teenager have we finally arrived at a simpler, more sustainable system. We have found that as we consistently hold our children to certain tasks, eventually we get less pushback. Our children have begun to accept work as a requirement, rather than balking at it, as if daily chores were a preposterous, new request every time.

One summer day, a teenage neighbor and his friend brought over a bike with a flat tire and asked if they could have a new inner tube. My husband told them they could earn one from him by picking a bucket of weeds. The young men sat down with dandelion pickers and began working. After about 5 minutes they had disappeared. According to my seven-year-old son (who had shocked me the previous day by earning over $10 picking weeds at the rate of a penny per root), they had gone home, saying, "This is too hard." At that moment, all the grumbling I had endured insisting my children work felt like a worthwhile trade for their developing stamina. Ultimately, we teach work because it does lead to productive change, both in the worker and his or her environment. When

God told Adam and Eve about weeds and working for their bread by the sweat of their brow, he included the profound phrase, "for thy sake" (Genesis 3:17).

Involving family members in household work not only helps it get done, but also provides each individual with a sense of meaningful contribution. Unfortunately, it takes work to teach work, and this can be a tiresome job. Initial investments may be high, but good results will likely follow. After my teenage son plopped onto the couch one day instead of starting his chores, I told him, "We rest from our labors *after* we perform them, not before." He smiled and reluctantly got going on his job. Sometimes it's not that easy. Other times, however, we may be happily surprised. My younger sons, who had come to view added responsibility as an honor or rite of passage, actually *asked* to be put on the job chart at about age four.* I remember how my fifth son Malachi beamed when he was officially added to the job rotation. The first morning he was in charge of cleaning the van, he went out early in the morning with a pail of water and a baby washcloth and washed the parts he could reach—even the tires.

How can parents teach children to accept or even enjoy work? Though our family certainly is not perfect in this area, our efforts have a taught us a few things. We have learned that:

• *With instruction, children can do quality work.* When we take a few minutes to demonstrate a task and provide the necessary tools, we set our children up to succeed. My husband, in particular, sets a high standard and sends the kids back to redo jobs that are incomplete or sloppy.

• *Working alongside our children and expressing appreciation can go a long way.* Instead of having my own separate agenda while my kids are doing chores, I often rotate between them and help. This seems to increase their stamina and their mood. If they are not working, however, they do not receive my periodic help; sometimes I tell them, "I'll start helping once you start working." I try to remember to thank my kids for their work and remind them to thank me for mine.

---

* Paradoxically, mischief-making may be one clue that a child is ready for more responsibility. Rather than indicating irresponsibility, sometimes it demonstrates that not all faculties are sufficiently or productively employed.

• *Clear expectations diminish conflict.* In our family, we usually hold to the expectation that the kids need to finish their work before receiving extra privileges. As a result, they usually get their work done. We found it helpful to communicate our expectations even more specifically for each job. My husband and I wrote out a checklist of cleaning specifications so each job was broken down into small definable tasks. When disputes arise about what it means to be "done" with a particular job, we can review the list instead of argue.

• *Our own attitude toward work matters.* Unfortunately, I tend to get instantly grumpy at the thought of doing big cleaning projects, but have tried to become a more cheerful worker. Once my son sweetly reminded me, saying, "But just think mom, shouldn't we be thankful we have all this stuff to pick up? It would be sad if we had nothing to play with." Finding ways to lighten the mood, such as racing against a timer, listening to music, or singing can help us face necessary tasks.

• *Work can be fun, but it can also be work.* We can be creative about making work fun, or at least memorable. I know one family who always listened to the Carpenters while doing Saturday chores and another who buried treasures in the garden for their kids to find as they weeded. Still, we must not mistakenly assume that our kids need to be constantly entertained or won over, or that somehow they should be absolved from all that is unpleasant. If we tie every job to an external reward or make every task a game, kids may miss seeing the inherent value in a job well done or the inherent enjoyment of the work itself.

Family chores are not the only way to teach children responsibility. Since modern society requires much less ongoing physical labor than agrarian society, the necessity of work may need to be taught in other ways. With no farm to tend, no cows to milk, no livestock to feed, one woman said, "Music is our cow." She had her children learn discipline and endurance through focused musical instrument practice. Another family has the tradition of going on a backpacking trip every year in the mountains. Even the small children carry some type of pack; they practice hiking with packs weeks ahead to get prepared. Whether families choose a musical instrument, a sport, a building project, or a backyard garden, children gain a chance to learn the "law of the harvest," discipline, teachability, cooperation, and confidence that can translate into other areas. Almost any arena can serve as its own microcosm holding the complete curriculum—the entirety of necessary lessons.

While not everyone needs to labor in the same way, a difference exists between children who have been taught to work and children who have not. Personally experiencing the positive fruits of hard work in some form strengthens children for future challenges. Goleman writes, "What seems to set apart those at the very top of competitive pursuits from others of roughly equal ability is the degree to which, beginning early in life, they can pursue an arduous practice routine for years and years."[3] Psychologist C. R. Snyder studied academic success of college freshman and found that levels of hope, "believing you have both the will and the way to accomplish your goals, whatever they may be," better correlated with grades than did SAT scores.[4] The work of psychologist Anders Ericsson from the mid 90's, which showed that elite performers in music, sports, and other competitive arenas often had put in over ten years of intense practice in their specialty area (often totaling >10,000 hours), also supports the notion that excellence hinges firmly on diligent work rather than just natural ability.[5]

At minimum, involving children in work teaches a skill; ideally it teaches a habit—one that can benefit them for life. As it has been wisely said, "Labor is the price of cleanliness, progress, and prosperity."[6] Over time, our children can come to see that "the privilege to work is a gift . . . the power to work is a blessing, [and] the love of work is success."[7]

Reflect or discuss:

1) How do I view work? How do my family members view it?

2) What systems for teaching and accomplishing work are already in place? In what ways are they effective or ineffective? What else may be needed?

3) What work needs to be done in my family? Who performs it or could realistically perform it? Are family members actively participating in helping the family function? How can strengths be utilized and weaknesses overcome in the work to be done? What types of work experiences would be most beneficial to my children?

A way to teach doctrine & instill values

I have heard some parents say, "I don't want to force my beliefs upon my children. When they get older they can decide what to believe." But failing to teach values is a tragic mistake, a profound missed opportunity. The scriptures set forth the parental duty to teach (Proverbs 22:6; Deuteronomy 6:7) and even specify the most important curriculum.[*]

Why is moral teaching so vital? As parents we point our children to God so they "know to what source they may look"[8] for proper guidance even in our absence. We help them know God's laws so they may qualify for His greatest blessings. Just as we would not want our children to miss the chance of an enriching opportunity, a scholarship, or a transfer of credit, we must not neglect to position them to receive the greatest promises, protections, and preparations available—those offered by God Himself. Many scriptural promises are extended as if-then clauses; they hinge upon specific action. Knowing these divine requirements and conditions will help our children develop throughout their lives. William Tyndale, a 15th century reformer who sought to make English copies of the Bible available to the common people, stated "The nature of God's word is, that whosoever read it, or hear it reasoned and disputed before him, it will begin immediately to make him every day better and better, till he be grown into a perfect man."[9] An ability to judge between right and wrong will protect our children—not from everything, but from many things.

Though we informally share values with our children in the process of daily living, scheduled teaching times are also important. In 19th century America, it was common for families to regularly gather for prayer and scripture study. How have so many let this powerful tradition go? Despite busy schedules, a wide age range of children, and sometimes less than enthusiastic participants, our family participates together in daily family prayer and scripture study, weekly "family night," and weekly church services. Sometimes our devotionals get chaotic—two kids start fighting over the prime spot on the couch, someone steps on someone else's scriptures, the baby protests at the sight of my lap being taken by his three-year-old brother—but we proceed anyway. It allows us on a regular basis to teach truths to our children. Recently we talked about how we are

---

[*] See Deuteronomy 5-6, Moses 6:57-68, 2 Nephi 31:14-21, Mosiah 4:15, D&C 68:25-31, D&C 93:40.

205

accountable to God for our choices and read from Hebrews 4, which teaches boldly that "the word of God is quick and powerful . . . and is a discerner of the thoughts and intents of the heart. Neither is there any creature that is not manifest in his sight." We had gathered for less than ten minutes and then went about our day—packing lunches, eating breakfast, scrambling off to the bus—but with greater grounding than we otherwise would have had.

Our "family nights" usually involve a song, prayer, lesson, treat, and shared activity. Sometimes they get scaled back to a brief discussion of a gospel topic over dinner, but most often we make more complete plans. One night, for example, we read an article entitled "Bind on thy Sandals," which told a story about a 4th string quarterback being unexpectedly called into the game and having to run out in stocking feet because he had taken his shoes off.[10] We discussed how continual preparation helps us meet our goals. We read a scripture from Ephesians: "Stand therefore having . . . thy feet shod with the preparation of the gospel of peace" (6:14-15). Each boy received a handmade "coupon" for a new pair of shoes for the coming school year. We ate a treat the boys had helped prepare and then played a game together in the backyard.

On Sundays we attend church as a family and set the day apart for service and worship. As it has through history, Sabbath observance serves as an important "sign" that we acknowledge and honor God (Ezekiel 20:20). Getting a family ready for church is no small task but, as I remind myself, a small price to pay for the associated blessings.[11] When I manage to prepare ahead, the Sabbath can be more reserved as a day of rest even for me as the mother. In order to experience a sense of renewal rather than tension or disappointment, I try to keep my expectations reasonable. I teach the kids about reverence and help facilitate it, but accept that small children will inevitably get restlessness in a long meeting. I bring a few items to help them sit still, such as coloring supplies, books with religious pictures, quiet toys, and a small snack, but take care that these do not themselves become disruptions. I have been relieved to observe that reverence, when cultivated, emerges as children's maturity and awareness grow. Some Sundays go better than others, yet despite the struggles, it comes down to the singular decision where as a family and individuals we "remember the Sabbath day, to keep it holy" (Exodus 20:8).

Reflect or discuss:

1) What is my source for moral truths? Which truths do I consider vital for my children to understand? What resources are available?

2) What family systems are already in place to teach values? What else may be needed?

A way to share time meaningfully

Sometimes I find myself longing to share meaningful time with my family to connect and enjoy one another. Since I spend most of my time at home, what is this longing about? I think of one particular cold Saturday morning when the kids each stumbled out of bed in turn and we all sat lazily on the couch wrapped in blankets talking and laughing. There was no planning beforehand and no pull from tasks after, just that comfortable, happy moment spontaneously unfolding. Also there are other special shared times I recall: certain fun outings and certain structured times of work or learning. Ultimately, the conditions leading to the standout memories are not always magical or predictable, yet they often occur when there is less rush and more focus on the present. Our lives must leave space for such moments to exist.

Less rush. Constant hurry tends to displace priorities. On certain mornings I have caught myself scolding a child for stopping to smile and talk to his baby brother instead of running out the door to school. If we're running late for bedtime, I get easily annoyed at anything my kids do besides going to bed—previously endearing acts become punishable offenses. When instead I choose to reset my expectations and acknowledge it predictably takes a certain number of minutes to get the kids in bed, the time can be restored to neutrality and all can move forward in a more positive way. Often processes are relatively incompressible and trying to rush them turns them instead into drawn out struggles. Though we must operate under time constraints, we can do so while staying loyal to higher purposes. Hurrying children along, when necessary, is more effectively pursued, figuratively speaking, with a pom-pom rather than a whip. As Steven Covey states, "[In relationships], 'slow' is 'fast' and 'fast' is 'slow.'"[12] The ability to follow the natural pace and rhythms of our children, the chance to enjoy unrushed transitions and spontaneous interactions—this is a wise and feasible choice, not an impossible luxury.

207

More focus. Sharing meaningful time with others is about focus. It requires taking time to "see, hear, [and] understand another person."[13] For example, stopping to sit on the floor with my toddler for even fifteen minutes while he plays blocks can allow for meaningful connection. Inviting one child along when I run an errand gives opportunity for talking along the way and, if nothing else, a common experience. I cannot fully control an interaction (even trying risks heightening the stress and pressure of it), but I can choose to extend my care and attention at a particular time and accept the interaction for what it is.

For a college class, I was once assigned to catalogue how every moment was spent in relation to my family. With this I realized that not every shared moment is created equally. I could be doing the dishes primarily to "do the dishes," during which time my awareness could be mostly closed off toward my kids, *or* I could do dishes as the secondary event as I talked to a child or splashed in the sink. Either way the dishes would get done. I found such greater satisfaction in choosing to focus on relationships rather than tasks. Although allowing my little son to stand pouring water from cup to bowl and back again while I did dishes often meant having water poured down the counter and a few swallowed sips of dishwater, it kept him engaged and happy while I accomplished my work.

It is unadvisable to pretend to our children they are the focus in moments they are not, or they will learn that "spending time" or "playing" constitutes a half-interested, distracted interaction. Sometimes efficiency must take precedence, but we should be conscious of our choices (rather than inadvertently or unnecessarily neglectful), acknowledging that when tasks are the focus, people may be left in shadow, and visa-versa.*

Choices. Recognizing decision points allows us to find power to choose our own lifestyle, giving room for change in areas we are unhappy. I have noticed that sometimes I plod along doing the opposite of what I want in the moment, when instead I could have been as effective (or more so) following my preferences. For example, sometimes when I want to play with the kids, I don't allow myself because of "having" to do dishes or laundry, and then feel sad to be missing out. Other times I am in the mood

---

* We may even consider verbalizing our intentions to give others accurate expectations. Sometimes I say to my kids, "I'm sorry, I can't listen very well right now because I have to concentrate on getting this done." Though I try to minimize such times, I feel less divided when I accept the situation for what it is and communicate truthfully about it.

208

to get something done, but feel guilty putting off the kids and so begrudgingly play with them. Because invariably we will play sometimes and work sometimes, why not at least more often do so without the inward mismatch? If we are playing with the kids, we can feel happy about that; if we are doing dishes, we can feel happy about that—certainly this is preferable to feeling guilty no matter what we choose. Similarly we can allow some flexibility in our children's schedules, so they can channel their energy in the direction it is already flowing. If their work gets done in reasonable time, why not let them choose whether to start with homework or practicing, and when to interject a needed break?

As writer Lin Yutang states, sometimes "the noble art of getting [the most important] things done" requires "the even nobler art of leaving [other] things undone."[14] We must be increasingly selective as our responsibilities grow. As I have had more children, for example, I have more work to do and more people with whom to regularly connect. I have had to purposefully build shared time into my routine, instead of only getting around to it after all else is said and done.

In a large family, experiencing each other as a group sometimes does not allow for more personalized interaction—it can feel somewhat like listening to static on the radio rather than tuning in. To bond individually with family members, I have established certain routines of connection, including brief bedside times and simple one-on-one outings. During a time when scheduling was too complicated for outings, I bought a large bag of pancake mix and made special early morning breakfasts to share with one family member at a time. My husband and I also try to go on a date a few times a month. Though these individual bonding times don't always happen, they happen enough to maintain relationships and help family members feel special.

Group activities also have their place—family vacations, family outings to a park, family walks. These activities will be unique to each family and will change as the family changes. Though children of different ages and personalities experience the activities differently (and sometimes I feel I am only watching from the sidelines with a baby in my arms or chasing a busy toddler), we have built special memories. I also enjoy reading books as a family. It may take us months to finish one book, but I love this time of gathering and impromptu discussion.[15]

As we schedule activities "in" or "out," we would also wisely leave a portion of time unscheduled. A large city rarely sits directly against a nature preserve—a space of transition must exist so an ecosystem is not disrupted.[16] Similarly, a comfortable margin must be left around our family time to protect it. If we leave some time open, we can more easily enjoy and share the plans we do have, allowing the sharing to take precedence over the tasks at hand. Though each family member will have unique memories, ensuring some amount of shared time will allow at least parts of it be special and remembered to someone.

Time perspectives. Some have introduced the distinction between two different aspects of time: Kronos (clock time) and Kairos (a certain readiness or ripeness of the moment that is more sensed than measured). Much of family life occurs on Kairos rather than Kronos time—the readiness of a meal, teaching opportunities, growth, birth, and death. Being in tune with underlying timelines and family rhythms allows for readiness and acceptance, whereas some would look only to clocks and calendars and miss the true significance of moments. Luke 12:54-56 highlights our potential for such lack of awareness: "When ye see a cloud rise out of the west, straightway ye say, There cometh a shower; and so it is. And when ye see the south wind blow, ye say, There will be heat; and it cometh to pass. . . .Ye can discern the face of the sky and of the earth; but how is it that ye do not discern this time?" The way we view and spend time not only reflects our values, but shapes them, simultaneously mirroring and forecasting.

Reflect or discuss:

1) Does your family regularly share meaningful time? What could be done to insure this?

2) Are connections between each family member strong? Which relationships could use additional attention or nourishment? How could this be accomplished?

34~ TRUE MEASURES

Once on a vacation to visit my husband's family in northern Idaho, we hiked Tubb's Hill, adjacent to Lake Coeur d'Alene. To me it seemed the hike kept going and going—partly from the baby getting heavy in his carrier and partly from the stress of maintaining vigilance over the exact whereabouts of my other five boys along the rocky, steep edges of the trail. I wondered aloud when we would ever get to the top. My husband smiled and said that this hike had no "top"—the path just circled around the hill and soon we'd arrive back where we started. Like my experience on Tubb's Hill, we often don't know the shape of certain journeys or their meaning until we've taken them. Despite our greatest parenting efforts, often results will seem inconsistent or non-existent even though we are truly making progress.

We nurture our children best when we feel hopeful and confident as parents. This becomes more likely when we know where we are headed. It has been said that, "If you can't measure something, you can't understand it. If you can't understand it, you can't control it. If you can't control it, you can't improve it."[17] Measuring alone does not fix, but is the first step in turning observations into applied insight.

Good mothering is not about appearances or superficial comparisons—there are "weightier matters" than these (see Matthew 23:23). Olympic runner Emil Zatopek, known for his seeming inefficient form, once said, "I shall learn to have a better style once they start judging races according to their beauty. So long as it's a question of speed then my attention will be directed to seeing how fast I can cover the ground."[18] The core measures of mothering relate more to wisdom and faithfulness than anything an external person could see or judge.

Even as we look at our own situations, we must judge carefully. The most obedient, pleasant, or easy child in a room of a hundred may not be the healthiest or happiest. Many developmentally normal stages are difficult to bear. Many quirky and "problematic" traits in our children are closely linked with their greatest strengths. We must allow for typical follies of childhood, lack of maturity, and evidence of lessons only half-learned ("in process"), while still finishing those lessons. With proper perspective, we can delight in each stage: allowing childishness to give way to maturity without robbing "childlike" innocence and joy; teaching carefulness, while allowing for spills as coordination develops; teaching manners, while allowing for refreshingly honest, spontaneous reactions; teaching goal setting, while allowing our children to savor the present moment; teaching focus, while not blinding them to the wonders all around them; and teaching responsibility, while allowing them to enjoy the unique position of having little. Though we are working to "raise" our children—an effort that proceeds "against gravity" (against certain natural tendencies within our children and ourselves), we must remember and delight in the fact that, for the time being, they *are* children after all. As acknowledged in the collection of essays entitled, *Your Children will Raise You*,[19] the raising goes both ways.

When certain approaches seem not to be working, we must discern whether to change direction or press on through the difficulty. This depends on whether we have reached a dead end or a figurative mountain to climb that leads to a promised land. When judging the effectiveness of our methods, we can consider the following possibilities:

• *More work or attention may be needed in a given area.* Legendary runner Juma Ikangaa stated, "The will to win is nothing without the will to prepare."[20] Desired outcomes often require significant background work.

• *It may be just too early to see results.* Sometimes patient persistence is required; as stated in the scriptures, "much lies in futurity."[21]

• *Change naturally brings resistance, especially when it involves increased demands or a higher standard.* An adjustment period may be required for all involved—this is not a signal to give up. Changes central to our progress or survival may feel difficult or foreign at first, but history is full of examples of those who have endured change and transformed their lives for the better. We as parents need to be resilient despite protests, and resistance (while being open to continued improvement even if suggested by or inspired by a child's reaction). Without paying too much heed to the critics, we can listen enough to learn from them.

• *Problems may be at the receiving end.* While we can work to adjust methods to address true needs of our children and to achieve the best "fit," at least two parties are involved (and usually more). Sometimes children choose not to accept or receive important lessons (yet).

• *The system may be one the family has outgrown.* What worked in the past may need adjustment to incorporate new stages and contexts. For example, my go-with-the-flow, responsive parenting model that had worked when I had one or two or three children, became outmoded with six and seven. There were too many kids pulling different ways, and without my own sense of direction (planned agenda) for the day, I found myself feeling paralyzed and ineffective. I had to establish greater structure in several areas to enable myself to accomplish the basic tasks for family functioning.

• *Our expectations may be too high or rigid.* A good system works much of the time, but is rarely 100% effective. With the multiple and spontaneous demands that arise in family life, we have to operate with some flexibility. We must balance previously planned work with needs that come up "in the moment." These ongoing interjections to the plan are a part of the reality of the present moment and should not be flatly disregarded or universally viewed as an interruption; however, they also should not be automatically allowed to bulldoze previous decisions without consideration. Steven Covey stated, "To ignore the unexpected (even if it were possible) would be to live without opportunity, spontaneity, and the rich moments of which "life" is made."[22]

• *In any system, we must reserve the right to revise.* If a system is not working, we can change it. Kids are resilient and can adapt to positive changes that we as parents see as beneficial.

Because we often cannot completely control outcomes, measuring inputs, such as diligent effort, may more accurately reflect success than outputs. In general, measurement is most meaningful when it occurs in areas where we have some control. We can seek to teach diligently and with inspiration, but can't guarantee engagement; we can love, but cannot control others' receptivity.

True measures accurately account for all factors and see beyond the illusion of appearances. Wise judgment resembles a godly perspective: "For the Lord seeth not as a man seeth; for man looketh on the outward appearance, but the Lord looketh on the heart" (1 Samuel 16:7). True measures favor intrinsic success ("primary greatness") over extrinsic success ("secondary greatness").[23] Julie Beck, leader in the LDS Relief Society, has said,

> We are doing well when we develop attributes of Christ and strive to obey His gospel with exactness. We are doing well when we seek to improve ourselves and do our best. We are doing well when we increase faith and personal righteousness,

213

strengthen families and homes, and seek out and help others who are in need. We know we are successful if we live so that we qualify for, receive, and know how to follow the Spirit. When we have done our very best, we may still experience disappointments, but we will not be disappointed in ourselves. We can feel certain that the Lord is pleased when we feel the Spirit working through us. Peace, joy, and hope are available to those who measure success properly.[24]

Whether fitting solutions appear quirky or brilliant to others bears little importance. As Emerson has said, "My life is for itself and not for a spectacle. . . . What I must do, is all that concerns me, not what the people think. . . . It is the harder, because you will always find those who think they know what is your duty better than you know it. It is easy in the world to live after the world's opinion; it is easy in solitude to live after our own; but the great [person is one] . . . who in the midst of the crowd keeps with perfect sweetness the independence of solitude."[25] We are accountable to God, ourselves, and our families, not to onlookers. To be a wise mother in the private sector is our greatest challenge.

Though, at times, the worth of certain methods or approaches may be in question, *our* worth never is. God wants us to succeed at mothering and will help us grow to "fill the measure of [our] creation" (D&C 88:19, 25).

Reflect or discuss:

1) On a daily basis, how do you measure your success? For you, what are the "true measures"?

2) How will you know when your family is functioning well? What qualities or important outcomes will be present?

IX. INSPIRED INSTRUCTION

On teaching effectively

Teaching is one main way we nurture as mothers. While previous chapters explore what to teach, this section will focus on how. One can know theory, but the true challenge lies in the implementation.

The background work of effective parental teaching involves a loving relationship, true principles, and divine inspiration. These foundational aspects, though perhaps not continually or perfectly in place, warrant our first attention before other methodologies will prove useful. When struggles arise, we must revisit these—relationship, principle, and inspiration—to inspect and repair as needed.

Relationship, correct principles, and inspiration

Effective parental teaching rests more on relationship than particular technique—we could bumble the words, but with humble intent and love teach powerful lessons. Recently I volunteered to bring a dinner to a friend struggling with health issues. After I made the dinner and packaged it to bring, it looked smaller than I anticipated. And the soup didn't turn out quite as good as usual. I started feeling self-critical and angry, but then stopped myself. The meal was not about me "carrying off" a production, it was about expressing care. I hoped my friend could enjoy the soup I had to offer and feel the love behind it.* Similarly in parenting, our ability to teach relies more upon our underlying feelings and intents and less upon the exact details of what we do and say.

Advanced parenting skills are tools, but only through relationship do we maintain our influence. Love is what carries our lessons "from the heart, to the heart" of our children. Upon what is relationship built? Among other things, goodwill, valuing, paying attention, respectful communication, care, devotion, and shared time. I refer not to surface relationships, but enduring ones—not smoothness in the moment gained by appeasing or pandering to all wishes, but doing justice to the long-term relationship. Sometimes the parental role requires us to invest in a child's future self, despite the momentary unpleasantness or discomfort of needed lessons.

---

* That very night my friend sent this email: "Thank you for the dinner tonight. Tasty and healthy both. I appreciate your thoughtfulness."

A great religious educator has taught, "The study of the doctrines of the gospel will improve behavior quicker than talking about behavior will improve behavior."[1] Since it is often our children's behavior we are working to modify, teaching them true principles alone will have great effect. Still, taking one step back, *our* behavior as parents will also improve as we study doctrine. Specifically, what doctrinal principles relate to teaching? The sources I reference below come primarily from my own LDS faith tradition, but I consider them wise and generally applicable.

• Content matters: certain lessons parents have the duty to teach. We are to teach "of the Lord"—the "peaceable things of the kingdom" (3 Ne 22:13, D&C 36:2).[2]

• Our power or influence as teachers comes by correct method (mostly, having the right state of heart) not automatically by our office as parents. We are to teach "by persuasion, by long-suffering, by gentleness and meekness, and by love unfeigned; by kindness, and pure knowledge" (D&C 121:41-42).

• Our lessons have more power when we are applying (or working to apply) them personally, "without hypocrisy, and without guile" (D&C 121:42). D&C 11:21 states, "Seek not to declare my word, first seek to obtain my word, and then shall your tongue be loosed."

• In teaching, saying words may not be enough; we must work to assure our children *understand* (D&C 68:25). This may require endurance and the use of multiple methods. Psalms 119:34 states, "Give me understanding, and I shall keep thy law."

• We must be diligent (D&C 88:78).

• All teaching ultimately occurs through the medium of the Holy Ghost (D&C 42:14; D&C 28:1, 4; D&C 43:15 –16; D&C 50:17-22). It is a two-way process, with lessons offered and received.

Whether referred to as the Holy Ghost, the Holy Spirit, the Spirit of God, or some other name, most religious individuals acknowledge the reality of and possibility for divine direction in their lives. Inspiration rounds out the limited perspective afforded by direct observation and common sense alone. Only though inspiration can we know our children's hearts and teach them individually tailored lessons. Only through inspiration and choice do our children receive our lessons: "For when [one] speaketh by the power of the Holy Ghost the power of the Holy

Ghost carrieth it unto the hearts of the children."[3] Qualifying for and utilizing this "unspeakable," priceless gift (see 2 Corinthians 9:15, D&C 121:26), will increase our chances for effective teaching. A most important aspect of our work "will be [our] own daily spiritual preparation, including prayer, scripture study, and obedience to the commandments."[4]

Many of us have had the experience of being awakened even by a very soft stirring or call of a child with a particular need. I remember once being suddenly awoken in the middle of the night by my son just standing silently at my bedside. Similarly, the Holy Ghost as the divine communicator speaks deep to the soul in ways that are hard to ignore; "But behold, it was a still voice of perfect mildness, as if it had been a whisper, and it did pierce even to the very soul" (Hel 5: 30). As mothers, we need to listen to the Spirit and go "straightway" (Mark 1:18), "regardless of fears or any inconvenience."[5]

The basic parenting tools are simple tools

In the scriptures we are taught that often "miracles [are] worked by small means" (Alma 37:41) and that "out of small things proceedeth that which is great" (D&C 64:33). In James 3:4, we are also told that great ships are "turned about with a very small helm." Similarly, seemingly simple approaches can powerfully impact the behavior of children.

It is not the complex, sophisticated strategies required to preserve or rescue most families, but rather the basic parenting tools put to use. Still, the words "basic" and "simple" don't necessarily mean easy and automatic. Simple things are often more elusive than the deeper mysteries. For example, though to love God and love our neighbors are foundational commandments (Matthew 22:36-40), the apostle Paul acknowledges that one could possess eloquence, faith, and knowledge of all the mysteries of God, yet still lack this basic love (1 Corinthians 13:1-3). Sometimes the most obvious and simple lessons are the ones we miss, resist, or ignore; perhaps they themselves are the greatest mysteries.

With the relative peace, prosperity, health, safety, and opportunity that most of us enjoy, we forget that children thrive on few and simple things. Poet Robert Louis Stevenson wrote,

> Happy hearts and happy faces,
> Happy play in grassy places—
> That was how, in ancient ages,
> Children grew to kings and sages.[6]

218

Knowing that nature itself can provide hours of exploration and discovery without another single toy, that the Bible has been a near-sole text for brilliant scholars of the past, and that historically, children have survived on turnips, potatoes and cornmeal, I'd still like to provide more where I can—but I must be sure the additional items are enhancing rather than detracting. For instance, allowing much time spent on video games, overscheduling with "enrichments," and serving junk food more than occasionally would be "additions" that result in net negative effects. The mere satisfying of a want or wish does not have any bearing on whether something is truly good or not. As parents, we have the difficult task of trying to teach our children to prize the right things, even when it means teaching a taste (or at least tolerance) for seeming unpleasant things that we know bring rewards (like work) and disallowing many seeming pleasures that lead to less ideal ends (like limiting certain types of media).

Educators Rachel and Oliver de Mille describe the first lessons of childhood as the "core phase," during which children optimally learn "right and wrong . . . relationships, family values, family routines and responsibilities . . . accountability, and the value and love of work . . . [which are] best learned through daily experiences in home life."[7] "Parenting" occurs naturally as we live side-by-side with our children teaching and exemplifying moral principles, providing mentorship and apprenticeship, and giving inspired guidance and correction.

We provide for our children's needs while, over time, teaching them to secure those needs. At different stages, our role in teaching our children will change. In the New Testament, Jesus admonished his disciples, "Feed my lambs . . . Feed my sheep." (John 21:15-16). Young lambs would be nursed or bottle-fed, while sheep are guided to specific pastures and allowed to graze. As we "teach correct principles," our children will, to a growing degree, be capable of "govern[ing] themselves."[8]

Establishing order

In order to be the parent, one has to "be the parent"—or in other words, take on the leadership role. Benjamin Franklin said, "Let thy child's first lesson be obedience, and the second will be what thou wilt."[9] If obedience is not taught, few other lessons can follow. While most parents would agree with this outwardly, many modern parents have an underlying ambivalence about obedience: we want our children to be teachable, but want to support initiative and independent spirit; we want our children to

219

be religious and faithful, but don't want to create blind followers, we want them to listen to us, but sometimes wonder if we're right. Insisting on obedience can be tiring and difficult; we don't want to spank or yell or fight, but then are at loss about *how* to insist.

I once asked an experienced mother advice on a parenting issue and she said, "I don't know what to tell you. The kids are different now than when my children or I were young. We never would have dreamed of talking back or blatantly misbehaving." Though she may have selective memory, unique parenting challenges arise in every era. The apostle Paul wrote, "This know also, that in the last days perilous times shall come. For men shall be lovers of their own selves, covetous, boasters, proud, blasphemers, disobedient to parents, unthankful, unholy, without natural affection, trucebreakers, false accusers, incontinent, fierce, despisers of those that are good, traitors, heady, highminded, lovers of pleasures more than lovers of God" (2 Tim 3:1-4). We will need wisdom and strength to counteract such tendencies.

Often, wise parenting does not bring popularity in the moment, but rather may be received with criticism, crying, screaming and struggle. As the nursery rhyme goes,

> Little boy blue,
> Come blow your horn,
> The sheep's in the meadow,
> The cow's in the corn.
> Where is the boy
> Who looks after the sheep?
> He's under the haystack,
> Fast asleep.
> Will you wake him?
> No, not I,
> For if I do,
> He's sure to cry.[10]

As parents, we can't afford to leave "little boy blue" sleeping under the haystack, though it would be much less hassle. To quote another nursery rhyme, while it is true that "All work and no play makes Jack a dull boy," it has also been frankly stated that "All play and no work makes Jack a useless boy."[11]

Clues that things may be "out of order" or upside down at home may include: children with no specific responsibilities, children showing

220

consistent disregard for parental direction, or children displaying demandingness and ingratitude. What can be done? Some specific strategies will be addressed later in the chapter, but the first step is "stepping up" to the parental role. In a recent LDS General Conference, Elder Lawrence stated, "What the world really needs is courageous parenting from mothers and fathers who are not afraid to speak up and take a stand." He goes on to say that we must value our children's lasting well-being more than their "temporary goodwill"—to have the courage to say "no" to destructive influences and "yes" to ennobling ones (putting forth the mental, physical, and emotional work to make the right things happen—and persisting despite protests).[12]

As parents we need to feel not only "permission" but encouragement to teach the best truths we know. Of course, our children will rewrite it in their own words, according to their experience, and may come to some different and even better conclusions on some points, but to give anything less than our best effort to teach truth is ultimate parental neglect. We would love interactions to remain continually pleasant, but this wish does not erase our charge to "raise up children in light and truth" (D&C 93:40). While forceful or overbearing methods weaken relationships and diminish our influence over time, gentle consistency and firmness strengthen relationships and influence. At times, we may have to sacrifice one type of relationship for another—friend for mentor, superficial for deep, momentary for lasting. We may need to choose to be a parent rather than a pal.

Obedience is not just a matter of convenience for those in charge, but rather an important gateway to a child's future learning and leadership. LDS Church President Thomas S. Monson states, "A knowledge of truth and the answers to our greatest questions come to us as we are obedient to the commandments of God. We learn obedience throughout our lives. Beginning when we are very young, those responsible for our care set forth guidelines and rules to ensure our safety. Life would be simpler for all of us if we would obey such rules completely. Many of us, however, learn through experience the wisdom of being obedient."[13] Mothering with full faculty will depend upon *our* living according to the best we know. At times our children will choose to learn by their own experience rather than our direction. This may lead to a degree of suffering on their (and our) part, but as we ourselves are striving to be obedient and faithful, we can remain their worthy guides.[14]

While it is best to keep rules simple and not overbearing (based on principles such as respecting others, respecting property, etc.), certain small enforcements send the message a parent "means business" and can prevent bigger infractions. In his book *The Tipping Point: How Little Things Can Make a Big Difference*, Malcolm Gladwell points out that New York City crime rates dropped when police began enforcing small violations such as fare-skipping on the subways.[15] At my house, I notice that requiring a specific standard of behavior at the dinner table, such as staying in seats through the meal, polite requests (using please and thank you), and keeping volumes down, helps to circumvent other problems. Sometimes I forget this and catch myself acting upon all sorts of demanding, rude requests: "I want . . ." "Give me . . .", "No, not that!" In such cases I stop myself (sometimes mid-stride) and say, "Wait a minute. Let's try this again. What is a more polite way to say that?"

Two helpful tools in teaching obedience are the "when-then" statement taught by various parent educators (*"when* your toys are picked up, *then* you may go to the park") and simple follow through. When out on errands with a misbehaving or whining child, we often make empty threats like, "If you don't stop that, we're leaving!" But then we don't leave, because we ourselves can't bear the inconvenience of a particular errand undone. There may be some tasks that can't be abandoned (or times when a child is purposefully trying to foil the task) where different strategies are needed, but usually, if children see we truly will not tolerate a certain behavior—if we show we will not move forward without it gone[*]—that behavior will extinguish.

Setting the stage: preparing the learner and the environment

Optimizing our environments and ourselves through balanced, healthy habits increases the likelihood for learning and good behavior. Everyone thinks and acts better when their physical and emotional needs are met—even parents. In addition to basic needs, we likely have noticed individualized conditions conducive to each family member's optimal functioning. Some may be particularly sensitive to hunger or lack of sleep, others may interact better after having the chance to talk or emotionally

---

[*] I mean this in the context of reasonableness. Of course, we do not need to be paralyzed from doing needed tasks, thereby placing the child in control. Instead, we act on our own terms, insisting upon respectful treatment.

connect, others may feel best after having fulfilled certain personal tasks (like practicing an instrument or exercising). As we take these observations into account, we can more effectively support each other in being at our best.

In our families, we can foster healthy eating, necessary sleep, and physical activity. What I spoke of in earlier chapters regarding sleep warrants further emphasis here. Proper sleep improves overall mood, concentration, energy, engagement, self-control, accuracy, and productivity. The scriptures tell us, "Retire to thy bed early, that ye may not be weary; arise early, that your bodies and your minds may be invigorated" (D&C 88:124). As alluded to in Ecclesiastes 5:12, being active in the day also improves sleep: "The sleep of a laboring man is sweet." Entire textbooks and parenting books focus on the scientific and practical issues relating to sleep, but one simple practice is to honor bedtime as a family. Activities that consistently displace bedtime may not be worth it.

Similarly, daytime schedules that leave no breathing room and require multiple rapid transitions also disrupt the sense of well-being. A mother once told me that many years ago she went to the pediatrician because her three-year-old daughter had developed an eye twitch. Upon inquiring, the pediatrician learned that the young girl was enrolled in multiple classes and activities and advised they scale back. The mother canceled many of the commitments and within a very short time the eye twitch stopped. Not surprisingly, the girl developed into a talented, bright, well-adjusted person despite missing those classes as a three-year-old and now is a mother herself.

I don't know who bears the stress of overscheduling more, the parents or the children, but it steals precious time and sours the interactions that do remain. Our kids need time to run and play and dream. We need time as families for spontaneous interchange—to laugh, to talk, to work side-by-side, or sometimes to do nothing but let a morning or afternoon unfold.

Though we strive for inner balance that transcends circumstance, with the reality of multiple external demands, not every day will feel balanced. I remember tax day 2013 when unfortunately I had left my mom's taxes until April 15th. With a new baby, a toddler, and a preschooler at home, this was a set-up for an unbalanced, stressful day. What do we do at such times? Certainly these are not days for nature walks or teaching the ABC's, but we do teach survival—that some things have to get done that may not be fun or convenient. On such days we can:

> 1) focus on the task at hand (meeting other needs at the bare necessity level) and suspend our awareness of the likely aftermath
>
> 2) build in some morale boosters for ourselves and the kids, such as breaks and healthy rewards
>
> 3) express appreciation ("I dragged you all over town yesterday running errands. Thank you so much for being my patient companion through all that!")
>
> 4) find balance the next day ("I chose everything yesterday, let's do something you want to do today")—something simple and reasonable for both, not a big production for mom to orchestrate

The aftermath of tax day 2013 included a messy house, a late dinner, and nail polish poured on the carpet. I tried to boost my morale by turning on the radio. Fittingly, the song playing was "Venus, Bringer of Peace" by Gustav Holst. I don't remember thanking my kids, but I hope I did. I must have restored balance to some degree, because the taxes got sent and life moved on.

Now back to learning environments. Children naturally learn, explore, notice, and ask. If we set up our homes to be rich with learning materials, like good books and simple creative supplies, and allow these things to be in use, our children will keep themselves busy with their own initiatives and projects. (Though I stocked a craft drawer with colorful supplies, my boys seem to prefer cardboard, packaging, and trinkets they themselves find outside for building and collecting). Providing primary experiences in multiple arenas expands the mind and brings lessons to life. Having time and patience for our children's questions invites deeper thinking and more questions (though the best answer may be another question or a resource in which to find the answer). As mentioned earlier, even our décor can hold symbols and communicate what we value. This can be subtle or overt. In our home we display art, family pictures, and have a white board where we write a scripture of the week that the kids can memorize for a small prize. There is much to explore and notice in nature, even in our own backyards or neighborhoods; there are things to touch, see, hear, smell, and even sometimes taste, like raspberries or fresh peas from the garden.

224

Even a square foot of lawn holds worlds of information to explore and analyze if our minds are tuned into it.[16]

Learning is modeled when parents too are scholars, not necessarily in the formal sense, and not to the point of distraction, but making a sincere study of worthwhile subjects—ones we'd be happy for our own children to pursue. We ourselves can read the classics, develop skills, and productively work. Though it may be slow going with certain books or projects given our many responsibilities, continued effort will set an example. Our children will learn from all we do and are—our routines, our choices, our character.

An additional element in creating a learning environment involves sensitivity to setting and timing. In our homes and interactions, a climate of emotional safety where a child needn't continually filter out or reject messages for self-protection fosters better receptivity. Several factors contribute to a sense of underlying respect and safety within a family. Ideally, we will avoid labeling, name-calling, sarcastic teasing, put-downs, threats, and harsh or rude talk; we will teach from a framework of love, not irritation; we will choose to emphasize strengths and efforts rather than mistakes and outcomes; we will ensure that enough quality time is being shared to communicate true care; we will foster unity in our marriages and thereby diminish overall familial conflict. I have heard the analogy made comparing parental teaching to ironing: we are trying to get out the wrinkles, but sometimes our children are more nylon than linen. We need to recognize how able in a given moment they are to endure correction and correct to the degree they can bear, ideally one-to-one.[17] Over time we can help build their resilience and teachability.

Reflect or discuss:

1) Which foundational aspects of teaching need most attention right now: improving relationships, returning to basics, relying on inspiration, or something else? What is one needed action step?

2) In what ways could you continue to reinforce the importance of obedience?

3) What small change could you make that would improve the learning environment at home?

36~ Noticing & Utilizing Teaching Moments: Part I

One morning in May, our family gathered at the Lake Harriet Rose Garden for professional pictures. For the last several years we had settled for backyard poses taken by neighbors and candid shots taken with our cheap, digital Nikon. Finally, we took the opportunity to hire our friend, a photographer and artist. She was carefully posing us, ushering us from a bridge overlooking a stream to a nearby rock formation with newly sprouting greenery. In this directed, high-stake hour of time, we needed our children's cooperation, but we needed it naturally given. At times the photographer told one of us to lift a chin, tilt a head, or move closer together; at other times she noted certain aspects of our natural positioning and gave encouraging comments—"Yes! Stay just like that!" Most often, however, she didn't say a thing; she just watched and clicked when the time was right—that is her business. Before we thought to tell him otherwise, my five-year-old picked a yellow blossom and said, "Here mom, this is for you." It matched my necklace perfectly and I put the flower behind my ear.

Just as the photographer established the setting and then stood ready to capture photos, we as parents establish a learning environment and then work to capture teaching moments. Lessons arise all around us and usually do not need to be forced or heavily orchestrated—they are handed to us and hold rich potential if we utilize them. These teaching opportunities occur ahead of time, in the moment, after the fact, and on an ongoing basis. Like seeds to the wind, more potentials exist than we bring to fruition, but some we catch and help take root.

BEFORE
Give proper expectations ahead of time. When we let our children know what *they* can expect of new situations and what *we* expect of them, things tend to go much better. Clearly communicating expectations ahead of time often circumvents problems and removes the need for later consequences or reprimand. When my husband and I take the kids to a new or important setting, we often have a little talk with them beforehand (sometimes even in the parking lot), "Now, we are going to a place where. . . (describe the setting). This is what you can expect . . . (what will happen there). Let's

review how to behave." The people who know us will attest to the fact that sometimes our children appear to have missed the lesson—but when we've "taught ahead," things always go better than they could have.[*] Even when an infraction has occurred, teaching ahead for *next* time can also replace scolding in the moment. "I saw _____. Let's review and practice what is expected so you can do better next time." It is also possible to convert a possible "post" teaching moment into "pre" message to give next time—rather than pointing out failings, we can use them to know the instruction required to improve similar scenarios in the future. Often this breeds less defensiveness and less sense of fault or blame.

Preparing children by providing information eases transitions—particularly when we focus on the positive aspects (the best-case scenario) of the upcoming situation or event. When our family was considering the possibility of moving to another state, the kids became sudden advocates after we took time to learn specific features of the town and even a possible house to buy that came with a chicken coop. We didn't end up moving, but I learned how engagement and cooperation increase when we fill blank unknowns with positive, specific information.

As parents, we can influence our children by setting them up for success, but this does not guarantee it—children still maintain accountability to use developmentally appropriate judgment and common sense even in areas where they have not been prepared or forewarned.

Overdone preparations can also backfire; often less is more. One Mother's Day, I decided I wanted to give my kids each a gift to tell them how I appreciated being their mother. I sewed little activity bags for them to use in church and placed craft items and snacks inside for that day's church meeting. Over time I was disappointed to discover that the kids behaved less well scrambling for their bags, comparing snacks, and fighting over items inside than they had with a simple pad of paper or nothing at all. I tried to tell them how I wanted the bags to be a help rather than a distraction, but eventually "bagged" the Sunday bag idea altogether. Though sometimes I feel under prepared, with "no scrip, no bread, no

---

[*] Note: If a child is being particularly belligerent or contrary, it may be best NOT to say how important a particular setting is and best NOT to arm them with the knowledge of how to cause embarrassment or disruption. Even better, avoid going out at such times—but when it cannot be avoided, hold your breath and hope for the best.

money in [my] purse" (Mark 6:8), I find that God does provide and kids can too. Ultimately, children's needs are simple—having much more than the necessities becomes useless baggage to be lugged about by parents. Their pleasures are often better secured by their own resourcefulness and initiative rather than prepackaged and provided.

Provide Clarity. We often tell our children what *not* to do without specifying what we'd like them to do instead. Sometimes we as parents haven't thought through a situation to exactly know our own wishes. When we have mixed feelings about an issue, we tend to send mixed messages. Sometimes we feel ambivalence toward a specific behavior because we know its appropriateness varies based on context. For example, in some contexts my kids get goofy and silly and I laugh along, however, when we are in a formal setting like at church or a concert, sometimes they resist or disbelieve my prohibitions because I have allowed the casual behavior before. When rules change according to context, the nuances will need to be clearly articulated or discerned over time.

Once I was driving with my kids between Minneapolis and Chicago and decided to stop for dinner. After having been cooped up in the car for hours, the kids got into the restaurant and went completely wild. I felt embarrassed, frustrated, and overrun. We finished our dinner, piled back in the car, and while I drove along I-90 trying to "keep myself together," I thought about what went wrong and what I'd like instead. Though the generalities of proper behavior in public seemed quite obvious to me, I realized I had never specifically verbalized my expectations to my children. (I hadn't even formalized them within myself, but kept having disappointing, frustrating experiences.) In the course of an hour of focused contemplation, I came up with four words to capture my expectations for my children in public: Calm, Polite, Purposeful, and Together. Having the benefit of a captive audience in the car, I introduced these four ideas and specified what I meant by each: we would not be bouncing off the walls and touching everything; we would use polite words (like please and thank you) and polite tones; we would stick to the purpose of the outing; we would stay physically together and unified—not running in all directions after personal whims or interests, not interfering with the enjoyment of other family members by teasing or rudeness. Then we debriefed about our most recent experience at dinner: "If this is what I'd like to see, how did we do in each area with our last stop. How can we do better?" Though

228

subsequent outings have not been perfect, providing clear expectations brought about instant and significant improvement.

Part of clarity is congruence—making language and action match our true expectations. For example, phrasing an intended directive as a question implies a choice: saying, "Will you stop jumping on the couch?" means something different than "No jumping on the couch." Even tacking on the seemingly innocent word "Okay?" to the end of a directive changes it to a mere request subject to a child's approval. All this being said, however, children can often discern what we mean even if we don't get the words exactly right and are accountable to act according to their understanding.

Avoid threats and bribes in the set-up. Threats and bribes seed improper behavioral motives rooted in self-interest rather than integrity. Inflation occurs with both, becoming burdensome, unreasonable, and potentially destructive. For example, when an original threat brings insufficient result, parents tend to amplify it, putting themselves in a bind of either not following through or being unreasonably harsh. (In such a position, it is often better to rescind or revise a threat than feel obligated to act against better judgment). Similarly, when an initial bribe brings insufficient results, parents tend to enlarge the promise, in effect giving the child increased reward for greater or prolonged resistance. Preferable methods may include reminding children of underlying principles or family policies, helping them think through likely results of certain choices, and communicating confidence. For example, a parent may say, "Remember, those who finish their morning jobs keep their privileges," or "How will you feel this afternoon if you don't qualify to go?" or "I know you can make a wise choice." With consequences or rewards, much depends on presentation and "set up." Very distinct from bribes, known incentives can be useful—particularly if carefully communicated so not perceived as a way to purchase compliance or indirectly used as a threat (a privilege to be rescinded).

DURING

Instruct and reframe, even in the moment. Behavior gives outward clues to a child's inner workings. Observations inform our developing hypotheses about a child's maturity, understanding, and insight. (We may or may not be right, but it is a place to start). When misbehavior occurs, we can step back to consider what underlying problem or deficit may have contributed and focus our efforts at the heart of the matter. Rather than a personal affront, misbehavior is often a clue to a needed lesson; we can neutrally observe it, then calmly take the needed action. For example, if a child is disappointingly unappreciative or rude, rather than "flopping" in despair or "flaring" in anger, we can *teach* (give insight or perspective where we perceive it to be lacking).

I once heard a story about a hard working farm family in the early 1900's who decided devote some of their earnings to purchase electricity for their home. That year they had a very poor harvest and very little to live on. For Thanksgiving dinner they could only gather turnips and a jack rabbit. At first, the disappointed children refused to eat. Their father, instead of despairing or scolding, went to the attic to retrieve an old oil lamp. He turned off the lights and lit the lamp to remind the children how dark it had been before. The family's whole attitude shifted and suddenly their small meal seemed like a feast.[18] Giving insight is much more preferable to collapsing in injury and hurt; it builds bonds and wisdom both.

Teach (and learn) from sources beyond yourself. Most worthwhile rules or standards have roots in true principles—they are not just arbitrary or "made-up." Our teaching gains strength and credibility when we share primary sources (at least from time to time). We can prepare ourselves to be ready for teaching moments by identifying main trouble behaviors and then studying to find helpful references. Previously, I felt some reservations about pulling out the scriptures when the kids were "in trouble." I didn't want them to resent the scriptures or associate them with lecturing, but as I have chosen to utilize them more it has not turned out that way.

A few years ago, I made a list of about twenty items that were recurrent problems in our family. I then translated these to the corresponding *desired* behaviors and found scriptural passages related to each word pair. In addition to helping me feel fortified and validated, using the scriptures to teach has helped the kids see more connection between family rules and larger truths. It also models the use of scriptures to find answers. One scripture I have repeatedly directed our children to read is Ephesians 4:29-32: "Let no corrupt communication proceed out of your mouth, but that which is good to the use of edifying . . . and grieve not the Holy Spirit of God . . . let all bitterness, and wrath, and anger, and clamour, and evil speaking, be put away from you . . . and be ye kind one to another, tenderhearted, forgiving one another, even as God for Christ's sake hath forgiven you." Sometimes in place of another potential consequence, I have allowed the kids the option of memorizing an assigned scripture. Occasionally we have playfully applied a short phrase to suit specific family purposes, such as, "Arise and make thy bed" (Acts 9:34).

Daily personal and family scripture study allows guaranteed, built-in spiritual teaching. Through exposure to true principles and through the Holy Ghost, all family members will gain applicable insights to help with current challenges and individual consciences will be stirred. As in Shakespeare's play *Hamlet*, in which Hamlet scripts his own play to awaken the conscience of his uncle Claudius, having true scenarios depicted before us invites introspection. At times we do not know our children's private challenges, but exposing them to truths daily will give them wisdom, comfort and guidance to address many of them. [19] We can solidify scriptural teachings by sharing our personal experience of their truthfulness and by applying them to our own lives.

Even taking a step back from doctrines, we gain insight by studying teaching methods themselves utilized in the scriptures. In the New Testament, we observe Jesus' masterful teaching through the use of metaphor, stories, questions, and personal connection. [20] We see high accountability, yet mercy extended in such a way to inspire the best in others.

Recognize what is in your jurisdiction and what is not. As the saying goes, "You can lead a horse to water but you can't make him drink." Similarly, you can tuck a child in bed, but can't make him sleep; you can set before the child a healthy plate, but can't make him eat; you can lead a child to the potty but can't make him pee or poop in it. Notice, however, that though you can't make a child eat, sleep, or go to the bathroom, there are many things you *can* do: you can decide which foods to offer and when, you can establish a "lights out" time, you can help encourage and teach potty training skills. As parents, we will feel and be more effective when we stop trying to demand the unenforceable and enforce the unreasonable (or the reasonable in unreasonable ways).

This brings us to the question of reasonableness. Some parents try to increase their realm of control, but thereby shrink the arena in which the child can practice self-regulation. Over-controlling now may lead to poor regulation later. Yet conversely, children who have not been taught disciplined habits may struggle later while developing them (or may never

231

independently arrive at them). Some parents expect too little, some parents expect too much—either interferes with development.

It *is* reasonable that parents, actively involved in providing for children's needs, expect some things from them in return. We must rely on intuition and inspiration to know what is reasonable to expect of a given child. Though sometimes children demonstrate sudden leaps in maturity, usually their growth is more incremental. As in the biblical parable of the indentured servant, sometimes we suddenly ask for full "payment" or performance of our children just because we ourselves are fed up or desperate (Matt 18:28-30). Ideally, we would maintain evenness in our expectation, matching the slope of our children's natural growth rather than jarred by our sporadic stress levels. Children are keen to true injustice or hypocrisy. It is generally reasonable to expect behavior consistent with their current level of development and insight, but not behavior better than our own.

Respond early and appropriately. Proactive noticing—the assessing and attending to needs when issues are small—allows repair before the spiraling escalation. For example, prior to a full-blown tantrum, a frustrated or disappointed toddler first may exhibit a downcast expression, then some whining, then perhaps a displeased gesture (like a stomp)—all these are possible points of notice and rescue ("catching" points). Similarly, our children exhibit all sorts of indicators in all sorts of areas where they could benefit from further teaching and help. With increased maturity, they will learn how to catch and rescue themselves, but in the meantime, we too will be there to intervene as necessary.

Terrible behavior can be powerful—it usually continues only when it carries its intended weight, when it is inadvertently allowed by parents to be "effective." When we avoid letting poor behavior accomplish its desired effect,[*] it tends to stop. If a behavior is meant to shock, we can seem unaffected; if meant to perturb, we can ignore. Of course even in attention-getting contexts, we do need to intervene when behavior is dangerous or destructive, but with resolute calm—only to the point of stopping the danger or destructiveness. For example, a thrashing toddler who is hitting his head on the tile can be carefully lifted and moved to the carpet (without commands or attempts to prevent the thrashing).

---

[*] Sometimes the effect may not initially be intended/desired, but when children see the first power in it, they often repeat it.

Debriefing can occur later: "Remember when you were mad and you hit your head? I did not like that—it made me sad to see you hurt yourself because you are special to me. Next time you are mad, what could you do instead of that?" Acceptable ways to communicate or display negative emotions can be discussed.

The best responses are focused, wise, and fitting. Sometimes we must filter our observations to concentrate first on the most essential lesson, trusting that many problems take care of themselves with time, and many others resolve with persistent gentle correction. Our children may not apply all our lessons simultaneously. For example, if I have asked a child to take out the garbage and he grumbles while doing so, perhaps I should kindly thank him, rather than criticize his attitude. Sometimes we must ignore the "delivery," and focus instead on the task at hand.

Though attitude or manner may be left for subsequent lessons, ideally we will eventually get to them; our children too can be held accountable for appropriate responses. I was reminded of this once when my son opened our van door into a new Lexus in the adjacent parking spot. He was embarrassed and a bit scared, but I asked him to apologize to the owner who was also just getting out. He sheepishly did so and began going away while I stood with the driver looking for possible damages. She said she didn't care about a small scratch, but she called my son back and requested he look her in the eye, act serious, and express sincere regret. I had felt satisfied that he personally apologized at all, but this woman reminded me that more advanced lessons were still needed. Time and circumstance will allow multiple opportunities to get to these.

As mothers, we communicate value by what we choose to focus or insist upon and by what we ignore (whether from unawareness, resignation, true acceptance, or strategic de-emphasis). Still, lest we get overanxious about finding a single "right" response, there are usually multiple effective ways to teach the same lesson. For example, on the subject of cleaning bedrooms, I know one mother who lets her kids determine the state of their own rooms, one mother who requires her kids' rooms be clean before they can have any privileges, and another mother who tidies the whole house herself. Who is to say which children will grow up to keep their homes cleaner—the ones who learn more organically over time through experiencing both order and disorder, the ones who have practiced the skill of cleanliness, or the ones who have witnessed and gotten used to the high standard of order maintained by their mother?

233

Wise responses take into account intended outcomes. One man tells a story of his grandmother who, as a young mother, had sent her son into town to buy eggs. When he returned with mostly broken eggs, the mother's friend suggested he be severely reprimanded for his carelessness. "Instead, Grandmother calmly and wisely said, 'No, that will not make the eggs whole again. We will simply use what we can and make some pancakes that we can enjoy together.'" He goes on to say, "When we learn to handle the small and simple daily things in a wise and inspired way, the result is a positive influence that will solidify harmony in our souls and build up and strengthen those around us."[21] As we maintain perspective and communicate encouragement, comfort and truth, we will positively influence our families.

Truth can more readily be found when our minds are calm. Eastern meditation practices advocate having a "mind like water."[22] Peaceful, still water reflects the landscape without distortion. Water does ripple when disturbed, but only to the degree matching the perturbation. Similarly, the appropriate parental response in a given situation is neither too lenient nor too harsh. It involves discerning and matching the seriousness of our response with the gravity of the grievance—correcting to the degree that teaches, but no more.[23] Psychologist Haim Ginott states, "A child needs to learn from his parents to distinguish between events that are merely unpleasant and annoying and those that are tragic and catastrophic. Many parents react to a broken egg as to a broken leg, to a shattered window as to a shattered heart."[24] If we discipline our own reactions and avoid fueling reactionary responses by joining them, the stress of any incident will more quickly dissipate. In most conditions, fires that are not fed will soon die out; even the strongest emotions, if not fed by escalating thought or action, often pass or diminish even in the course of a few moments. When possible, we can debrief later, when children are more receptive.

Children often respond better to encouragement than streams of criticisms or warnings. Imagine yourself on a balance beam. Under which conditions would you perform best? With a running negative commentary, "You are tipping to the right . . . now you are tipping to the left—you are going to fall! I see you wobbling again," or positive encouragement: "Stay with it, you are almost there. You can do this! You are maintaining your center."?

Open **yourself** *to be taught in the moment.* Especially as kids mature, they will give important feedback about what works for them. For us parents, it is easy to push against this and proceed as we had planned, but we may do better to at least consider what is being suggested. A few times my oldest son has said things like, "That's not helping me," or "Mom, could you stop now? I don't need you to tell me that." Others have said, "Mom, you aren't listening to me," or "You are not being fair." Though I may feel like insisting that yes I *am* listening and that life may not be fair, sometimes I realize they are right. And they are always right that they *feel* these things when they say they do—to deny that is to reinforce the feeling further—to bind them to it in stubborn necessity. Ultimately in a family we teach each other how to best teach us, love us, and care for us. Taking cues (especially overtly stated ones) from others allows us to match our approach with their needs more rapidly and consistently. Of course, kids may want to turn off any correction or explanation immediately, thinking they "don't need to hear it" even when they do. In such a scenario a parent may reasonably say, "No, I feel this needs to be said" or, "Tell me what you think I want you to know from this experience, then if there is anything I feel like I need to add, I will do that when you are finished."

When we think ahead and pay attention in the moment for teaching opportunities, many problems can be averted or immediately addressed before they grow.

Reflect or discuss:

1) Recall a time when you have successfully utilized a teaching moment with each of your children. What made the interaction effective?

2) In a scenario where problem behaviors repeatedly occur, consider what lesson may still need to be taught. Notice the improvements that come with proactively addressing this issue.

3) In general, how could you make better use of teaching moments beforehand or in the moment?

37~ NOTICING & UTILIZING TEACHING MOMENTS: PART II

Sometimes behavioral issues arise unexpectedly or occur too fast to handle in the moment. That's okay—it's not too late! Processing an event after the fact gives everyone a chance to cool off and think. Also, some of our most important parental lessons occur naturally in an ongoing way as our children live and grow alongside us.

AFTER

Allow or create proper consequences. We typically call the natural results attached to specific choices "natural consequences." As long as these are not too distant, too abstract, too harsh or too dangerous, we can get out of the way and let these speak for themselves. Unless modification is necessary, interference is counterproductive, either erasing or overdoing the lesson. Rescuing too automatically or frequently negates the need for a child to improve or change. Conversely, once a child has experienced a consequence, though some discussion or processing may facilitate resolution, additional lectures or anger only detract from the lesson by fostering resistance. Sometimes it takes time to see evidence of a lesson learned; during this waiting period we must refrain from heaping on added punishments to rush the satisfaction of results. A child experiencing a reasonable consequence for misbehavior is paying his debt and does not need a fullness of parental wrath hanging over him.

Love withdrawal (shunning, prolonged exclusion, silence, refused attention) can be very damaging to relationships. However, respectful communication of disapproval or crossed boundaries has a definite place in teaching. Authentic responses may at times include the conveyance of negative emotions, such as an irritated look or a statement like, "That bothers me, please stop." While we do not reject our children, certain behaviors are worth rejecting, even to provide social cuing that will assist children to have future successful relationships.

When natural consequences are either insufficient or inappropriate, revised consequences become necessary. Here we find ourselves standing in the unenviable position between our children and full justice[25] (having created a buffer from or a channel to it), sometimes bearing the brunt of their displeasure and resistance. A child may not see relevance in cleaning up after himself—at present he may not care about the mess that surrounds him—so a consequence must be chosen he does care about. When a child loses winter gloves, particularly in a cold climate like Minnesota, the harshness of the natural consequence (having bare hands) warrants substitution—perhaps having the child work to pay for replacement gloves. Crafting proper consequences requires parental resourcefulness, creativity, and wisdom; enacting them requires fortitude and faith. This constitutes one of parenting's finest arts.

Effective leverage items to influence a child's behavior usually are things the child cares about but the parent sees as optional. Imposed consequences are usually a privilege removed (something dispensable to the parent but meaningful to the child) or a responsibility added (something productive but less pleasant). Consequences should be clearly and simply stated, such as, "No _(privilege to be removed)_ until _(desired behavior)_ " or "Because _(problem which occurred)_ you will need to _(additional responsibility)_." It should be something enforceable and may require extra supervision to ensure follow-through. Taking the time and energy required to enforce consequences is an investment for the future that pays high relative returns.

While idle threats weaken boundaries, actions confirm them. Sometimes the most effective consequences don't need to be verbalized but are just demonstrated: for example, without saying anything, a mother may pull over the car, stop speech mid-phrase, turn off a movie, or remove a toy. Usually kids will figure out what they need to do and straighten up fast.

When consequences aren't working, perhaps they are not the right consequences *or* haven't had enough time to "work their work." Or perhaps we have not yet set them in place. I remember one particular day feeling powerless as I watched my son persist in disregarding my direction: I had asked him to clean his room, but hours later he still had not. I mentioned my struggle to a wise friend and she asked, "What is he doing instead of listening?" He was playing amid mounds of toys. She said, "Then take the toys." Previously I hadn't taken the toys because that would necessitate me picking them up instead of him. But my action set him in motion. I selectively confiscated toys he cared more about first and then stepped away once he was actively working. Once his room was clean, I offered him the chance to earn back lost toys by doing work for me to

237

compensate for the time and effort I had invested (but at a high rate of exchange, lest he think it a worthwhile trade for the future).

Not every imperfect behavior warrants intervention or attention. An overcorrected child may feel paralyzed, discouraged, or resentful. We ultimately want to correct in love, in a way that will effectively bring needed change—not just offer a for-the-record expression of disapproval. The scriptures direct us to "reprove [correct with kindly intent] betimes [early, speedily, and occasionally] . . . *when moved upon by Holy Ghost* (D&C 121: 43 emph. added). Though we are told that the fruits of the spirit are "love, joy [and] peace" (Gal 5:22), sometimes we must begin with the vegetables of the spirit—saying and doing what needs to be said and done, even when less palatable.

Each situation is unique, but generally, correction may be *less needed* when:
- the child has made an honest mistake and is already suffering for it (the realization is there)
- the child is already working to fix it (i.e. in process of cleaning up a mess)
- the problem will naturally resolve itself with time or maturity
- it is of little or no consequence
- a behavior is merely bothersome but involves no moral error.

Correction may be *more needed* when:
- the child's action is hurtful to himself or others (or potentially so)
- the child clearly lacks insight into a significant problem
- the child has purposefully caused damage
- deception or disregard is involved
- the problem becomes a pattern.

In many cases, change requires repeated, consistent correction over time. Even if child ultimately disregards parental instruction in a given area, our role is to offer it.

The way we offer correction matters. The table on the following page characterizes more and less effective ways of offering feedback to our children.

Less effective ways to offer correction:	Explanation:	More effective ways to offer correction:
Focusing on undesired behaviors	Attention rewards and reinforces behavior; it becomes self-fulfilling, since we see what we look for.	Stating, focusing on, and looking for glimpses of the desired behavior.
Heaping on or blasting with correction.	Since the manner of correction is rejected, so is the message; we decrease our own credibility.	Addressing one thing at a time, using respectful language/delivery.
Routinely missing important opportunities for correction.	Regardless of cause (busyness, distraction, oversight or discouragement), this communicates that current behaviors are acceptable.	Being attentive to behavior, consistently holding to a clear standard.
Correcting verbally without action or follow through (i.e. asking, "Do you want me to take you home?" when you have no real intention of doing so.)	Without supporting action, verbal correction is meaningless and undermines parental authority. Constant criticism clouds interactions with unpleasantness.	Taking action that reinforces parental expectation.
Correcting with negative labels or characterizations. (i.e. statements like, "You should've said thank you. You are ungrateful and rude.")	Labels do not inspire improvement, but diminish hope and likelihood for change.	Avoiding negative labels or fixed thoughts; seeing children as you hope them to become.

When provided in the optimal way, correction is more likely to be received—either accepted as a useful idea, or even naturally incorporated without being perceived as correction at all.

One year, after growing tired of sloppily made and unmade beds, I held a "How to make a bed" instructional session for my boys. Between St. Patrick's Day and Easter, each child who made his bed according to specification received three jellybeans on his pillow from the "Easter Bunny." Sometimes instead of jellybeans, I left a little note from the bunny saying, "More neatly please." The kids all knew I was the bunny, but the ability to talk about the bunny's judgments in third person, even jokingly, diffused resistance and defensiveness. Even my teenaged boys played along. Even after Easter came and went, the boys did better at making their beds, I knew the skill had been taught, and no scolding had been required.

Natural rewards or added incentives can also "speak for themselves" if offered in neutrality and with consistent follow-through. For example, a child may come to notice and appreciate the extra free time naturally afforded by efficient completion of chores. We may also choose to offer additional benefits, either before or after the fact, such as allowing all who are finished with chores an extra privilege, such as participation in a fun outing. Though negative feelings may initially arise in those who have not earned a particular reward, if acknowledged with compassion, these often translate into motivation for the future. Rather than emphasizing losses to those who have missed out, we can express a hope in, and provide, future opportunities for success. While not all family fun should hinge upon compliance (or we may unintentionally reinforce emerging distance in relationships with struggling children), reinforcement of positive behavior is fitting.

Invite reentry and resolution. In parenting, a balance exists between justice and mercy: both can inspire change. In every given situation we may ask ourselves, "What response will inspire the desired change?" At times, well-placed absolution (even before a full debt be paid) can instill a deeper dedication or conviction to change than fully meted justice. However, if we are unconvinced a lesson has been fully learned, offenses have been recurrent, or children seek to escape consequences without an apparent change of heart (seemingly for their own ease and convenience), full follow through is often the wiser course. Though predetermined timelines for reentry (such as a two-minute "time-out") give a sense of order, they should not override our observations of readiness. For example, I have pronounced a "two minute time-out," only to observe in the next 10 seconds a child achieve a complete change of heart—apologizing, hugging

240

a brother, and happy. Do I forbid reentry until the remaining 110 seconds have passed? Similarly, I have seen a child fume for over an hour; do I invite this walking volcano back because he has paid his two minutes? I prefer to base reentry on true readiness—often determined by the child. I say, "*When* you are ready to [apologize and reform behavior in specifically stated ways], *then* you may rejoin us." If the child's return is obviously premature (i.e. they say they are ready but do not exhibit readiness), I send them back to do more internal work. To me, a solid apology involves specific acknowledgment of wrong (I'm sorry *for* . . .) and demonstrated change.

Forgiveness is essential to family happiness. If we say we believe in God's mercy, we should behave in our relationships as if we do. Mercy involves extending to others (especially our own family members) fresh chances to improve and change. Of course, wisdom is required: though forgiveness may be granted in an instant, trust must be rebuilt and trustworthiness proven *over time.*[*] Elder Nelson taught, "Rich meaning is found in study of the word *atonement* in the Semitic languages of Old Testament times. In Hebrew, the basic word for atonement is *kaphar,* a verb that means 'to cover' or 'to forgive.' Closely related is the Aramaic and Arabic word *kafat,* meaning 'a close embrace.'"[26] Chastisement properly given is a loving act—arriving full circle as an invitation to "come" not a rejection or casting away. As parents we would take care to not damage or destroy bridges of return. Rather, like the wise father of the prodigal son, who seeing his returning son "a great way off . . . had compassion, and ran, and fell on his neck, and kissed him" (Luke 15:20), may we maintain hope and readiness for reconciliation.

Reward appropriately. The greatest reward we could give our children— our full dedication—has already been given. As the father states to his faithful son in the above parable, "Thou art ever with me, and all that I have is thine" (Luke 15:31). Further outward rewards to instill loyalties or purchase compliance should not be necessary. Still, appropriate rewards can delight, encourage, communicate appreciation, and build bonds. Even God, who has already provided us with all we possess, rewards and blesses. Examining his perfect generosity (even in our limited way) gives insight into parenting. How does he give so abundantly—such that our "cup

---

[*] See scriptural examples: Matthew 24:45-46, 25:21 and Luke 16:10, 19:17.

runneth over" (Psalms 23:5)—without fostering entitlement or merely self-interested loyalty?

Looking to the scriptures (and likely our own personal experience) we observe that:

• God gives fitting, individualized blessings. He provides what is most needed, not necessarily granting our shortsighted wishes. His gifts are often not flashy or indulgent, but deeply meaningful, based on His intimate knowledge of us. (See Matt 6:25-33, Matt 7:7-11).

• God always rewards good, but in unpredictable ways and on an unpredictable timetable. Sometimes His reward is a sense of divine approval, other times a tangible, direct blessing; sometimes it comes now, sometimes later. Even though He has set up certain "if-then" clauses[*] that clearly communicate specific blessings for specific behaviors, the blessings come on His terms. This allows good to remain its own reward and fosters pure motives.

• God gives generously, sometimes granting more than is expected or imagined. (See I Kings 3:5-14, Helaman 10:4-10, Ether 3:4-13).

• God allows us to forfeit rewards. If rewards came regardless of merit, motivation to choose and behave well would diminish. (See 2 Ne 2:5-11, Genesis 25:29-34).

Unless my children are struggling in an area, I don't tend to reward them for meeting my underlying expectations. For example, I've never paid them for assigned household chores or good grades. I allow inherent rewards to be their motivation, hoping they will learn to see the deeper rewards and appropriately value them. When I do give rewards, they tend to be simple, celebratory, and sporadic. At times when the kids have set important goals, we have chosen some way to celebrate when they reach the goal. On weekends when the kids have bigger chores, sometimes I plan an outing or make a treat for which those who have done their work may qualify. If I did this every week, it would seem my obligation rather than a surprise bonus. I try to reward in ways that do not overshadow intrinsic benefits and do not teach bad habits or false concepts. For example, though many associate food with celebration, overindulgence or frequent unhealthy treats send the wrong message.

---

[*] For examples of if-then blessings see Exodus 20:12 (honoring parents), Isaiah 58 (fasting and observing the Sabbath), D&C 89, esp vs. 18-21 (healthy habits).

242

In his book *Punished by Rewards*, Alfie Kohn addresses how the wrong kind of rewards can paradoxically sabotage our best intents. Even certain types of praise can stifle, increase stress, or taint motives. The best praise is sincere, spontaneous, and specific (describing observations rather than evaluating or generalizing based on them). In another of his books, *Unconditional Parenting*, Kohn states, "Instead of [traditional praise]: try saying nothing (and just paying attention); describing, rather than evaluating what you see ["Look how he stopped crying right when you shared!"]; inviting reflection ["How did you do that?"]; asking, rather than judging."[27]

In our "age of entitlement," low accountability, and inflated rewards, teaching our children to value doing the right things for the right reasons becomes an increasing challenge. My kids have asked, "Why does my friend get to play video games for hours every day during the summer when I have to do all this and only get a little computer time?" and "Why does my friend get a $20 allowance every week without having any jobs to do and I do jobs every day without getting paid?" Unfortunately, even if we have chosen not to motivate by external rewards (like bribing with treats for good behavior, as if it is a commodity for us to "purchase"), it has become so prevalent that it likely will encroach upon our parenting practices, even if indirectly. If teachers at school or church offer treats for good behavior, we may seem stingy or withholding not to. If they offer large treats, our occasional modest incentives may pale in comparison. It is hard to prohibit others in using tools with such immediate, surface efficacy, particularly those who are likely well-meaning and kind enough to help instruct our children, but we can communicate concerns and avoid a token economy at home.

ONGOING

Live worthy of emulation; exemplify. When my children were all very young, unarguably innocent, cuddly, and redirectable, it was easier to know that I was being a good mother. I felt all I had to do was love them—this was enough! Yet later, I still loved them, but my effectiveness was less clear: though most of my time and effort was dedicated to them, sometimes they didn't listen or seem very receptive. This loving was more complicated.

Children will not be forced down a path, but they can be shown the way. I frequently examine my life even to the detail asking in what ways I could better exemplify the standards I want my children to embrace, for this is my work as a mother. I have found it less effective, for example, to chase my kids around in my pajamas telling them to get dressed, to angrily tell them to stop fighting, or to expect them to keep time commitments when I struggle to keep mine. Though parents have multiple responsibilities and perfect mastery should not be prerequisite to teaching children a true principle, our effectiveness as teachers increases as we seek that mastery. Not only do we gain credibility, but we also gain qualification—practical wisdom about best methods and potential pitfalls. With any behavioral learning, first comes theoretical knowledge, then choice and discipline. Though we can teach theory, we cannot effectively invite, persuade, or challenge our children to greater levels of disciplined choice than we ourselves are willing to reach. We don't exemplify perfection, but can demonstrate process (sincere effort and improvement).

Provide lessons that keep teaching. Current school curriculums place less value on memorization; perhaps acknowledging the relative flood of information and easy-access reference materials, society tends not to require it. Yet our minds seek to be filled and do become filled with something. What will be running through our children's minds in quiet moments—what phrases will they have to call upon? Hopefully, more than impoverished rhymes from commercial jingles, quotes from movies, or less-than-uplifting popular song lyrics.

As a family, committing uplifting songs, scriptures, quotes, and poems to memory not only creates bonds, but stores lasting lessons. Several meaningful lessons from my childhood have come from songs. Many nights our mom would sing to us after my sister and I crawled into our beds. There was a song about a kitten that taught about being kind and gentle, a song about a poor man who was honest, a song about sticking together as a family "through all kinds of weather." The words of another song said, "When you're all alone and blue, no one to tell your troubles to, remember me, I'm the one who loves you." Even now when my mom has difficulty remembering some things, she remembers the words to all these songs. My mother also instilled within me a love of hymns. At various times in my life, hymns have lifted and sustained me. It has been as if certain phrases were highlighted to my heart as personal promises or reminders or prayers:

> . . . *As thy days may demand, so thy succor shall be* ("How Firm A Foundation," #85) . . . *By a whisper sow we blessings; by a breath we*

244

scatter strife. In our words and thoughts and actions lie the seeds of death and life ("We are Sowing," #216) . . . *Oh, refresh us, oh, refresh us, traveling through this wilderness* ("Lord Dismiss Us with Thy Blessing," #167).[28]

When I was in labor with my sixth child, one help to me was replaying in my mind John Rutter's choral setting of Psalm 23: *The Lord is my shepherd, therefore can I lack nothing. He shall lead me in a green pasture and lead me forth beside the waters of comfort* . . .

Regarding the power of memorized scripture, Elder Scott of the LDS Church has said, "Scriptures are like packets of light that illuminate our minds and give place to guidance and inspiration from on high . . . they can be stalwart friends that are not limited by geography or calendar. They are always available when needed. . . Learning, pondering, searching and memorizing scriptures is like filling a filing cabinet with friends, values, and truths that can be called upon anytime, anywhere in the world. . . To memorize a scripture is to forge a new friendship. It is like discovering a new individual who can help in time of need, give inspiration and comfort, and be a source of motivation for needed change."[29] At our house we have a white board where we write a scripture or quote of the week related to our family night lesson. The kids are invited to memorize these for an M&M per word. Whether or not these scriptures land in long-term memory, the kids are gaining a deeper familiarity with the words and concepts.

My son's second grade class memorized and recited poetry on a monthly basis. The year culminated with a poetry celebration in which they recited a poem for parents entitled, "Keep a Poem in Your Pocket"[30] by Beatrice Schenk de Regniers. It talks of how lines of poetry provide words and pictures that serve as companions, lullabies, and dreams. What a gift this teacher had given her students through the year, with all those memorized lines!

Build uplifting connections. Along with connecting our children to ideas, we can connect them to people who will inspire and support them through their lives—especially family members, both past and present. My mother often told wonderful stories from her childhood that contained built-in lessons. One year for a gift I wrote three of the stories into a book for my children—one about my mom trying to give chickens a bath and the gentle way her mother corrected her, one about her sneaking after her older siblings to school because she wanted so much to go, one about an adventure at the zoo showing that situations tend to work out in the end. My children listen to these stories with rapt attention and ask to read them again and again. I say, "Do you know that the hero in these "Little Benita" stories is your grandma? These are things that happened to her. She used to be young like you!" When children know their extended families and their roots, they have context and connection. Author Alex Haley has said, "When [an elder] dies, it is as if a library has burned to the ground."[31] The people around us—family members, community members, figures from history—hold riches of knowledge and experience that can provide inspiring examples to our children.

The connection we can most directly influence is the one between our children and ourselves. Memories we build together provide lasting lessons that become foundational for all other learning.

Reflect or discuss:

1) Consider how you currently use consequences and rewards to teach your children. Do you have any new ideas to use them more effectively?

2) What meaningful lessons do you remember receiving during childhood that have stayed with you?

38~ PROVIDING UNDERSTANDING AND HONORING CHOICE

Teach toward understanding

The hoped for outcome in parental teaching is that our children will understand. Psalms 119:34 states, "Give me understanding and I will keep thy law."[32] When children are disobedient, it is often because they don't yet fully understand the principles behind the behaviors we are trying to teach. When they begin to show natural dependability, it evidences a growing understanding.[33]

How do we increase the likelihood that our children will understand important principles?

• *We can allow them to learn by experience.* Ideally, our children will most often learn by experiencing the benefits of choosing wisely rather than the pitfalls of choosing poorly, but both increase insight.[34] As they live according to truth, they will learn it (see John 7:17). When we allow our children in an age-appropriate way to "experiment upon the word" even while under our watch (see Alma 32:27), their initial hypothesis matters less than their ultimate conclusions.

• *We can offer consistent, repeated lessons.* Learning is often gradual and takes time (see D&C 98:12). The moment of true understanding is not often externally predictable. In our families, as we establish faithful habits, like family prayer, family scripture study, and regular church attendance, we will increase the odds of reaching our children when they are ready to learn.

• *We can keep developmental levels and maturity in mind as we teach.* One instance when I failed to do this, I said to my toddler son, "You need to make it to your potty—you don't want to be wearing diapers in college!" Later in the day he came to me and said, "Mommy, what's college?"

• *We can allow learning to come full circle, acknowledging real-life illustrations and examples when they occur.* When we see related applications of a principle we have taught, we can say, "*This* is just what we were talking about!" An example of this is a story told in chapter 29 (shortly after discussing the importance of quickly obeying, the boys saw the benefits of doing so as it prevented us from getting a parking ticket).

247

• *We can know our children well and be tuned into them.* When my first son began to speak, my husband and I delighted to note the subtle distinctions between his words. Though no casual observer would have noticed the difference (or deciphered any particular meaning), he consistently said "mah" for mom, "muh" for mountain, and "mahw" for mouse. The scriptures say that "the Lord God giveth light unto the understanding; for he speaketh unto men according to their language, unto their understanding" (2 Ne 31:3). In order to teach our children in their own language, first we need to know it.

Outward obedience does not always indicate understanding, but rather may be the result of coercion or intimidation. These strategies, however, do not last. Parenting author Alfie Kohn writes, "Some erroneously judge the success of a technique by how children *behave*, regardless of how they feel about complying with a given request, or, for that matter how they come to regard the person who succeeded in getting them to do so. . . . [E]ven disciplinary techniques that seem to 'work' often turn out to be much less successful when judged by more meaningful criteria. The child's commitment to a given behavior is often shallow and the behavior is therefore short-lived."[35]

A scripture applicable to effective parenting often quoted in the LDS Church states, "No power or influence can or ought to be maintained. . . only by persuasion, by long-suffering, by gentleness and meekness, and by love unfeigned; by kindness, and pure knowledge, which shall greatly enlarge thy soul without hypocrisy, and without guile" (D&C 121:41-42). Though parental duty originates from role, parental influence grows from relationship. This scripture also indicates that effective teaching will occur in a multiplicity of ways—sometimes by longsuffering (long endurance or perseverance), sometimes by gentleness and meekness (standing back, softening or withholding reproof), sometimes by sincere love (displaying enduring care and loyalty), sometimes by kindness (mercy extended or service rendered), sometimes by knowledge (wise, inspired action), or by a combination of these.

Kohn states, "The kids who do what they're told are likely to be those whose parents *don't* rely on power and instead have developed a warm and secure relationship with them. They have parents who treat them with respect, minimize the use of control, and make a point of offering reasons and explanations for what they ask."[36] Not surprisingly, research has borne out the effectiveness of parental use of persuasion and reasoning over more controlling styles[37]—it produces true understanding, fosters relationship, and minimizes resistance and resentment.

Use "gentle persuasion"

Gentle persuasion involves guided choice. Using creativity, reasoning, and personal knowledge of a child, parents present true options in a way that encourages a certain ideal course.

On a cold Minnesota morning I was walking with my six-year-old son to school and wanted him to wear his hat and mittens. He insisted he did not need them. I could have scolded him or ordered him to put them on, but instead employed gentle persuasion. I knew my son liked stories and that he liked science, so I utilized these. I said, "I have a question for you. I know you are good at science, so let's see how you do. If you saw a shallow puddle on the ground or a big body of water, like Lake Superior, which would more readily freeze to ice on a cold day?" Of course, he said the small puddle. I told him that ears and fingertips were kind of like that small puddle—that they could actually get frostbitten if uncovered in the cold. We walked in silence for a few moments and then he reached for his hat and mittens and put them on. There was no resistance to following the course of action I desired of him because he himself had chosen it. Also, because I employed truth and reason, he gained useful knowledge. In contrast, though some may consider deceit and manipulation to be useful in the moment, they do not build wisdom or trust and should be avoided.

Gentle persuasion can even be used with very young children. Recently, my one-year-old son was screaming and struggling as I tried to wash food off his face. Instead of pinning him down and forcing the issue, I took him in front of the mirror and showed him his messy face. After this, he held completely still and interestedly watched me wash his face.

Older toddlers and preschoolers are getting big enough and strong enough that physical redirection can be an unpleasant challenge. Engaging in play can be especially helpful at this stage. Two illustrative examples are playfully "chasing" a child to where you want them to go or challenging a child to a clean-up race. These are much more pleasant than the common alternatives of wrestling and carrying a crying child or demanding, threatening and scolding an unhelpful child.

Utilizing distraction, humor, or surprise can also interrupt protests. Once when my 18-month-old son was thrashing around resisting a diaper change, I put on a silly red and black checkered cap with ear flaps; my son immediately stopped crying and stared at me. Then, rather than the battle-of-wills that would have occurred, we both laughed while I changed his diaper.

Offering children appropriate choices also tends to significantly decrease resistance. One summer I arranged for my four older boys to participate in a week-long, two-hour-a-day Vocal Academy with a gifted teacher. Since the Mormon Tabernacle Choir happened to be touring our city that weekend and I had been able to get a few tickets, I decided we'd have a drawing at the end of the week to see which boys could attend. It all seemed perfect—that is, until I announced my plan and one son adamantly refused to participate. I wanted to insist, but knew it would likely ruin the experience for all of us. I also admitted to myself that, though I valued the opportunity, it was not vital enough to mandate. I told my son that the choice was his, but I asked him to make a decision-square to identify the positives and negatives related to each choice. It looked something like this (I include it with his permission):

	Positives	Negatives
Summer voice class	-in drawing for Tabernacle Choir concert tickets -might get a treat after the concert	-don't like to sing
No summer voice class	-stay home -wouldn't have to sing	-no chance for concert tickets -might feel left out

His motives to participate were mostly based on external rewards, but I could accept that. He vacillated for several minutes, but I challenged him to make a choice and stick to it without complaint. I was happy he ultimately chose to be in the voice class, but even happier that *he* had been the one to choose it. This eliminated most of the need to further coax, persuade, or struggle. He overall seemed to enjoy his experience and even happened to win the drawing for one of the concert tickets.

When our children become teenagers, guiding their choices using gentle persuasion becomes even more vital. Though we can still shape their environment when they are with us, more aspects of life are in their

250

control. We can no longer continually supervise, we can no longer set up a physical gate between them and potential dangers, we can no longer sling them over our shoulder and carry them to safety. Our influence on their behavior relies almost completely on previous instructions, ongoing dialogue, and an established relationship.

Foster teachability

When I was a little girl, my parents asked me if I wanted violin lessons. As far as I was concerned, I had seen my dad practice his viola and play in concerts, and this was enough. I told them, "I don't need lessons. All you do is go up and down [with the bow]."

The limited experience and beautiful, built-in confidence of children often leads them to resist lessons of multiple kinds. How can we get around it? As addressed above, offering appropriate choices tends to increase engagement, but other strategies also can help. We help increase our children's motivation to learn when we successfully:

- expand vision (help children see pertinence, application, and possibilities)
- provide clarity (break instructions into smaller, specified steps, while being careful not to rob them of the opportunity at times to figure things out themselves).
- evoke curiosity (cause them to wonder, ask questions, and discover)
- increase the quality of the lessons (ensure adequate teacher preparation)
- invite active, meaningful participation
- communicate confidence and hope in the learner (ego-strengthening)
- keep the context pleasant
- match lessons with learner readiness (in terms of level, timing, context)—children in an agreeable mood are less likely to reject ideas or requirements
- utilize both novelty and familiarity to seed interest

Novelty tends to attract attention; familiarity influences preferences—our children will naturally gravitate toward things they have experienced before in a positive context. Recently I took my younger boys to a children's concert offered by the Minnesota Orchestra. The night before,

251

I previewed the program and let them listen to excerpts of the songs they would be hearing the next day. At the concert, they were captivated by various novelties—the design of the hall, the energy of the crowd and live performers, certain striking melodies and rhythms—but their recognition of specific pieces deepened their experience by adding a layer of personal connection. They were not just observers of a great orchestra, but that orchestra was playing *their* songs—ones they had heard before in their own living room. Psychologist Robert Zajonc and others have studied how familiarity influences our preferences, often termed the "mere exposure effect."

As parents, we can also model receptivity. For example, rather than being universally rigid or abruptly dismissive, we can give fair hearing to dissenting opinions or alternative perspectives within the family and respectfully consider them.

Reflect or discuss:

1) The next time one of your children behaves differently than you'd like, ask yourself if there is an underlying principle they have not yet understood. Instead of focusing on the specific behavior, consider how you can teach the principle in a way that will reach that particular child.

2) How do you give your children the opportunity to practice making developmentally appropriate choices?

3) Do you recall times you have successfully guided your children to choose well (used "gentle persuasion")? In your experience, has this worked better than forced compliance?

39~ Holding on to struggling children

In the New Testament, a certain rich man approaches Jesus, saying, "What shall I do to inherit eternal life? All [the commandments] have I kept from my youth up." Jesus truthfully tells him the next needed step for growth, but—at least for that moment—he doesn't want to do it and goes away sorrowing (Luke 18:18-23). At times our children too will go away sorrowing when we have told them what they most needed to hear. How is it that mothers know these things? Through long observation of our children and through the inspiration that comes to us in the line of duty. President Packer has stated that even considering all the didactic hours of formal instruction that occur, "the greatest teaching in the church is done by the mothers."[38]

In Matthew 6, we learn how God so carefully provides for the lilies of the field and the fowls of the air (6:26, 28), yet even these have initiative to take. Fowls must gather food (often flying miles and miles to optimal locations to do so) and produce and care for their young. Lilies do the work of being a flower: pushing up through the soil, engaging in photosynthesis, and putting forth seeds (6:26, 28). Notwithstanding divine care and parental care, certain work exists for our children alone to do— it can be no other way. Learning will always be partly up to them.

Some children resist teaching, reject help, refuse responsibility, and travel down wayward paths. As parents, we'd choose a safer and more pleasant route for our children, edged by important boundaries. When children insist on testing rules personally, they do still learn—but often in a more painful way than we would have hoped. Our brave first mother Eve, in tasting of the fruit of knowledge, consented to this profound experiential learning. And it was fittingly she—no other could rightly permit it—because no one like a mother suffers along with a suffering child. Whether Eve fully realized it initially or not, only by opening this possibility to experiential learning could the *other* tree in the garden, "whose fruit was desirable to make one happy," ever be validly approached by any of her children. She later says, "Were it not for our transgression we never should have had seed, and never should have known good and evil, and the joy of our redemption, and the eternal life which God giveth unto all the obedient" (Moses 5:11).

What can effectively be done to reclaim children who wander? Though our children may turn from us, causing suffering, we must turn *toward* them— to observe and learn, to gain the information to guide change, and to extend love. However poorly a child has behaved, poor behavior of reactionary parents does little to win children back. As parents we can get into cycles of scolding: a child makes poor choices, we express strong disapproval (pushing the child further from our influence), then the child perceives himself to be untrusted and unsupported, feels resistance and resentment, and continues behaving poorly or even worsens his behavior. Chasing down or berating often sends children running further away, whereas noticing good is an invitation to come. An LDS hymn states,

> Know this, that every soul is free
> To choose his life and what he'll be;
> For this eternal truth is giv'n:
> That God will force no man to heav'n.
> He'll call, persuade, direct aright,
> And bless with wisdom, love, and light,
> In nameless ways be good and kind,
> But never force the human mind.[39]

All through the scriptures we see examples of God attempting to reclaim his children. In the commandments we find God's teachings, but in the stories we learn of God's teaching methods. For example, in the scriptural account of Jonah, we see how God actively guides Jonah's path, while preserving his agency. The Lord gives Jonah direction, observes his response, "hedge[s] up the way" (Hosea 2:6) when he is off track, rescues just the right amount, and provides insight. Though noting the preservation of Ninevah, the story is more about the tutoring of Jonah. The book begins with a directive: "Arise, go to Ninevah." But Jonah runs another way "from the presence of the Lord." God sends a "great wind" to toss the ship carrying Jonah. Recognizing Jonah as the source of the tempest, the other travelers reluctantly cast Jonah into the sea. The Lord prepares a great fish to swallow Jonah to contain and redirect him. While in the fish's belly, Jonah has a change of heart and recommits to follow God. Once again he is told, "Arise, go unto Ninevah." This time Jonah goes, but still without full vision or understanding. He preaches repentance, but when the people repent and God forgives them, Jonah

254

resents it. God then provides Jonah an illustrative experience with a withered shade plant, drawing parallel between the value of the plant to Jonah and the value of the people of Ninevah to God.

The story of Jonah shows how thoroughly God invests in teaching his children. Because of this, we are not alone in our attempts to teach and guide *our* children. God is also there, affecting outcomes, instructing, and extending rescue—for them and for us. Early church leaders taught,

> Though some of the sheep may wander, the eye of the Shepherd is upon them, and sooner or later they will feel the tentacles of Divine Providence reaching out after them and drawing them back to the fold. Either in this life or the life to come, they will return. They will have to pay their debt to justice; they will suffer for their sins; and may tread a thorny path; but if it leads them at last, like the penitent Prodigal, to a loving and forgiving father's heart and home, the painful experience will not have been in vain. Pray for your careless and disobedient children; hold on to them with your faith. Hope on, trust on, till you see the salvation of God.[40]

If this "debt to justice" provides schooling (though perhaps at a heavier price than we'd like), it may be a worthwhile tuition.

One way we demonstrate continued hope in our children is by loving them despite their weaknesses. As discussed earlier, often weaknesses are the flip-side of strengths—positive traits underdeveloped or misapplied—illustrated by the pairs below:

Negative characterization	Just as true (and better to focus on)
Devious	Curious, inventive
Overactive	Energetic
Emotional	Aware, sensitive
Inattentive	Imaginative, active inner world
Stubborn, difficult to transition	Dedicated to the task at hand, persistent
Bossy	Confident to lead
Nonsocial, oblivious	Independent
Obnoxious, inappropriate	Able to see humor, lightness, ironies
Over-serious	Respectful
Passive	Flexible
Perfectionistic, demanding	Conscientious, committed

At times we fixate on negative interpretations and become blinded to positive acts, thereby, ironically, impeding growth.

Once my son said of a kindergarten classmate, "He is a bad boy." (I had also heard other students in the class refer to him this way—all likely echoing sentiments expressed by school staff.) At the time I corrected my son saying, "Who says he is bad? Maybe he has done things he is not supposed to do, but that doesn't mean he himself is bad. Maybe no one has taught him how to act." A few weeks later, when I visited my son's class to help with a party, I got a chance to meet the boy. My toddler, who had tagged along, dumped out a box of toys in the classroom play area and this boy stepped out of his chair to help pick up the items. I thanked him for being attentive and thoughtful and he seemed happy and glowing. Then his teacher noticed he was out of his seat and sternly corrected him. He appeared deflated and didn't react well to her further directions to get on his boots and snow pants. By the end of the interaction, he was lying in a heap crying with the principal standing over him. I kept thinking of this boy and felt the events that transpired could have been much different. I spoke to the teacher expressing my concern. How was this five-year-old to improve if everyone had already decided he was "bad"? She dismissed my comment, saying, "You do not know him like I do." She was right— but I didn't want to know the boy like she did.

What a gift it would be to view each event and interaction freshly, without baggage of the past? As parents we must be wise, extending trust to the degree our children prove themselves trust*worthy*, but always leaving the door to improvement open and inviting. When our children peer into this door toward possible change and reconciliation, what will they see in us? An angry, exasperated, or resentful parent? An overanxious parent, fretfully waiting? A resigned parent, withering from defeat? If rather we stood in loving assurance, still actively pursuing personal growth, this would be a more welcoming sight.

When I have allowed myself to feel paralyzed by non-compliance in my children, we all seem to come to a standstill. In contrast, when I begin to take action, modeling the behaviors, attitudes, and progress I wish to see in them, we begin to move forward. Regardless of current or eventual outcomes, good parents "are those who have lovingly, prayerfully, and earnestly tried to teach their children by example and precept 'to pray, and to walk uprightly before the Lord.'"[41]

How do we rebuild trust in damaged relationships or make important changes, even if it means raising expectations or removing previous freedoms? We can start by just starting—by applying positive changes and beginning to carry things out differently. Though we may have to endure initial resistance and backsliding, if we persist, the new ways will likely take hold.

The greatest hope for continued influence rests in fostering relationship. With children, one natural relationship builder is play. This applies to children of all ages, though it looks differently at each stage. Running, laughing, pretending, or just sharing an activity the child chooses can magically reduce tension. Psychologist Lawrence Cohen addresses this topic beautifully in his book, *Playful Parenting*.[42]

If we recognize the need to repair or fortify our relationship with a given child, positive mental, physical, and spiritual work may also be required. We may ask ourselves: Are my thoughts of this child fair, loving, and hopeful? Do any important commitments remain unmet or could any new actions be taken to communicate love to this child? Do I need a change of heart? Have I prayed for guidance? We may consider arranging shared time—ideally, a simple activity with low conflict potential, on their turf. We may ask to sit down beside them and join them in an activity already underway, or extend an invitation based on our knowledge of their interests or current situation. Ultimately, when children are already struggling, they need *connection* more than *correction*. Sometimes reconnection itself solves the problem; if not, it still needs to come first.

Once my young son was very angry about perceived injustices and threatened to run away. I couldn't seem to comfort him or reason with him and I worried he might endanger himself by actually following through. I pulled him aside and asked him, "Can I run away with you? How about tomorrow morning? I'll talk to Dad so he won't worry." The next morning we woke up early, walked to the store and bought a donut, and then went to the park and sat and talked. We talked about why he had felt like running away, and I expressed why I wouldn't want him to (I'd worry, I'd miss him, it may not be safe). We returned quietly as the other kids were waking up and my son's divided feelings had melted away. As children get older, problems and conflict may have higher stakes, but the concept of maintaining influence through relationship still applies.

As we teach our children with inspiration in the context of a loving relationship, we set our children in motion along a path to "walk in the light" (Isaiah 2:5). The proverb states, "Train up a child in the way he should go: and when he is old, he will not depart from it" (22:6). Though this scripture says nothing of the time *between* old age and youth, it is only "through faith and patience [we] inherit the promises"—those results and blessings "afar off," but real (see Hebrews 6:12, 11:13).

As a wise teacher once remarked, "When we follow the Savior out of love, others will follow us out of love."[43] By great love we will draw our children to us. With time their understanding will come, as in the bright morning and without a storm of any kind the dews naturally appear.

> *For as the rain cometh down, and the snow from heaven, and returneth not thither, but watereth the earth, and make it bring forth and bud . . . so shall my word be that goeth forth out of my mouth: it shall not return unto me void, but it shall accomplish that which I please, and it shall prosper in the thing whereto I sent it.* (Isaiah 55:10-11)

Reflect or discuss:

1) Consider simplifying and clearly communicating your "family rules." Brainstorm all rules you want kids to live by, large and small, and then boil them down to four or five representative ones (discard, broaden or combine as necessary).

2) To prepare for situations where natural consequences are less obvious, less immediate, or too severe, brainstorm potential imposed consequences with which you feel comfortable. (Review section above on consequences prior to beginning).

3) When a teaching interaction hasn't gone well, write to debrief: What happened? What factors contributed? How do you wish you would have responded differently?

X. A JOYFUL MOTHER OF CHILDREN
On finding abundance

40~ PROCESS AND PARADOX

My three year old has spent the last month-and-a-half chasing butterflies. Last year he had little awareness of them; this year they are the fleeting brightness of color and his deepest wish. Though having caught only one (that an older brother first cornered for him), his hope is fresh at every new chance. I thought I'd wait and buy him a butterfly net for his birthday, but then I changed my mind: *now* is the season for butterflies.

With one swoop of his new net my son caught a Painted Lady or, as the field guide said, "*Vanessa cardui.*" The moment held preeminent delight: he laughed and shrieked in pure, disbelieving joy and called his brothers over to see. But there will be more butterflies this season and others.

Joy is not an emotion for the end only; it is to be found in processes, not just in culminating moments. Unfortunately, as adults, some of us have forgotten how to be happy. A few years ago I rediscovered an old book from the mid-80's called *Teaching Children Joy* by Richard and Linda Eyre. The book's basic premise, that sharing joys with preschoolers—spiritual, physical, mental, emotional and social joys—was more important than early academic drilling, caused me to realize that *I* (more than any of my children) needed to relearn how to more fully experience joy. Because of distraction and stress, I had become less able to enjoy the day-to-day experience of being a mother.

For all of us, times of dulled attention not only diminish our capacity and influence for good, but also constitute a sad wastefulness—an imposed blindness, deafness, and numbness though no true impairment exists. I wash plastic bread bags to get a second use out of them and insist my kids eat their crusts; how could I so easily waste the delights that are before me?

After finding the Eyre's book, I invited a friend to have a "joy school" experience, utilizing the suggested outline. Each week for about three months we focused on a new joy: "the joy of the body," "the joy of the earth," "the joy of spontaneous delight."[1] We wrote back and forth about our discoveries. This exercise heightened my attention to joy for a season, but as before, there came cycles of forgetting and remembering.

The first week I wrote: "This week I focused on joys from my five senses—taste, smell, touch, hearing, and sight. I tried to really taste my food, to smell it cooking, to feel the warmth and softness of Gabriel [my newborn] as I held him, to listen to beautiful music, to really look at my children and how beautiful they are. I lay on the grass holding Gabriel in the warmth of the sunshine and the coolness of the wind and looked at the blue sky. I love to see the gentle power of the wind as it blows the clouds so smoothly and steadily across the sky." I realized it had been a long time since I had allowed myself to deeply experience such things. My friend wrote of a walk in the leaves, being caught off-guard by a beautiful sunset, of listening to her grandson's voice as he practiced new words. She wrote, "Enjoyed being outside on Saturday at the barn. . . . Inhaled the aromas of the barn, the sound of the horses whinnying a hello. Took time to rub their velvet noses and scratch their ears. Noticed that their coats were getting thick and shaggy for the winter. . . . Bought new seed for the bird feeders and sat in the sun and watched the numerous birds come to feed. The chickadees are my favorite with their dive-bombing antics and song."[2]

We can notice and invite joy, but cannot force it. As is often quoted, "Happiness is like a butterfly: the more you chase it, the more it will elude you, but if you turn your attention to other things, it will come and sit softly on your shoulder."[3] Joy comes in many ways: in meaningful participation; in relationships; in gaining insight; in valuing true things; in observing, sharing in, and contributing to the joy of others; in momentary delights. Not an elusive, fleeting thing to chase after, joy is right here, made from the raw materials discussed in this book: vision, loving service, truth, committed relationships, growth, developing gifts, sacredness, effectiveness, and teaching (sections 1-9).

If joy is deep satisfaction and peace, perhaps its value comes less in the experience of it than the path that naturally brings it. Joy eludes us only when we want the sensation without the expense, losing sight of how path and product are connected, or when we want it exclusively, as an isolated emotion.

We rarely catch solitary joys, independent of other emotions. Poet and philosopher Kahlil Gibran writes, "Your joy is your sorrow unmasked. . . . Some of you say, 'Joy is greater than sorrow,' and others say, 'Nay, sorrow is the greater.' But I say unto you, they are inseparable."[4]

One scriptural discourse states, "Men are, that they might have joy," or in other words, joy is God's ultimate wish for us. The same chapter also reads, "It must needs be, that there is an opposition in all things. If not so. . . . all things must have vanished away."[5] Therefore, it may be as true to

261

say that a full life experience by necessity gives us disappointments and sorrow wrapped in with the joys, and only by such contrast does joy gain definition.

An experience wrapped in both joy and sorrow for me has been caring for my aging mother. Recently I attended a luncheon for those serving as family caregivers, at which we discussed our joys and difficulties. Each attendee was given a single rose and one elderly gentleman fittingly observed, "You can tell it's real because it has thorns." This man had kind, wrinkled eyes and rough hands—a former railroad worker who now cared for his wife with Parkinson's disease. One author has wisely stated, "I will love the sun for it warms my bones; yet I will love the rain for it cleanses my spirit. I will love the light for it shows me the way, yet I will love the dark for it shows me the stars. I will welcome happiness for it enlarges my heart; yet I will endure sadness for it opens my soul."[6]

Reflect or Discuss:

1) Which life experiences have shaped you the most? Were they difficult experiences, joyful experiences, or both?

2) When was the last time you felt a sense of joy? What were you doing at the time?

3) Have any thoughts come to mind about how you could more fully or more often experience joy?

41~ Choosing to invite, notice, and gather joy

Though some aspects of life may be outside our control, certain choices and actions facilitate greater enjoyment and satisfaction. We cannot effectively chase or force joy, but we can invite, notice, and gather it in our daily lives.

Invite

We invite joy into our lives as we accept another invitation already extended to us by God: "Draw near unto me and I will draw near unto you" (D&C 88:63). We draw near to God by knowing Him, following Him, and praying to Him. As God's Spirit increases in our lives, increased joy comes as a spontaneous "fruit" (Galatians 5:22). Tasting of God's love, "fill[s] [our] soul[s] with exceeding great joy."[7]

An elderly friend named Queta once told me of her experience walking down a dusty road in Mexico on a hot day. The sun was beating down and shining in her eyes, so she prayed for a cloud to come shade her. The sky remained clear, but as she turned the corner, there in the road was an old straw hat. She picked it up and put it on, offering a prayer of thanks as she continued walking. Her story reminded me of a morning I walked to work and was caught in a sudden downpour. I prayed that the rain would stop, but instead, a city bus pulled over and the driver offered me a free ride. In such experiences we find joy not only in the blessings themselves—the shade, the dryness or warmth, the need met—but in the central reminder they give: that God is there. Though tangible or immediate rescue does not always come, remembering past glimpses of God's awareness and love will carry us.

Our joy cannot be contingent upon fleeting things outside our control, such as the smoothness of events, the cooperation of others, perfect outcomes, or accomplished tasks. Our joy must be rooted in deeper things. Lasting joy connects more to process than outcome, more to people than things, more to giving than getting; it is an underlying mode of peaceful cherishing enriched by spontaneous delights. In motherhood, our joy can be inherent, not a separate miracle. Writer and anthropologist from the mid 1900's, Dorothy Lee describes,

As I sewed this Christmas Eve, I was suddenly astonished to discover that I had started to add an entirely unpremeditated and unnecessary edging of embroidery; and, simultaneously, I was aware of a deep enjoyment in what I was doing. . . . There was no justification for my work; yet it was the source of such a deep satisfaction, that the late hour and my fatigue had ceased to exist for me. . . . What gave meaning to my work was the medium in which I was working—the medium of love, in a broad sense. So far, my rationalization and justification of my work had obscured this meaning, had cut me off from my own social context. It suddenly became clear to me that it did not matter whether I was scrubbing the kitchen floor or darning stockings or zipping up snowsuits; these all had meaning, not in themselves, but in terms of the situation of which they were a part.[8]

The medium of love is a wellspring of joy and satisfaction in motherhood. Mothers have countless opportunities to access this source: every small kindness, every met need can serve as a running rivulet.

Notice

We will have a greater capacity for joy as we are more childlike—more curious and present, and less focused on past or future. Ralph Waldo Emerson states,

These roses under my window make no reference to former roses or to better ones; they are for what they are; they exist with God to-day. There is no time to them. There is simply the rose; it is perfect in every moment of its existence. Before a leaf-bud has burst, its whole life acts; in the full-blown flower, there is no more; in the leafless root, there is no less. Its nature is satisfied, and it satisfies nature in all moments alike. But man postpones or remembers; he does not live in the present, but with reverted eye laments the past, or, heedless of the riches that surround him, stands on tiptoe to foresee the future. He cannot be happy and strong until he too lives with nature in the present, above time.[9]

I remember watching my son at ice-skating lessons. Another parent on the stands referred to him, saying, "Look at that little boy. He keeps falling down, but he keeps getting up and still has a smile on his face!" To my young son, the ups and downs were nothing of themselves, only parts of the full adventure and experience. Psychologist Virginia Satir profoundly wrote, "Life is not the way it's supposed to be. It's the way it is. The way you cope with it is what makes the difference . . . the event does not determine how to respond to the event. That is a purely personal matter. The way in which we respond will direct and influence the event more than the event itself."[10]

Coming to terms with "what is," we can observe it peacefully rather than turning away. Simple inward statements of fact can neutralize situations. For example, when a laundry pile has been spilled over by a child too young to help clean it up, I can let go of the context as I refold it and simply say in my mind, "I am folding laundry." While wiping up an inconvenient spill that is holding me back, I can say, "I am wiping the floor." Psychologist Jon Kabat-Zinn would call this "non-judgmental moment-to-moment awareness." He asks the profound questions, *Is your awareness of anger angry? Is your awareness of sadness sad?*[11] Many find that being "in awareness" (the place of noticing and observing) is a safe-harbor from tension and emotional reactions. It a potential space for learning and for happiness.

We notice the details of life through our five senses—rich colors, melodies, textures, aromas and flavors. My three-year-old son sits in his pajamas and a pair of winter gloves, holding a broken rubber band, strumming it over the bucket. I would have considered the bucket out of place and the rubber band as garbage, but to him they are music. The sound intrigues him and he creates it again and again. He looks up and smiles. His face shines—his skin is perfect and smooth, his eyes blue like slate, his lashes dark and long. How often have I looked at him without really seeing? He climbs on my lap and leans against me. How often has he perched here without it inwardly registering? So many small moments of sensation are there, yet unclaimed.

As we do notice and claim these moments, we gain comfort and joy. Only within awareness can gratitude arise. Gratitude nurtures joy and enables it to grow to a fullness. It has been said that, "Gratitude is the mother of both goodness and happiness."[12] In her book *Simple Abundance*, Sarah Ban Breathnach notes, "Both abundance and lack exist simultaneously in our lives, as parallel realities. It is always our conscious choice which secret garden we will tend. . . . When we choose not to focus on what's missing in our lives but are grateful for the abundance that's present—love, health, family, friends, work, the joys of nature and personal pursuits that bring us pleasure—the wasteland of illusion falls away and we experience Heaven on earth."[13] Similarly connecting gratitude with abundance, D&C 78:19 states, "The kingdom is yours and the blessings thereof are yours, and the riches of eternity are yours. And he who receiveth all things with thanksgiving shall be made glorious; and the things of this earth shall be added unto him, even an hundred fold, yea, more."

Gather

Though not all of life is pleasant or positive, we gather what is most sweet and significant to create our pervading experience. Mormon pioneer Jane Johnston recorded in her journal, "We had nothing to sweeten anything until the Lord sent honey dew, which we gathered from the bushes until we got all the sweets we wanted." In our lives, we discriminately select memories, experiences, and insights to focus upon as a prized, defining distillate. In parenting, our selective focus or attention determines where we channel our energy. As we look for the strengths in our children and emphasize the positive in the experiences we share, this becomes self-fulfilling.

As we select, we also deselect, de-emphasize, and let go. We claim what is central and meaningful and let go of unnecessary elaborations and distractions. For meals, celebrations, and family outings, I am learning to choose realistic simplicity over extensive productions. For example, on the boys' last day of school, though I initially imagined welcoming them to a clean house and homemade rhubarb pie, as the day wore on I revised the plan to a mostly clean house and chocolate chip cookies. Then, since the baby needed to nurse when I would have had to bake the cookies, I simplified further to a half of a grapefruit and a warm welcome. Prov 17:1 reads, "Better is a dry morsel, and quietness therewith, than a house full of sacrifices with strife."

Dr. Kabat-Zinn, a pioneer in mindfulness, describes parenthood as an opportunity gain insight and let go of unnecessary attachments. He compares children to master teachers "whose presence and actions were guaranteed to push every button and challenge every belief and limit." He goes on to say of parenting,

Like any long retreat, there [are] easy periods and harder periods, wonderful moments and deeply painful ones. . . . The list of situations in which your equanimity and clarity will be sorely challenged and you will find yourself 'losing it' is endless. There is simply no escape, no hiding, no dissimilation that will serve either them or you. Your children will see it all from the inside and up close: your foibles, idiosyncrasies, warts and pimples, your shortcomings, your inconsistencies, and your failures. These trials are not impediments to either parenting or mindfulness practice. They *are* the practice, if you can remember to see it this way. Otherwise, your life as a parent can become one very long and unsatisfying burden, in which your lack of strength and clarity of purpose may lead to forgetting to honor or even see the inner goodness of your children and yourself.[14]

Rather than fixate on imperfections or regrets, we can celebrate our growing insights and move forward. God mercifully has set up families where both parents and children can mutually progress. And we *do* progress.

Just as we invite, notice, and gather joy in the context of our parental role, God also delights to invite, notice and gather *us*. Despite our imperfections, He extends toward us an "arm of mercy" (Jacob 6:5); He attends to details—the lilies, the birds, the hairs of the head (Matt 6:28, 31-32; Alma 40:23); He says, "As a shepherd, so will I seek out my sheep" (Ezekiel 34:12). *We* are His joy. As we help in His work, reaching out to others—particularly our own children, our joy increases further. Jacob 5:71 states, "If ye labor with your might *with me* ye shall have joy in the fruit which I shall lay up unto myself." (ital. added).

Reflect or discuss:

1) How can giving attention to your five senses help you experience joy?

2) Is the path to happiness more one of seeking or accepting?

3) In what ways have you come to know God is aware of you? How have you felt His influence in your life?

42~ ABUNDANCE

Abundance can be found in the smallest of things. In the bright blueness of a patch of sky, in the warmth of the sun, in a bird singing two clear notes. Any physical or spiritual joy experienced with reverence contains a fullness: comforts or pleasures of the five senses, moments of arrival, fulfillment in creative or productive work, and the reverent connectedness of relationship. Of all of these joys, our closeness to God and family are the most enduring. Unlike fleeting comforts or culminating moments, love exists independent of condition or circumstance.

Though love lasts, it changes. All trivial things that call to us, that would distract and pull us away from these central relationships, we must willfully ignore. As one woman wrote of nagging housework, "Quiet down cobwebs, dust go to sleep, I'm rocking my baby, and babies don't keep."[15] Marie Bellet, singer, songwriter, and mother of nine, has a song entitled, "Mother You are Worried About Many, Many Things." The lyrics acknowledge that what our children are asking for or needing from us is often different and much simpler than what we are trying to provide: our relaxed presence rather than packed schedules, playfulness instead of continual fretting, simple preparations instead of costly elaborations.[16] We will capture a greater abundance of joy as we accept invitations to play with, hold, and listen to our children.

The folksong *Turn Around* notes how we just "turn around" and are suddenly struck that our children are older and then "going out of the door."[17] The double meaning in this is a mother's pleading for her growing child to "turn around" and come back. The triple meaning is that we as mothers also must "turn around"—to look at, notice, and fully experience our children *now*. This turning can and does go both ways.

The summer that my mom, my sister, and I all agreed it was time to clear out her house and move my family in just preceded my mom's first massive stroke. For six or seven years up until then, my mom had been dividing her time between my sister's house and my house because she could no longer live on her own. With her declining health, we acknowledged that this may be her last opportunity to move back "home." One early morning after I had stayed overnight frantically cleaning in efforts to prepare her house for our return, I received a phone call from my sister that my mom was in the ICU. More than ever before, I felt

268

worried, panicked, and lost at the thought of losing my mother; I felt like my very roots to this earth would be severed and I would just float away.

I drove home to nurse the baby and arrange travel details to visit my mother. As I rushed around, my six-year-old son Malachi said, "Mom, did you eat? I will make you some food." He toasted me four slices of bread to make me two grape jelly sandwiches—"one for now, one for later"—and gave me a radish from our garden. As I gathered my things and headed out the door, he asked, "Mom, am I old enough to run down the road to wave while you drive away?" I said he could run along on the grass to the end of the block and he ran, waving earnestly and smiling. He saved me. I knew I wouldn't float away. I was caught like a runaway kite in my own safe branches—in this new family tree I am growing. My own sweet son caught me.

The Book of Malachi in the Old Testament says, "Behold, I will send you Elijah the prophet . . . And he shall turn the heart of the fathers [and mothers] to the children, and the heart of the children to their fathers [and mothers]" (4:5-6). To those who have nurtured us and to those we nurture, our hearts are turning.

Though some joys are bittersweet, others are pure sweetness. Finding homemade cards on my pillow, noticing treasures on long neighborhood walks, reading stories on the couch, laughing at inside jokes, watching ideas, abilities and dreams emerge. I used to color the pictures, now I receive them; I once dawdled along, now I patiently wait at the corner; I was once lifted, held, and carried, now I am the carrier—the "joyful mother of children" (Psalm 113:9).

"Faithful nurturing" is devoted, dedicated motherhood, but it is not only this. Faithful nurturing acknowledges God and trusts his perfect ability to make all things right—even our own imperfect ability. In this place of trust and reverence, here again is abundance.

In a recent year, the spring thaw came to Minnesota later than usual so the growing season was more limited. My neighbor and I would ask each other over the fence, "Have you planted yet?" We both were waiting for more favorable weather reports. When I did plant, I was distracted and hurried and didn't prepare the soil as I should have. Some seeds never came up, likely because they were buried too deeply or too shallowly in the clumpy soil. Beans came up, but rabbits ate them despite the fence. The winter squash was hearty, as usual, but overtook space for certain other plants. An early frost limited our tomato crop. Despite these non-ideal conditions and the imperfect investment we ourselves had made, I was struck by the abundant harvest we received. Certain neighbors were leaving town for several weeks and offered us picking rights in their large garden if we'd water while they were gone. Other neighbors, having grown tired of their fruit trees, generously shared cherries and apples. Ultimately, though our personal harvest had been less than I hoped, we ended up with produce to spare. Similarly, in parenting, God blesses us for our efforts and helps supply what we lack. His goodness and mercy follow us all the days of our lives, He prepares a table before us, and our cups fill to the brim and run over (Psalms 23:5-6). Again and again in motherhood this scripture comes to pass.

During the Passover feast, a Jewish holiday commemorating God's deliverance of the children of Israel from Egyptian bondage, one of my favorite traditions is singing *Dayenu*, a song which celebrates God's wonderful generosity. It names blessing after blessing, one by one, and then there is the chorus of clapping and singing over and over, "Day-dayenu, Day-dayenu . . . ." Dayenu literally means, "It would have been enough." If God had just given us one of these things, it would have been enough, but He has given us so much more.

This is the generosity of God; there is no end to it. With God, we are not just conquerors, but *"more* than conquers" (Romans 8:37); He doesn't just fill our cup, but it "runneth over" (Ps 23:5); He opens the windows of heaven and pours out blessings such that "there shall not be room to receive it" (Mal 3:10); His peace "passeth understanding" (Phil 4:7); though we may pass through "light affliction," we gain an "eternal weight of glory" (2 Corinthians 4:17); He offers "joy unspeakable" (I Peter 1:6-8). Particularly as we too are generous, generosity will be extended to us, "good measure, pressed down, and shaken together, and running over" (Luke 6:38). The scriptures invite us: "Feast upon that which perish not" (2 Nephi 9:51), "Feast upon the words of Christ" (2 Nephi 32:3), "Feast upon [God's] love" (Jacob 3:2). "Verily I say unto you, ye are little children, and ye have not as yet understood how great blessings the Father hath in his own hands prepared for you" (D&C 78:17).

Certain personal and supernal joys, such as the pieces of this world we uniquely love, enrich our existence with a resonating, enlivening connection. They are gifts straight from God. My mother's love of music has propelled her even through below-zero weather, ice, and snowstorms to get to a good concert—particularly one put on by the Minnesota

Orchestra. I recall her pushing her walker through several inches of sparkling, newly fallen snow (insisting it was "*not* beautiful"), cursing good-naturedly all the way, and then climbing (with great effort and help) into our 15-passenger van to attend a concert celebrating the Minnesota Orchestra's Grammy nomination for their recording of Sibelius Symphonies 2 & 5. I went to the concert full of worries—wondering about the roads, finding parking, being late; worrying about the future, my husband's employment, a possible move, etc. etc. Because of the weather, they delayed the concert and we walked in just as they closed the doors. The head usher had refused entry until late seating, but the ticket taker waved us in anyway.

At intermission, my mom said she wished we could see a certain orchestra member—an old friend—and he walked out just at that moment to cross our path in the crowd. Our silent prayers and wishes were granted at every turn; we experienced a parting of the Red Sea and a calming of the waters. For their encore piece the orchestra played Sibelius' *Finlandia*, which tune has been made into the hymn, *Be Still My Soul*. The reminder of the hymn prompted me to look up the words when I got home—to read them right then despite knowing I had to wake up very early the next morning. These are the words of the second verse:

> Be still, my soul:
> Thy God doth undertake
> To guide the future as he has the past.
> Thy hope, thy confidence let nothing shake;
> All now mysterious shall be bright at last.
> Be still, my soul:
> The waves and winds still know
> His voice who ruled them while he dwelt below.[18]

The third verse talks of life after death, with "sorrow forgot[ten], love's purest joys restored." Though we may not have a "fullness" of joy yet, trusting God clears out the worry, the fear, the unresolved regret, the despair—those things antithetical to joy.

Trusting in God's timing and care brings true joy. God does not open the way for us only once; nor are we presented with a singular opportunity to trust Him. For the children of Israel, God parted not only the Red Sea (Exodus 14: 13-16, 21-22), but also the river Jordan (Joshua 3:13, 17). In the latter case, the Lord promised that the river would be halted "*as soon as the soles of the feet . . . rest[ed] in the waters*" (3:13, ital. added); trust had to precede the miracle. We arrive at the water's edge multiple times, but through this come to know God's love and deliverance. As we note and commemorate such miracles, generations can be blessed. Joshua directed his people, "Take ye up every man of you a stone upon his shoulder, according unto the number of the tribes of the children of Israel: That this may be a sign unto you, that when your children ask their fathers in time to come, saying, What mean ye by these stones? Then shall ye answer them, That the waters of Jordan were cut off before the ark of the covenant of the Lord; when it passed over Jordan . . . and these stones shall be for a memorial unto the children of Israel forever" (4:5-7).

I have a dish full of stones on my dresser: the heart-shaped rock (introduced in chapter 4) and many others. One is smooth and fits perfectly in my hand, another looks like an elf shoe. Some were found on the shores of Lake Superior, others in the local creek bed, and still others in our very own backyard. Most were gifts from my children and have outlasted the flowers. They are small, handheld monuments from this treasured time of motherhood.

Reflect or discuss:

1) In what ways have you felt God's generosity in your life?

2) When have you been most able to experience the joy of motherhood?

3) What helps you "turn your heart" to your children?

4) What is the most important idea that has come to you while reading this book?

CONCLUSION

As has been stated by a wise teacher, "There is so much more to say . . . but some things one must learn individually and alone, taught by the Spirit."[1] After eight years, I have come to an end of my focused endeavor to write this book. It has taken such a ghastly amount of time because it happened only in pieces—early mornings and late nights in exchange for sleep, or sometimes in sudden daytime or nighttime bursts—because it would have been a great act of hypocrisy to miss mothering only to write about it.

There is slight relief but also sadness to part with these ideas and questions that have become companions to me, with which I've had such continual interface. Admittedly, on some days these same ideas and questions have puzzled, overwhelmed, or exasperated me. Some writing stages were too much like housework or remodeling to be enjoyable to me: deciding what to keep and what to get rid of, finding the right place for what was to be kept, and tearing out whole sections. I would not have spent such effort on anything except as a labor of love—loving the act of writing itself, loving my children now and their future adult selves, and anyone else who may someday ask, "How did you do it?" Writing, mothering, or any major undertaking proceeds only because of committed diligence—as we "work with all [our] intelligence and love."[2]

Like children, words don't always cooperate and publishers too have their independent will. All along the way, I have not held complete control of outcomes. The amount of work I put in didn't always correlate to product; sometimes a section taking hours or days of work ultimately had to be completely rewritten. Similarly, in parenting, our efforts don't guarantee good outcomes, but increase their likelihood. Work must be done day by day, unfailingly, "Let[ting] patience have her perfect work" (James 1:4).

Once when presenting at a conference during medical school I stayed with my cousin in San Francisco. She told me how relieved she felt in having waxed her kitchen floor. Because she worked full time, she had little chance to complete the whole project, so she waxed one square per night. One large square of ten small squares every day for weeks—but this was how she was able to wax her floor. This book, similarly, has been

273

completed in squares and rectangles: paragraphs, lines, and words, day by day.

Though I know now, initially when I decided to write this book, I didn't have any idea how long it would take (that a book's gestation could be 3 times longer than an elephant's!). The time of most focused parenting is also finite, but more predictable in duration. By the time my youngest will likely leave home, I will have spent about 30 years of my life in the more active phases of raising children. Any slight relief in completion of this phase will be mixed with the hope in beginnings and the sadness in endings, which has accompanied each passing, treasured stage.

The art of both writing and parenting are highly personalized. Though we find community and insight in writing groups, parenting groups, or play groups, the real work of writing or parenting falls squarely on the author or parents themselves. It is accomplished in quiet, even unexpected hours, in thought and then dialogue, in courageous acts. Wallace Stegner writes, "The man who publishes a book is a man with a sending set, but no receiver, broadcasting messages into space without ever knowing whether they have reached any ears. . .This is not a statement of public neglect. It is an acknowledgment that the writing of books is a private, not a public, art."[3] Parenting too is a private art—part triumph, part tragedy, with most details never to be published or known. Even within the realm of home, the effects of our efforts—their ultimate endings—may for now be hidden to us. Stegner observes that, unlike musicians, actors, or even painters and sculptors (who could attend their own exhibition), "[a writer is] rarely privileged to watch the faces of his readers as they read. Reading is private, even solitary, as a rule. . . . The natural audience of the novelist is not a crowd, but single individuals in armchairs. . . and they can't be safely imagined or predicted."[4] Can we really predict who are children are? Often we don't even have the luxury to be present at the sacred moment when the lessons we have taught sink in. In fact, we most often teach to our children's future selves. For now, we see initial reactions, but not final ones.

In the end—naturally—our children will likely turn out very much like us, but different too. Stegner continues, "What all this comes to is that the writer, who must write *out of* his special culture because it is all he has, can hardly write *for* his special culture. . . He must write, eventually, for the man in the armchair . . .[who] will turn out, I suspect, to be someone very like the writer himself. . .Yet the man in the armchair (or the lady in the chaise longue) is someone *other*, too, and that makes all the difference. . . I have said somewhere else that a work of literature is not primarily a gem, but a lens, a thing to look through, and that one thing we get by looking through it is a sense of acquaintance with the best in the man who wrote it."[5]

Our children, as the ultimate "receivers" of our parenting, will likely emerge as a representation of the "best" in us. Yet, ours is a shared authorship. Three simultaneous creations occur: by parents, by the child him or herself, and by God. As parents we contribute our best, but can only influence rather than dictate outcomes.

In our families, we are simultaneously bound to each other now, but also to who each family member is in process of becoming. This is where our strength is spent—and through its spending, gained: within the surrounding, encircling arms of family. We are linked by generations past, present, and future. Our families will be our personal and sacred triumphs.

In the LDS faith, the culminating ordinance is the "sealing" of individuals to their families for eternity. I have kneeled before the temple altar twice to be eternally bound to a family—once as a child to be sealed to my parents and sister and then, as an adult, to be sealed to my husband and future children. Were these culminating events, or only beginnings? Speaking of the sealing rooms of some LDS temples, Elder Packer describes,

> Opposite walls are adorned with large mirrors so that one may stand near the altar and view on either side a corridor of diminishing images. It gives one the feeling of looking into infinity; into the eternities. For the images in that corridor never end. You can see as far as you can see, and you have the feeling that if you could move to the limit of your vision, you yet could see on 'forever.'[6]

We glimpse eternity looking in our children's eyes; as we view their current selves, we see reflections of their infancy and projections of who they will become.

Words endure for a time, but "Family is a gift that lasts forever." To this story there is no ending, only turning pages.

Summary

As mothers, we nurture by:
1. Establishing vision
2. Exercising charity
3. Cherishing moments
4. Remaining available
5. Fostering gifts
6. Nourishing growth
7. Making home a sanctuary
8. Creating systems
9. Utilizing teaching moments and
10. Appreciating the big and small joys of everyday.

May God bless you in your mothering journey. –MW

ACKNOWLEDGMENTS

Without the help of my sister, Laurie, this book would not exist. In fact, I consider it partly hers. Though I wrote it, many of the insights are ones we arrived at together in discussing daily issues of parenting and life. These ideas built upon one another and became something new—we could no better separate them than one could separate the ingredients in a baked loaf of bread. Laurie and I have ongoing conversations about trusting God, seeing our families as our most important work, using our gifts to fulfill the purposes of our lives, providing enriching environments for our children, finding balancing between cherishing current stages while seeking growth, and many other topics. We arrived at certain similar insights independently, after having had parallel experiences and drawing similar conclusions. Our shared history and perspectives lead us along very connected paths.

Certain realizations originated with Laurie—she related them to me and they became my realizations too. With permission, I include some of these in my book and reference Laurie in the text where possible. She also contributed: insights about listening to our own inner reactions to draw boundaries (chapter 7), the metaphor of optical illusions and flipping perspectives (chapter 10); the idea that when people feel desperate they need soothing rather than scolding (chapter 13); and the recommendation for the opening quote of section II, "The moment is vast" (chapter 13). She shared uplifting quotes and scriptures with me, some of which I include in the book: the quote about "magic" from *The Secret Garden,* the concept that "trying again" is a holy act (from a talk by Elder Christofferson), D&C 8:1-5 about the gift of revelation, D&C 123:17 about doing all that is in our power and trusting God, and I Thessalonians 5:21 about holding fast to what is good. Laurie also pointed me toward various inspiring Suzuki resources, which I reference in chapters 24, 25, and 35, as well as *The Caregiver Helpbook,* which helped us navigate issues related to caring for our mom. Laurie read through my drafts at the earliest stages and has been a continual voice of encouragement and wisdom. She astutely called my attention to redundancies, contradictions, and oversimplifications. She has been a mentor to me in life as well as in my writing.

Other helpful readers and advisors were Sharon Janzen, Pat Dooley, Natalie Goodson, Jayne Pearl, and my husband Jason. Emily Allen and JoAnn Jolley also donated time to provide feedback.

I am grateful to my children and husband for sharing life's journey with me. I appreciate my kids giving permission to have stories about them included in this book. I assure each of my sons that they are equally loved and cherished, even if I happen to share more stories about one than another (I'm sure they are counting pages already!).

I am thankful to my own loving mother who, more than anyone, taught me how to nurture others.

I am grateful to God, who makes comfort, peace, and inspiration available to us all.

REFERENCES AND NOTES

INTRODUCTION
[1] Erdrich, Louise. "Writings from a Birth Year" in *Your Children Will Raise You: The Joys, Challenges, and Life Lessons of Motherhood.* ed Eden Steinberg. Boston: Trumpeter, 2005. p 4

I. ATTRIBUTES OF MOTHERHOOD
[1] "Across the Great Divide" by Kate Wolf. Recorded by Nanci Griffith on her album *Other Voices, Other Rooms,* Elektra, 1993.
[2] The children's choir version is arranged by Nick Page. More recently I found another version for soprano voice composed by Chester Biscardi. This perhaps more representatively captures my position as a grown child looking back. http://chesterbiscardi.com/listen.php?id=9
[3] Dag Hammarskjold qtd in *The Caregiver Helpbook: Powerful Tools for Caregivers.* 2nd ed. Portland: Legacy Caregiver Services, 2006. p 32
[4] Emerson, Ralph Waldo. "Spiritual Laws." *The Essays of Ralph Waldo Emerson.* Cambridge, Belknap Press, 1979. 92
[5] Saint-Exupéry, Antoine de. *The Little Prince.* San Diego, Harcourt Brace & Company, 1934. p 73-74
[6] Saint-Exupery. *The Little Prince.* p 65
[7] "I Want to Be a Mother" by Janeen Brady on album *Songs for a Mormon Child.* Covenant, 2000.
[8] Allen, James. *As a Man Thinketh.* White Plains: Peter Pauper Press, (non-copyrighted). p 51
[9] Proverbs 29:18
[10] Pearce, Virginia. *A Heart Like His: Making Space for God's Love in Your Life.* Salt Lake: Deseret Book, 2006. p 18

II. BOUNDLESS CHARITY
[1] The scriptures are filled with examples of individuals experiencing God's love in personal ways. See Psalm 23, Jeremiah 1:4-8, John 8:1-11, John 9:1-38, John 13:4-15, 3 Ne 17:15-17, Moses 7:41, 47. See also "Eternally Encircled in His Love" by Bonnie Parkin. *Ensign,* Nov 2006.
[2] *A Simple Path* compiled by Lucinda Vardey. New York: Balantine Books, 1995.
[3] Two Book of Mormon prophets, Alma and Nephi, provide an example of humbly accepting the contexts in which they are called to serve, despite acknowledging wishes for greater success or influence. See Alma 29:1, 3 and Hel 7:7-9. (It is interesting to note that though Alma did not realize it at the time, his preaching recorded in the Book of Mormon *has* gone forth to a wide, global audience. Often service in our "small" spheres has much broader reach than we can imagine.)
[4] Qtd by Elder Bednar in *Increase in Learning.* Salt Lake: Deseret Book, 2011. p 58
[5] Porter, Eleanor. *Pollyanna.* London: Harrap, (orig 1927) 1974. p 121
[6] Kohn, Alfie. *Unconditional Parenting.* Atria Books: NY, 2005. p 11

7 See also Genesis 43:30, 45:2, 45:14-15, 46:29.
8 Costa, Claudio R. "Don't Leave for Tomorrow What You Can Do Today." *Ensign,* Nov 2007.
9 See D&C 88:125 and D&C 124:116 (emphasis added).
10 "The Infinite Power of Hope." *Ensign,* Nov 2008.
11 *Arriving at Your Own Door* New York, Hyperion: 2007. p 72
12 Ueshiba, Morihei. (trans./ed. John Stevens) *The Art of Peace.* Boston: Shambhala: 2010. p 4
13 The discourse *Divine Love* by Russel M. Nelson (*Ensign,* Feb 2003) clarifies that God's love is perfect, but His favor and blessings are conditional.
14 Lindbergh, Anne Morrow *Gift from the Sea.* New York: Pantheon Books, 1955, 1975. p 118
15 Lewis, C. S. *Mere Christianity.* New York: HarperSanFrancisco, 1980 (1952). p 86
16 *The Caregiver Helpbook,* p 62
17 *The Sacred Poets of the Nineteenth Century.* Miles, Alfred H. ed. 1907 (cited on bartleby.com).
18 Credited to Rev. John Watson, pseudonym Ian MacLaren.
19 *Teachings of the Presidents of the Church: Spencer W. Kimball.* Salt Lake City, The Church of Jesus Christ of Latter-day Saints: 2006. p 82

III. MOMENTS OF MOTHERHOOD
1 Ballard, Russell M. "Daughters of God." *Ensign,* May 2008.
2 Original lyrics by Malvina Reynolds (though when I sang it, I adapted the words for boys).
3 Salt Lake City, Deseret Book, 2002. p 3
4 Yellowstone National Park website, "Old Faithful" wikipedia
5 Eyre, Linda. *I Didn't Plan to Be a Witch and Other Surprises of a Joyful Mother.* New York, Fireside: 1996. p 20
6 *The Nichomachean Ethics.* Ed Lesley Brown NY: Oxford UP, 2009. p 36
7 *The Caregiver Helpbook,* p 90
8 Ginott, Haim. *Between Parent and Child.* Macmillan Co: NY, 1965. p 50
9 *The Book of Mormon.* 1 Nephi chapter 8; 1 Nephi 11:21-23, 25, 36; 1 Nephi 12:17-18
10 see I Corinthians 13:5 KJV
11 Benson, Ezra Taft qtd in "Truths and Lies" by Jennifer Nuckols. *Ensign,* Oct 2009.
12 Goleman, Daniel. *Emotional Intelligence.* New York: Bantam, 2006 (1995). p 240
13 Seligman, Martin. *The Optimistic Child.* Boston: Houghton Mifflin, 2007. p 163
14 Seligman, pp 135, 297
15 Beever, Sue. *Happy Kids, Happy You.* Wales: Crown House Publishing: 2009. p 112-113
16 *Teachings of the Presidents of the Church: Brigham Young.* Salt Lake City: The Church of Jesus Christ of Latter-day Saints, 1997. p 186
17 Ginott, p 23

[18] Light edifies (D&C 52:16); frees (John 8:36), strengthens (Ephesians 3:16); brings the Spirit (Gal 5:22); (Spirit of Christ) invites to do good, believe in Christ, serve God (Moroni 7:16); teaches to pray (2 Ne 32:8); satisfies/fills (2 Ne 9:51, Alma 32:42); teaches truth (2 Ne 32:3, Nehemiah 9:20, Alma 41:14, Moroni 10:5). We are children of light (1 Thessalonians 5:5, 21).

[19] Darkness does not edify (D&C 50:23); enslaves (2 Ne 26:22), seeks to destroy (Helaman 8:28); mocks (Moses 7:26); breeds contention (3 Ne 11:29), diminishes inspiration (Alma 12;10-11), brings negative consequences (Alma 3:26-27); persuades to do evil, not believe in Christ, not serve God (Moroni 7:17); teaches to not pray (2 Ne 32:8); leaves hungry (2 Ne 27:3); turns heart from truth (D&C 78:10, D&C 93:39)

[20] See D&C 50: 2, 23-25, 41; D&C 88:6-13; Moses 1:12-24, Moroni 7: 15-16.

[21] Uchtdorf, Dieter. "The Infinite Power of Hope." *Ensign*, Nov 2008.

[22] Allen, James. *As a Man Thinketh*. White Plains: Peter Pauper Press, (public domain). p. 31

[23] Turner, Nancy. *These is My Words*.

[24] Recipe for Strawberry Rhubarb Jam: Pour 3 cups sugar over 5 cups coarsely chopped rhubarb and let stand for 4 hours. Boil mixture for 15 minutes (until rhubarb loses its shape). Stir in 3 oz. package of strawberry Jell-O powder and allow to cool 5 minutes. Ladle into storage containers and refrigerate or freeze.

[25] Smith, Stevie. *Collected Poems*. Comp by James MacGibbon. New York: New Directions Books, 1983. p 303

[26] Kimball, Spencer W. "The Abundant Life." *Tambuli*, June 1979. p 3

[27] Thoreau, Henry David. *Walden: 150th Anniversary Illustrated Edition of the American Classic*. Houghton Mifflin: Boston, 2004. p 53

[28] Maxwell, Neal A. "Jesus, the Perfect Mentor." *Ensign*, Feb 2001.

[29] See "The Divine Gift of Repentance" by D. Todd Christofferson. *Ensign*, Nov 2011.

[30] In remarks given by President Boyd K. Packer on June 23, 2013 in a broadcast entitled "Hastening the Work of Salvation." Available at www.lds.org.

[31] Blair, George. "The Carpenter of Nazareth" qtd in "Broken Things to Mend" by Jeffery R. Holland. *Ensign*, May 2006.

[32] Emphasis added.

[33] Diamant, Anita. *How to Be a Jewish Parent*. NY: Schocken Books, 2000. p 88-94

[34] Hamilton, Edith qtd in *Hour of Gold, Hour of Lead* by Anne Morrow Lindbergh. New York: Harcourt Brace Jovanovich, 1973. p 212. Orig. citation: *The Greek Way* 1993.

[35] See Helaman 13:4, 16:2; Mark 6:4.

[36] Lindbergh, Anne Morrow. *Hour of Gold, Hour of Lead: Diaries and Letters from Anne Morrow Lindbergh 1929-1932*. New York: Harcourt Brace Jovanovich, 1973. p 212

[37] Abraham 3:25

[38] Kimball, Spencer W. *Faith Precedes the Miracle*. Salt Lake: Deseret Book Co., 1973. pp. 97–98. (Also quoted in "Gifts of the Spirit" by James A Cullimore, October 1974, General Conference).

[39] 1 Ne 1:20. See also "The Tender Mercies of the Lord" by David Bednar *Ensign*, May 2005.

[40] *Hymns of the Church of Jesus Christ of Latter-day Saints.* Salt Lake: Deseret Book, 1985.

[41] Maxwell, Neal A. "Enduring Well." *Ensign*, Apr 1999.

[42] D&C 93:24, 26

[43] *In Their Own Words: Women and the Story of Nauvoo* by Carol Cornwall Madsen. Salt Lake: Deseret Book, 1994. p 164

[44] thesecomefromtrees.blogspot.com

[45] See also Helaman 5:12, Helaman chapter 12, Moroni 10: 3, Deut 6:7-9.

[46] Beck, Julie B. "And Upon the Handmaids in Those Days Will I Pour Out My Spirit." *Ensign*, April 2010.

[47] Hanley, Victoria. *The Seer and the Sword.* New York: Dell, 2000. p 40

[48] Edgeworth, Maria qtd in *To a Child Love is Spelled T-I-M-E.* Mac Anderson and Lance Wubbels. New York: Warner Faith, 2004. p 18

[49] Dickinson, Emily. *The Complete Poems of Emily Dickinson.* Ed. Thomas H. Johnson. Boston: Little, Brown and Co., 1960. p 307

[50] New York: Golden Books, 1997. p 27

[51] See Luke 15:17.

[52] Townley, Roderick. "Fred's Shoes: the Meaning of Transitions in *Mister Rogers' Neighborhood*" in *Mister Rogers' Neighborhood: Children, Television, and Fred Rogers.* Ed. Mark Collins and Margaret Kimmel. Pittsburgh: University of Pittsburgh Press, 1996. p 68

[53] Diamant, Anita. *How to Be a Jewish Parent.* NY: Schocken Books, 2000. p 51-2

[54] Covey, Stephen. *The 7 Habits of Highly Effective Families.* NY: Golden Books, 1997. p 22

[55] Thoreau, p 85

IV. STAYING POWER

[1] Dickinson, Emily. *The Complete Poems of Emily Dickinson.* Ed. Thomas H. Johnson. Boston: Little, Brown and Co., 1960. p 597

[2] Lee, Dorothy. *Freedom and Culture,* Englewood Cliffs, N.J.: Prentice-Hall, pp. 29–30

[3] This concept of modeling a *process* came from my sister. She acknowledged that when we do not measure up to ideals and our efforts to change are met with setbacks and obstacles, it is easy to feel discouraged. She was once comforted by the realization that repeated attempts to change, instead of being a "shabby, last place gift," showed a process that was the "most real and applicable model of all." She commented that that even when we make repeated mistakes, all is not lost because we can still model something—repentance, hope, and change over time.

[4] *All the Places to Love* by Patricia MacLachlan. New York: Harper Collins, 1994.

[5] See 2 Nephi 9:28-29. The Church of Jesus Christ of Latter Day Saints teaches both men and women to be devoted to family. For further related reading, see "Women of the Church" by Gordon B. Hinckley, *Ensign,* Nov 1996; "The Moral Force of Women" by Todd Christofferson, *Ensign,* Nov 2013; and "Education" in *Eternal Marriage Student Manual* 2003, p 77-8 (all available at lds.org).

[6] Comments such as "Are these all yours?" "You must have a very handsome husband!" and, "You're a doctor—haven't you figured out where babies come from?"

[7] www.bls.gov/news.release/archives/famee_04262013.pdf "Employment Characteristics of Families Summary"

[8] Penny, Agnes. *Your Vocation of Love: A spiritual companion for Catholic mothers.* Rockford: Tan Books and Publishers, 2006.

[9] David O. McKay (quoting from J. E. McCullough, *Home: The Savior of Civilization* [1924], p 42) *Conference Report,* Apr. 1935. p 116

[10] Bible Dictionary in *The Holy Bible: King James Version.* Salt Lake: The Church of Jesus Christ of Latter-day Saints, 1979.

[11] Hinckley, Gordon B. "Rise to the Stature of the Divine Within You." *Ensign,* Nov 1989.

[12] Kimball, Spencer W. "The Role of Righteous Women" *Ensign,* Nov 1979.

[13] Qtd in *Motherhood Matters: Joyful Reminders of the Divinity, Reality, and Rewards of Motherhood* by Connie Sokol. Springville: Cedar Fort, 2012. p 87

[14] *Mere Christianity.* New York: Harper San Francisco, 1980 (1952). p 107, 109

[15] Helaman 13: 33 & 35

[16] excerpts from "Testimony of the Prophet Joseph Smith" (4th from last paragraph) prefacing *The Book of Mormon.* Salt Lake: The Church of Jesus Christ of Latter-day Saints, 1981 (1830).

V. FRUIT

[1] 1 Ne 15:36

[2] Smith, Joseph. *Teachings of the Presidents of the Church: Joseph Smith.* Salt Lake: The Church of Jesus Christ of Latter-day Saints, 2007. p 394

[3] *Gospel Principles* manual chapter 37 "Family Responsibilities." Salt Lake: The Church of Jesus Christ of Latter-day Saints, 2011. p 215

[4] *Your Two-Year-Old: Terrible or Tender* by Louise Bates Ames. New York: Dell, 1976.

[5] See "Milk and Honey Motherhood" in *All God's Critters God a Place in the Choir* by Laurel Thatcher Ulrich and Emma Lou Thayne. Salt Lake: Aspen Books, 1995.

[6] Alma 32: 37-43

[7] D&C 123:15-17

[8] *Emily Dickinson Collected Poems*, ed. Peter Siegenthaler. Philadelphia: Courage Books, 1991. p 219

[9] Gallwey, Tim. *The Inner Game of Tennis.* New York: Random House, 2008 (1974). p 21

[10] Emerson, Ralph Waldo. "Spiritual Laws" *The Essays of Ralph Waldo Emerson.* Cambridge: Belknap Press, 1987. p 85

[11] *Frog and Toad Together* by Arnold Lobel. New York: Harper Collins, 1971.

[12] Qtd in *Paranoid Parenting: Why Ignoring the Experts May Be Best for Your Child* by Frank Furedi. Chicago: Chicago Review Press, 2002. p 67

[13] Weissbourd, Richard. *The Parents We Mean to Be.* Boston: Houghton Mifflin Harcourt: 2009. p 57

[14] Bowen, Shane M. "Agency and Accountability." *The New Era* Sept 2012. p 8

[15] Latham, Glenn. *What's a Parent to Do?* Salt Lake: Deseret Book, 1997. p 99

[16] Ginott, Haim. *Between Parent and Child.* Macmillan Co: NY, 1965. p 23

[17] *The Lost Art of Listening* New York: Guilford Press, 1995. p 62-3

[18] See Helaman 10:4-5, Isaiah 58:9, Jeremiah 14:10, 12; John 9:31; Mosiah 11:24.

[19] Uchtdorf, Dieter F. "The Infinite Power of Hope." *Ensign,* Nov 2008.

[20] *The Caregiver Helpbook: Powerful Tools for Caregivers.* 2nd ed. Portland: Legacy Caregiver Services, 2006. p 66

[21] See also Hebrews 6:12 & Hymn #217 "Come Let Us Anew" *Hymns of the Church of Jesus Christ of Latter-day Saints.* Salt Lake: Deseret Book, 1985.

[22] Hymn #216 "We Are Sowing," *Hymns of the Church of Jesus Christ of Latter-day Saints.* Salt Lake: Deseret Book, 1985.

[23] Hymn #163 "Lord Dismiss Us with Thy Blessing," *Hymns of the Church of Jesus Christ of Latter-day Saints.* Salt Lake: Deseret Book, 1985.

[24] Stephen Covey qtd in *The 7 Habits of Happy Kids* by Sean Covey. NY: Simon and Schuster, 2008. p 93

[25] Stapley, Delbert l. "Teaching Righteousness at Home." *Ensign,* Oct 2012. p 64

[26] Weissbourd, Rick. *The Parents We Mean to Be: How Well-Intentioned Parents Undermine Children's Moral and Emotional Development.* Boston, Houghton Mifflin Harcourt: 2009. p 1-2

[27] Ibid. p 3

[28] *Children Learn What They Live: Parenting to Instill Values* by Dorothy Law Nolte and Rachel Harris. New York: Workman, 1998. p vi

[29] One aspect of LDS theology that sets it apart from other denominations is the rejection of "original sin." The third of thirteen "Articles of Faith" (or statements of belief) says, "We believe that men will be punished for their own sins and not for Adam's transgression." Like any children, we experience effects of our parents' choices (we are subject to the conditions of mortality because of the Fall), but we are not made guilty by them. We are held accountable our own mistakes, but can overcome these through Christ's Atonement. See also Moroni 7:16.

[30] See Kohlberg's six stages of moral development in *The Growth of Interpersonal Understanding: Developmental and Clinical Analysis* by Robert Selman. New York: Academic Press, 1980, p 37-40. See also *Theories of Moral Development* by Rich, J. and J. DeVitis. Thomas Books, Springfield, 1985, p 88-9.

[31] From *The Secret Garden* by Frances Hodgson Burnett. New York: Scholastic, 2007 (1911). p 184

VI. THE BEST GIFTS

[1] Hymn # 145. "Prayer is the Soul's Sincere Desire." *Hymns of the Church of Jesus Christ of Latter-day Saints.* Salt Lake: Deseret Book, 1985.

[2] Langton, Jane *The Fledgling* New York: Harper Trophy, 1980. p 5, 10

[3] Ibid. p 16

[4] Ueland, Brenda. *If you Want to Write.* St. Paul: Graywolf Press, 2007 (1938). p 5-6

[5] See Doctrine &Covenants 46:11-26, 1 Corinthians 12: 3-11; see also "There Are Many Gifts" by Marvin J. Ashton. *Ensign,* Nov 1987.

[6] Suzuki, Shinichi. *Nurtured by Love.* Miami, Warner Bros Publications, 1983. p 1-2

[7] Doctrine & Covenants 46:8-9, 12; see also Moroni 10:8.

[8] New York: Harper Trophy, 1978 (1950). p 108

[9] "There are Many Gifts" by Marvin J. Ashton. *Ensign,* Oct 1987.

[10] D&C 8:4. See also D&C 29:34, Ether 12:27.

[11] Suzuki, Shinichi. *Nurtured by Love.* Miami: Warner Bros. Publications, 1983. p 15

[12] "The Transforming Power of Faith and Character." *Ensign,* Nov 2010. See also D&C 11:20, D&C 6:13, and D&C 14:7.

[13] In an address to students at Brigham Young University, President Spencer W. Kimball asked the following: "It has been said that many of the great artists were . . . moral degenerates. In spite of their immorality they became great and celebrated artists. What could be the result if discovery were made of equal talent in [individuals] who were clean and free from the vices, and thus entitled to revelations?" ("The Gospel Vision of the Arts" *Ensign,* July 1977). See also "Happiness, Your Heritage" by Dieter F. Uchtdorf. *Ensign,* Nov 2008—an article on compassion and creativity.

[14] I am inspired by Laurie's perseverance and dedication. She decided early she wanted to play in a professional orchestra like our dad, and was very much on the trajectory to do so. She attended prestigious camps and festivals, including the Tanglewood Institute in Boston, and studied from the most renowned teachers in our area of the country, including Mary West. During her senior year of high school, riding to a cabin with friends from school orchestra, she was in a car accident that caused nerve damage in her arm. She did months of intense physical therapy and, despite initially only having enough arm strength for a few minutes of actual playing time interspersed with mental practicing and memorization work, she still practiced hours a day. Week by week she added minutes to her playing time, continued on to win a college performance scholarship, and completed her degree in violin performance and pedagogy. The deepest dreams don't easily go away; they persist even through hardship, "against all odds." Ideally, however, one wouldn't have to fight so hard.

[15] "The Countess of Covent Garden" by Charlene Renberg Winters. *BYU Magazine* Fall 2012. p 26-29

[16] Eyring, Henry B. "Help them Aim High" *Ensign,* Nov 2012.

[17] "The Night I Met Einstein" by Jerome Weidman. *Reader's Digest* Nov 1955. http://www.rd.com

[18] *Collected Dialogues of Plato* ed. Edith Hamilton et al. Princeton, Princeton UP, 1961. p 16-17

[19] Several scales exist to aid in prioritizing responsibilities: see "Good, Better, Best" by Elder Oaks *Ensign,* Nov 2007; essential, important, nice to do: "Choose Ye This Day to Serve the Lord" by Julie Beck. BYU Women's Conference Transcripts April 29, 2010 (available online at ce.byu.edu); the important/urgent decision square: *The 7 Habits of Highly Effective People* by Stephen Covey. NY: Fireside, 1989. p 151.

[20] *10,000 Hours: You Become What You Practice* by Phyllis Lane and Rodrigo Coelho, 2012.

[21] Presentation by Beth Cantrell "Nurturing the Individual: Rivers, Trails, and Time" Parents as Partners Online 2012 Series. suzukiassociation.org

[22] Ueland, Brenda. *If You Want To Write.* Saint Paul: Graywolf Press, 2007 (orig 1938). p 89-90

23 "Happiness, Your Heritage" by Dieter F. Uchtdorf. *Ensign,* Nov 2008.
24 Kimball, Spencer W. "Jesus the Perfect Leader." *Ensign,* Aug 1979.
25 Alcott, Louisa May. *Jo's Boys.* New York: Bantam Classic, (orig 1886) 2008. p 19
26 Ueland, Brenda. *If You Want To Write.* Saint Paul: Graywolf Press, 2007 (orig 1938). p 89-90
27 *A Room of One's Own.* San Diego: Harcourt, (1929) 1981. p 4
28 Ueland, Brenda. *If You Want To Write.* Saint Paul: Graywolf Press, 2007 (orig 1938). p 91-91
29 Ibid. p 89-90
30 Nightingale, Florence. "From Cassandra." *The Norton Anthology of English Literature.* Ed. M. H. Abrams et al. 6th ed. Vol. 2. New York: Norton, 1993. p 2284-2285
31 3 Ne 27:27
32 Article of Faith #13. *The Pearl of Great Price.* Salt Lake: The Church of Jesus Christ of Latter-day Saints, 1981.
33 *Letters of Emily Dickinson* ed. Mabel Loomis Todd. New York: Dover Books, 2003 (1894). p 253
34 Ibid. p *x*
35 Gardner, Peter. "Painting the Mormon Story." *BYU Magazine.* Winter 2008.
36 See D&C 88:36-40, 47, 51-68.
37 *This Day and Always* by Lloyd Newell. SLC: Deseret Book, 1999. p 18

VII. A TEMPLE HOUSE
1 Lyrics by Bernie Grossman.
2 Diamant, Anita. *How to Be a Jewish Parent.* NY: Schocken Books, 2000. p 17
3 D&C 127:1; see also Hebrews 3:4.
4 Ether 2:16
5 *Family Guidebook* (www.lds.org/manual/family-guidebook)
6 See Stevenson, Gary E. "Sacred Homes, Sacred Temples," *Ensign,* May 2009 and Faust, James E. "Standing in Holy Places," *Ensign,* May 2005.
7 "More Diligent and Concerned at Home." *Ensign,* Nov 2009.
8 http://eip.uindy.edu/crossings/publications/Interfaith%20Conversations-1.pdf
9 See Ether 12:4, Hel 5:12, 2 Ne 25:26.
10 Bednar, David. *Increase in Learning: Spiritual patterns for obtaining your own answers.* Salt Lake: Deseret Book, 2011. p 99
11 see Ether 12:4 and Hebrews 11
12 www.poets.org.
13 Several scriptures refer to the glory of the Lord filling a space: see Exodus 40:34, 1 Kgs 8:10-11; 2 Chronicles 5:14; Ezekiel 43:5, 44:4.
14 For further reading on this topic, see "A Matter of a Few Degrees" by Dieter F. Uchtdorf. *Ensign,* May 2008.
15 Trans from *Vetaher Libeynu (Purify Our Hearts),* prayer book p 35 qtd in *How to be a Jewish Parent* by Anita Diamant w/ Karen Kushner. Schocken Books, NY 2000. p 19-20
16 Qtd in *The Sabbath: The Day of Delight* by Abraham Millgram. Philadelphia: Jewish Publication Society of America, 1944. p 1. See also: Isaiah 58:13-14.

[17] www.jewfaq.org
[18] Millgram, Abraham. *The Sabbath: The Day of Delight.* Philadelphia: Jewish Publication Society of America, 1944. p 24-25
[19] Ibid. p 91
[20] Gay, Robert C. "What Shall a Man Give in Exchange for His Soul?" *Ensign,* Nov 2012. p 34-36; see also Alma 5:14-19.
[21] Reprint. New York: The New York Review Children's Collection, 2013.
[22] *Being the Mom: 10 Coping Strategies I Learned by Accident Because I Had Children on Purpose* Salt Lake City, Deseret Book, 2002. See "Strategy 10."
[23] *Children's Songbook,* p. 192. See https://www.lds.org/music/library/childrens-songbook/home?lang=eng
[24] Personal correspondence dated December 2, 1971.
[25] Ginott, Haim. Between Parent and Child. Macmillan Co: NY, 1965. p 49-50
[26] Ueshiba, Morihei. (trans./ed. John Stevens) *The Art of Peace.* Boston: Shambhala: 2010. p. 122
[27] *The Caregiver Helpbook: Powerful Tools for Caregivers.* 2nd ed. Portland: Legacy Caregiver Services, 2006. p 55
[28] "For Peace at Home" *Ensign,* May 2013.
[29] BYU Women's Conference Apr 29, 2010; see http://ce.byu.edu/cw/womensconference/pdf/archive/2010/JulieBBeck2010.pdf
[30] See "The Unspeakable Gift" by Joseph B. Wirthlin. *Ensign,* May 2003.
[31] McConkie, Bruce R, *A New Witness for the Articles of Faith* (1985), 253.
[32] See Hebrews 12:14, D&C 36:2, Galatians 5: 22, 2 Corinthians 13:11. See also "Reverence Invites Revelation" by Boyd K. Packer. *Ensign,* Nov 1991. p 21
[33] James 5:16, adapted

VIII. SYSTEMS AND MEASURES
[1] See Genesis 6:14-16, Exodus 25-27, 1 Chronicles 28:11-13.
[2] Feynman, Richard. *"What Do You Care What Other People Think?"* New York, W.W. Norton: 1988. p 12
[3] Goleman, Daniel. *Emotional Intelligence.* New York: Bantam, 2006 (1995). p 80
[4] Ibid. p 86
[5] Ericsson, Anders. "Expert Performance: Its structure and acquisition" in *American Psychologist* Aug 1994, vol 49, No 8. pp 725-747
[6] Hinckley, Gordon B. *Teachings of Gordon B. Hinckley.* Salt Lake: Deseret Book, 1997. p. 707
[7] Qtd in "Work and Personal Responsibility." *Gospel Principles.* Salt Lake: The Church of Jesus Christ of Latter-day Saints, 2009. p 160
[8] See 2 Ne 25:26.
[9] Tynsdale qtd in "The Miracle of the Holy Bible" by Russel M. Ballard. *Ensign,* May 2007.
[10] https://www.lds.org/general-conference/1978/04/bind-on-thy-sandals?lang=eng
[11] See Leviticus 26:1-4, 12; see also chapter 29 "Characteristics of a temple house."
[12] Covey, Stephen. *The 7 Habits of Highly Effective Families.* New York: Franklin Covey, 1997. p 22
[13] Satir, Virginia. *Making Contact.* Madison: Halcyon Publishing, 2011.

[14] Lin Yutang quoted by Dieter F. Uchtdorf in "As You Embark upon This New Era." BYU commencement address, May 2009. https://speeches.byu.edu/talks/dieter-f-uchtdorf_embark-upon-new-era/

[15] As much as I like reading together, I dislike the potential fragmentation that occurs with the overuse of media devices. They have their usefulness, but as a friend once observed, "I feel like the computer is a window from our house that everyone takes turn looking *out* of." In families where all have their own personal devices, interaction may be further diminished. In our family, we are selective about computer use and have chosen not to have a TV. Even with carefully selected programming, I consider it too much of a potential time sink—I'd rather do things than sit and watch other people do them.

[16] In one of our discussions about preserving family time, my sister reminded me about a part in Terry Tempest Williams' book *Refuge*. When a visitor from the Department of Energy visits the rocky wilderness where a nuclear waste repository is proposed and actually sees its beauty, she exclaims, "I had no idea." My sister drew the parallel that just like the blank space on the official's map, the last few empty places on our calendars just might be the space that allow the connections and peace that are too beautiful to trade in for some other purpose.

[17] Harrington, H. James. *Business Process Improvement*. New York: McGraw Hill, 1991. p 164

[18] Qtd in *The Perfect Mile* by Neal Bascomb. Boston: Houghton Mifflin Co., 2004. p 51

[19] Steinberg, Eden. *Your Children Will Raise You: The Joys, Challenges, and Life Lessons of Motherhood.* Boston: Trumpeter Books, 2005.

[20] Qtd by Sandrock, Michael. *Running with Legends: Training and Racing Insights from 21 Great Runners.* Champaign, Human Kinetics Publishers: 1996. (Also: Dalton "Return to Virtue")

[21] See D&C 123:15. See also "Our Duty to God: The Mission of Parents and Leaders to the Rising Generation" by Robert D. Hales. *Ensign*, Apr 2010.

[22] Covey qtd in *Getting Things Done: The Art of Stress Free Productivity* by David Allen. New York: Penguin Books, 2001. p 199

[23] See the discussion about "primary greatness" at the beginning of chapter 23 "Nurturing Goodness."

[24] Beck, Julie B. "And upon the Handmaids in Those days Will I Pour My Spirit" *Ensign,* May 2010.

[25] Emerson, Ralph Waldo. *The Essential Writings of Ralph Waldo Emerson.* New York: Classic Books International, 2010. p 27

IX. INSPIRED INSTRUCTION

[1] Packer, Boyd K. "Washed Clean" *Ensign,* May 1997.

[2] For ideas on important lessons for parents to teach, see Deuteronomy 5-6, Moses 6:57-68, 2 Nephi 31:14-21, Mosiah 4:15, D&C 68:25-31, D&C 93:40.

[3] 2 Ne 33:1 (see also vs 2-3).

[4] McConkie, David. "Teaching with the Power and Authority of God." *Ensign,* Nov 2013. See also D&C 11:20.

[5] Gay, Robert C. "What Shall a Man Give in Exchange for His Soul?" *Ensign,* Nov 2012.

[6] Stevenson, Robert Louis. "Good and Bad Children" in *A Child's Garden of Verses.* New York: Barnes and Noble, 1999 (orig 1957). p 41

[7] DeMille, Rachel "A Thomas Jefferson Education in our Home: Educating Through the Phases of Learning" Cedar City: George Wythe College Press, 2001.

[8] Joseph Smith qtd by John Taylor. *Millennial Star,* 15 Nov 1851. p 339

[9] Quoted in *Teachings of the Presidents of the Church: David O. McKay.* Salt Lake, The Church of Jesus Christ of Latter-day Saints, 2003. p 159

[10] In *Tomie dePaola's Mother Goose.* New York: G.P. Putnam's Sons, 1985. p. 25

[11] Clark, J. Reuben qtd by Harold B. Lee. "Administering True Charity" address delivered at the welfare agriculture meeting 5 Oct. 1968. Cited in *Ensign,* May 1981, p 88.

[12] Lawrence, Larry. "Courageous Parenting." LDS Gen Conference Oct 2010.

[13] Monson, Thomas S. "Obedience Brings Blessings" *Ensign,* May 2013. See also D&C 93:24, 26-28.

[14] See Hebrews 5:8-9.

[15] Boston: Little Brown and Co (Back Bay), 2000 (2002). p 146

[16] See "Observing Nature at Home" in *Tom Brown's Field Guide: Nature and Survival for Children.* New York: Berkley Books, 1989. p 81-89

[17] This analogy comes from a book entitled *Helping Parents Practice: Ideas for Making it Easier* by Suzuki instructor and psychotherapist Edmund Sprunger. Yes Publishing: St. Louis, 2005. p 18-19

[18] Monson, Thomas S. "The Divine Gift of Gratitude." *Ensign,* Nov 2010.

[19] See Hymn 277, "As I Search the Holy Scriptures." *Hymns of the Church of Jesus Christ of Latter-day Saints.* Salt Lake City: Deseret Book, 1985.

[20] *Teach Ye Diligently* by Boyd K. Packer is a wonderful teaching resource that examines these methods.

[21] "Rest Unto Your Souls" *Ensign,* Nov 2010.

[22] Allen, David. *Getting Things Done: The Art of Stress-Free Productivity.* New York: Penguin Books, 2001. p 10-11

[23] See Alma 42:29.

[24] Ginott, Haim. Between Parent and Child. Macmillan Co: NY, 1965. p 47

[25] See Mosiah 15:9.

[26] Nelson, Russell M. "The Atonement" *Ensign,* Nov 1996.

[27] *Unconditional Parenting.* Atria Books: NY, 2005. p 157 (bracketed items added)

[28] *Hymns of the Church of Jesus Christ of Latter-day Saints.* Salt Lake City: Deseret Book, 1985.

[29] "The Power of Scriptures." *Ensign,* Nov 2011.

[30] See http://home.nyc.gov/html/misc/html/poem/poem1b.html and https://www.poets.org/national-poetry-month/poem-your-pocket-day

[31] *Roots.* New York: Vanguard, 2007 (1974). p viii

[32] See also Psalms 119:18, 27, 105, 111, 165.

[33] See "Teaching our Children to Understand" by Cheryl Esplin. *Ensign,* May 2012.

[34] See "Choices" by James E. Faust. *Ensign,* May 2004.

[35] *Unconditional Parenting.* Atria Books: NY, 2005. p5-6

[36] Kohn, Alfie. *Unconditional Parenting.* Atria Books: NY, 2005. p 51-2
[37] Damon, William. *The Moral Child: Nurturing Children's Natural Moral Growth.* New York: Free Press, 1988. p 60-61
[38] "Hastening the Work of Salvation" Mission President's Fireside 2013; see lds.org
[39] *Hymns of the Church of Jesus Christ of Latter-day Saints.* Salt Lake City: Deseret Book, 1985. Hymn 240
[40] Orson F. Whitney (paraphrasing Joseph Smith) qtd in Faust, James E "Dear are the Sheep that Have Wandered" *Ensign,* May 2003.
[41] Faust, James E. "Dear Are the Sheep Who Have Wandered" *Ensign,* May 2003.
[42] *Playful Parenting: A Bold New Way to Nurture Close Connections, Solve Behavior Problems, and Encourage Children's Confidence* by Lawrence Cohen. New York: Ballantine Books, 2001.
[43] Bishop Richins addressing the Crystal Ward congregation (personal notes). See also D&C 121:45-46.

X. A JOYFUL MOTHER OF CHILDREN
[1] *Teaching Your Children Joy* by Richard and Linda Eyre. New York: Fireside, 1994. (1980)
[2] Personal correspondence with Mary Young dated 11/07/10. Used with permission.
[3] This quote is often attributed to Thoreau, but Hawthorne also made a very similar comment.
[4] *The Prophet.* Oxford: One World, 1998. p 40
[5] See 2 Ne 2:25 and 2 Ne 2:11-13.
[6] *Og Mandino: Three Volumes in One* NYC: Bonanza Books, 1981. p 52-4
[7] 1 Ne 8:12
[8] *Freedom and Culture,* Englewood Cliffs, N.J.: Prentice Hall, 1959. pp 27–38
[9] Emerson, Ralph Waldo. *The Essential Writings of Ralph Waldo Emerson.* New York: Classic Books International, 2010. p 34
[10] Virginia Satir qtd in *The Caregiver Helpbook: Powerful Tools for Caregivers.* 2nd ed. Portland: Legacy Caregiver Services, 2006. p 15
[11] *Coming to Our Senses.* New York, Hyperion: 2005. pp 88-90
[12] www.dennisprager.com
[13] *Simple Abundance: A Daybook of Comfort and Joy.* New York: Warner Books, 1995. p 219
[14] Kabat-Zinn, Jon "Parenting as Practice" in *Wherever You Go There You Are* New York, Hyperion: 1994. p 247-251
[15] From the often-quoted poem "Song for a Fifth Child" by Ruth Hulbert Hamilton.
[16] Bellet, Marie. *Lighten Up.* Ordinary Time Music, 2003. www.mariebellet.com/lyrics
[17] Lyrics by Malvina Reynolds, copyright 1957; multiple recordings.
[18] "Be Still, My Soul" in *Hymns of the Church of Jesus Christ of Latter-day Saints.* Salt Lake: Church of Jesus Christ of LDS, 1985. Hymn 124

CONCLUSION
[1] "The Candle of the Lord" by Boyd K Packer. *Ensign,* Jan 1983.

[2] Ueland, Brenda. *If You Want to Write.* St. Paul: Grey Wolf Press, 1938 (1987, 2007). p 8

[3] *Wallace Stegner: On Teaching and Writing Fiction* Lynn Stegner ed. Penguin Books: NY, 2002. p 82

[4] Ibid. p 83-84

[5] Ibid. p 90-91

[6] Packer, Boyd K. *The Holy Temple.* Salt Lake City: Deseret Book, 1980. p 4

Note: all scriptural references, General Conference addresses, *Ensign* articles, and hymn texts can be accessed on lds.org.

Made in the USA
Middletown, DE
27 May 2017